21:1 / March 2024

LABOR

Studies in Working-Class History

Labor and Science

Seth Rockman, Lissa Roberts, and Alexandra Hui, Coeditors

BOOK REVIEWS

Joining Forces: Labor History and the History of Science

Seth Rockman, Lissa Roberts, and Alexandra Hui

The study of work is flourishing in a corner of our discipline where few readers of *Labor* tread. In recent years, historians of science have begun to think about "science in action": that is, science as constituted by, and constituent of, work. Much of this work is situated in sites that aren't conventionally identified as "scientific" and carried out by actors who are not conventionally viewed as "scientists." Historians of science have turned their attention, for example, to the infrastructural labor that supports research, asking who carried the intrepid geologist's suitcases, washed the chemist's glassware, or watched the kids so that someone else could have an "aha" moment at the microscope. So too have they trained their focus on the scientific work done by distillers to develop product substitutions that evaded excise duties, by shipyard managers who introduced new standards to compartmentalize "mental" and "manual" labor, and by miners at Potosí who developed new ways to extract silver from ores. Historians of science have credited artisanal and agricultural laborers with investigative/constructive practices and forms of knowledge about the natural world that are more typically remembered as belonging to famous scientists and their "discoveries." They have embedded Taylorist fantasies of workplace discipline in the broader evolution of the human sciences and created deep intellectual genealogies for the "scientific racism" that has historically structured who does a society's most backbreaking labor.[1]

Historians of science have done all these things quite effectively, albeit with only the loosest engagement with the prevailing scholarship in the field of labor history. Citations to *Labor, International Labor and Working-Class History*, and *Labour/Le Travail* are few and far between on the pages of *Isis, History of Science*, and other

---

1. Emblematic scholarship might include Shapin, "Invisible Technician"; Roberts, Schaffer, and Dear, *Mindful Hand*; Smith, *Body of the Artisan*; Long, *Artisan/Practitioners*; Delbourgo, "Knowing World"; Bangham, Chacko, and Kaplan, *Invisible Labour in Modern Science*; Ashworth, "Practical Objectivity"; Hellawell, "'Best and Most Practical Philosophers'"; Cañizares-Esguerra, "On Ignored Global 'Scientific Revolutions'"; Leong, *Recipes and Everyday Knowledge*; Barnett, "Showing and Hiding"; d'Avignon, *Ritual Geology*; Williams, "Plantation Botany"; Bulstrode, "Black Metallurgists"; and Hogarth, *Medicalizing Blackness*.

Labor: Studies in Working-Class History, Volume 21, Issue 1
DOI 10.1215/15476715-10948868   © 2024 by Labor and Working-Class History Association

history of science journals. But of course, the conversational gap runs in both directions, and labor historians have generally steered clear of sites that are conventionally identified with science as locales for investigating worker resistance, class formation, and labor conflicts. With the exception of recent attention to the neoliberal university as fertile terrain for unionization, our field has not spent much time thinking about research as a job; about laboratories as workspaces; about the invisibilization of certain kinds of labor in the pursuit of particle physics, astronomy, or medicine; or about the deeply entangled presence of scientific work in networked sites of material production, ranging from plantations to factories, data centers, and power plants.[2] The creation of the "worker" as an object of scientific inquiry has been a long-standing concern for labor historians studying the factory shop floor and the plantation, but labor historians have been slower to mobilize the insights of STS (Science and Technology Studies) scholarship to analyze regimes of workplace surveillance and regimentation.[3] Similarly, labor historians have been less inclined to adopt the experiential research methodologies that have impelled historians of science to reconstruct laboratory instruments or get their hands dirty in pursuit of the tacit knowledge circulating in dyehouses, fields, and kitchens.[4]

In terms of instinct and sensibility, the two fields share a great deal. Each has vastly expanded its field of inquiry, such that the range of activities now understood as work or as science are numerous and capacious. Both fields recognize that "what counts" as work and science has always functioned both to reflect and produce power; in turn, contesting those definitions—historically and historiographically—is invariably political. Recent scholarship recognizes labor (in one case) and science (in the other) as performed, produced, and governed in a variety of settings by various practitioners across a spectrum of terms, and embedded within multiple political economies and ecological relationships. Scholars in both fields have explored the long process by which knowledge originating with artisans and laborers—embodied understandings of the natural world derived from toiling in a mine, tending to an orchard, or working at a kiln—came to be appropriated, codified, and claimed by gentlemen natural philosophers, statesmen, projectors, and, of course, managers.[5] The two fields have common preoccupations around topics like automation and concepts like extraction, while the concurrent and contingent histories of the plantation, the factory, and the laboratory provide both with a shared terrain for ongoing research.[6]

2. Shermer, "What's Really New about the Neoliberal University?"; Groeger, "In Higher Education, Neutrality Is Not an Option." There are, of course, notable exceptions to this generalization: see Rood, "Toward a Global Labor History of Science"; Brown and Klubock, "Environment and Labor"; and Doherty and Brown, "Labor Laid Waste."

3. Seow, "Psychology as Technology"; Robinson, "Military Medicine"; Auderset, "Manufacturing Agricultural Working Knowledge"; Roediger and Esch, *Production of Difference*.

4. Smith, *From Lived Experience.*

5. Montgomery, *Fall of the House of Labor*; Ash, "Expertise and the Modern State"; Klein, "Depersonalizing the Arcanum"; Fisher, *Enclosure of Knowledge*; Jones, "Stratifying Seamanship"; Felten, "History of Science."

6. Anthony, "Introduction to 'Working at the Margins'"; Jones-Imhotep, "Ghost Factories"; Resnikoff, "Myth of Black Obsolescence"; Murphy, "Translating the Vernacular"; Kumar, "Plantation Science."

Hoping to accelerate scholarly cross-fertilization between labor history and the history of science, this special issue of *Labor* stands alongside a special issue of *History of Science* and a dedicated "Focus" section in the journal *Isis*. These three coordinated publications emerged from a 2022 conference titled "Let's Get to Work: Bringing Labor History and the History of Science Together," generously hosted by Philadelphia's Science History Institute. The robust response to the call for papers confirmed our sense of this conversation's potential, even as (sorry to say) self-identified labor historians responded in far smaller numbers than did historians of science. The three postconference publications have sought to channel scholarly energy in several directions. The *Isis* issue contains something of a manifesto for a "labor history of science," urging historians of science to embrace the political dimensions of a project connecting the recovery of histories often labeled "hidden" to self-reflexive practices of community and care within the profession.[7] The *History of Science* issue begins with a substantial historiographical survey, noting the deliberate marginalization of labor questions from twentieth-century scholarship on scientific activity and then plotting out present and future research pathways; the issue also contains research articles that run from the early modern period to the present and explore worksites ranging from colonial New England apothecaries to British munitions factories and Burmese oilfields.[8]

While this special issue of *Labor* invites a broad range of readers, it especially seeks to guide labor historians in three specific directions: to bring more of their scholarly attention to sites of scientific work, both traditionally and nontraditionally defined; to borrow more productively from the analytical frames and methodologies that inform recent work in the history of science; and to recognize scientific work as integrated with other forms of work and practiced by a broad range of actors almost everywhere that labor takes place. On the first matter, the classic "labor question" of *who works for whom, on what terms, and to whose benefit* applies to science as readily as to any other arena in which markets and states allocate resources and set the rules under which capital and labor interact. Scientific work has consistently reflected the global division of labor and its attendant political economies, whether we are speaking of the enslaved Ibo man collecting botanical samples under violent compulsion for a European naturalist in Suriname or the Pakistani chemist working for a US corporation on a special visa that might be eliminated in the next Congress. Labor history's recent attention to capital flight, labor migration, and regimes of border policing has an immediate applicability to the organization of scientific labor, its embeddedness in regimes of racial difference, and the larger question of whose knowledge and labor is "cheap" and whose is not. Similarly, labor history's older investments in the history of "deskilling" remain relevant for grasping the changing—and always overlapping—boundaries of mental and menial labor, especially in light of advances in computing,

---

7. Hui, Roberts, and Rockman, "Let's Get to Work," with contributions from Gabriela Soto Laveaga, Harun Küçük, and Laura Stark.

8. Roberts, Rockman, and Hui, "Science and/as Work," with contributions from Zachary Dorner, Duygu Yildirim, Patricia Fara, Gadi Algazi, Chao Ren, Juyoung Lee, Patrick Anthony, Juliana Broad, Xan Chacko, and Judith Kaplan.

artificial intelligence, and robotics. As labor historians continue to explore class reproduction, economic stratification, and the struggle for workplace control, sites of science have a great deal to offer.

Three contributions to this issue highlight sites of scientific labor as fruitful spaces to explore major themes of labor history. A moderated conversation among five scholars whose research areas span trans-Siberian Russia, British New England and Jamaica, French colonial Senegal, and Hawaii considers the varieties of labor coercion operative in producing new botanical, medical, and geological knowledge in the seventeenth, eighteenth, and nineteenth centuries. Patrick Anthony, Jody Benjamin, Zachary Dorner, Nicholas Miller, and Kate Mulry shed new light on the interlocking dependencies and categories of difference that structured unfree labor more generally under imperialism, racial slavery, and state penal regimes. Their discussion also suggests the value of an earlier chronology to understandings of the more recent intersections of labor and science.

Later in the issue, Jonathan Victor Baldoza brings readers to Manila's Bureau of Science, where the hierarchical administration of scientific labor contributed to US imperial governance in the early twentieth-century Philippines. Science and the state both gravitated toward bureaucracies that shaped the nature and organization of research as well as working people's experiences under the conditions of empire. Baldoza's attention to "science as routine" is a powerful reminder that the mundane labor of preserving samples, maintaining equipment, and filing data constitutes an essential, if inglorious, dimension of knowledge production.

Marta Macedo situates the laboratory and the plantation in the same frame as she explores the transformation of São Tomé cocoa beans into Cadbury chocolates in the early twentieth century. The exploited labor of Angolan laborers made São Tomé into the world's foremost cocoa producer, but not without creating difficulties for English firms that prided themselves on their moral commitments. Cadbury's scientists provided a technical solution significantly less burdensome than policing labor recruitment in a Portuguese colony: new industrial food processing techniques that allowed Cadbury to source lower-quality beans from elsewhere without jeopardizing the confections that consumers found on store shelves. In this sense, a remote labor problem mobilized scientific activity thousands of miles away, the result of which was the further reconfiguration of global labor as cocoa farming took hold in Ghana. Macedo's essay also seeks to elaborate the "commodity history" genre with greater attention to the relationship of crop materiality to the organization of both labor and science.

Macedo's essay also points to a second goal of this special issue: to guide labor historians toward the analytical tools informing dynamic scholarship in the history of science and often embedded in the related field of STS. Macedo, for example, draws on the broader constellation of more-than-human frameworks that have proliferated in the wake of Bruno Latour's Actor-Network Theory several decades ago. Labor historians have encountered comparable moves in Thomas Andrews's *Killing for Coal* (2008) and other scholarship that sees history unfolding at (and through) the interaction of human and nonhuman agencies. Still, the insights of an expanded materiality remain to be fully explored with the field of labor history, especially relative to a materialist turn in the history of science that positions human, objects, instruments, and specimens in an epistemological feedback loop.[9] Similarly, the theorization of maintenance and repair within the history of science and technology aligns with labor historians' attention to reproductive labor but provides still-unfulfilled opportunities to think more critically at the intersection of work and sustainability.[10] And insofar as the history of science provides a basis for historicizing work as an object of inquiry within the behavioral and social sciences, labor historians can better connect the institutionalization of new academic disciplines to the emergence of metrics that would transform skill, strength, and expertise into "human resources" and "human capital."[11]

In their contribution to this issue, Salem Elzway and Jason Resnikoff revisit one of labor history's perennial topics: automation. Recognizing the idea of "automation" as a political claim rather than an objective description of reality (especially in light of the extent to which automation has not meaningfully diminished the amount of human work required for survival), they explore the ideological shield that "science" has provided to the claim that automation is inevitable. The article leans on the concept of technopolitics, an STS framework for understanding processes that mask political contingency vis-à-vis the presumptive irresistibility of "progress."

Similar STS-informed understandings of systems and infrastructure inform Trish Kahle's article on the electrical grid in the 1970s United States. Kahle's conceptualization of "energy work" offers a mechanism for writing women's unwaged domestic labor into accounts of how (to put it colloquially) the lights stay on. Looking closely at the service area of the Pennsylvania Power and Light Company during the energy crisis, Kahle notes that the imperative of conservation fell heavily on housewives whose baking, vacuuming, and washing—that is, their labor of (re)production— were reimagined *merely* as consumption. As such, women's labor was not merely devalued but also subject to an indirect form of labor discipline in the service of the overall health of the power grid.

Finally, Sibylle Marti asks readers to think critically about the political possibilities of statistics in the context of labor activism. The transformation of labor into a statistically knowable entity has its own particular history over the nineteenth and twentieth centuries, one entangled with the contested histories of statistics themselves. Some decades ago, Joan Scott alerted labor historians to the rhetorical character of statistical reports, and historians of science have devoted substantial attention to quantification as a mode of power.[12] As Marti shows, efforts to measure the informal sec-

---

9. Latour, *Reassembling the Social*; Andrews, *Killing for Coal*; Rosenthal, *Beyond Hawai'i*; Uekötter, "Should Agricultural Historians Care about the New Materialism?"; Fernando, "Seeing like the Sea"; Herzig and Subramaniam, "Labor in the Age of 'Bio-Everything.'"

10. Russell and Vinsel, "After Innovation"; Werrett, "Voyages of Maintenance."

11. Derkson, "Turning Men into Machines?"; Laemmli, "Taylorism Transfigured"; Scheffler, "Power of Exercise."

12. Scott, *Gender and the Politics of History*, 113–38; Bouk, Ackermann, and boyd, "Primer on Powerful Numbers."

tor undergirded the efforts of the ILO to promote "decent work" globally. However, the definitions and metrics for capturing the scope of informality changed as such work became increasingly prevalent in industrialized nations. By tracing debates over national accounting standards, Marti reveals that the production of informal sector statistics was just as fundamentally political as it was technical, opening space for "statactivism" among advocacy organizations eager to expand or contract the boundaries of informality in the service of transforming public policy.

Finally, the six contributions reflect science's omnipresence, integrated with virtually every other form of work and workplace in highly consequential ways. In an influential recent essay, the historian of science Steven Shapin encourages us to look for the "embedded science" that, for example, "saturate[s]" almost every aspect of a fast-food restaurant, from the laboratory-derived chemicals that flavor the food to the HVAC system, the vandalism-resistant design of the seating, and the biodegradability of the packaging. Any local McDonald's, explains Shapin, "sucks in huge amounts of scientific and technical expertise."[13] This expertise is overwhelmingly produced in the business sector: twice as many scientific researchers, technicians, and engineers are employed in private enterprise as in education (including universities) and government. In this sense, while labor historians should most definitely bring their analytical insights to the kinds of academic research so readily understood as science (a labor history of oceanography, anyone?), they must also recognize that "science-ing" is unfolding in almost every place where people labor and, accordingly, must read working people's experiences and political possibilities more generally as infused with and shaped by science in all its many instantiations.

SETH ROCKMAN is associate professor of history at Brown University and a member of *Labor*'s editorial committee. He completed work on this issue while a fellow at re:work, the Berlin-based research institute on global labor history and the human life cycle. His publications include *Scraping By: Wage Labor, Slavery, and Survival in Early Baltimore* (2009); the coedited volume *Slavery's Capitalism: A New History of American Economy Development* (2016, with Sven Beckert); *Der alte und der neue Materialismus in der Geschichte der Sklaverei* (2022); and *Plantation Goods: A Material History of American Slavery* (2024).

LISSA ROBERTS is editor-in-chief of *History of Science*, coeditor of the Cambridge University Press monograph series Science and History, and emeritus professor of history of science and technology in global context at University of Twente. Her many publications include *Compound Histories: Materials, Governance and Production, 1760–1840* (with Simon Werrett); *The Brokered World: Go-Betweens and Global Intelligence, 1770–1820* (with Simon Schaffer, Kapil Raj, and James Delbourgo); and *The Mindful Hand: Inquiry and Invention from the Late Renaissance to Early Industrialization* (with Simon Schaffer and Peter Dear).

13. Shapin, "Invisible Science," 36, 37.

ALEXANDRA HUI is associate professor of history at Mississippi State University and coeditor of the History of Science Society publications, including the journal *Isis*. She has published several scholarly articles and anthology chapters on the relationship between science, sound, music, and listening. Other publications include *The Psychophysical Ear: Musical Experiments, Experimental Sounds, 1840–1910* (2012), and she coedited *Testing Hearing: The Making of Modern Aurality* (2020) and the 2013 *Osiris* volume on music, sound, and the laboratory. Her two current projects are histories of background music and how scientists listen to the environment.

References

Andrews, Thomas G. *Killing for Coal: America's Deadliest Labor War.* Cambridge, MA: Harvard University Press, 2008.

Anthony, Patrick. "Introduction to 'Working at the Margins: Labor and the Politics of Participation in Natural History, 1700–1830.'" *Berichte zur Wissenschafts-Geschicht* 44 (2021): 115–36.

Ash, Eric. "Expertise and the Early Modern State." *Osiris* 25 (2010): 1–24.

Ashworth, William J. "Practical Objectivity: The Excise, State, and Production in Eighteenth-Century England." *Social Epistemology* 18 (2004): 181–97.

Auderset, Juri. "Manufacturing Agricultural Working Knowledge: The Scientific Study of Agricultural Work in Industrial Europe, 1920s–60s." *Rural History* 32 (2021): 233–48.

Bangham, Jenny, Xan Chacko, and Judith Kaplan, eds. *Invisible Labour in Modern Science.* Lanham, MD: Rowman and Littlefield, 2022.

Barnett, Lydia. "Showing and Hiding: The Flickering Visibility of Earth Workers in the Archives of Earth Science." *History of Science* 58 (2020): 245–74.

Bouk, Dan, Kevin Ackermann, and danah boyd. *A Primer on Powerful Numbers: Selected Readings in the Social Study of Public Data and Official Numbers. Data and Society*, March 2022. https://datasociety.net/library/a-primer-on-powerful-numbers-selected-readings -in-the-social-study-of-public-data-and-official-numbers/.

Brown, Kate, and Thomas Klubock. "Environment and Labor: Introduction." *International Labor and Working-Class History* 85 (2014): 4–9.

Bulstrode, Jenny. "Black Metallurgists and the Making of the Industrial Revolution." *History and Technology* 39 (2023): 1–41.

Cañizares-Esguerra, Jorge. "On Ignored Global 'Scientific Revolutions.'" *Journal of Early Modern History* 21 (2017): 420–32.

d'Avignon, Robyn. *A Ritual Geology: Gold and Subterranean Knowledge in Savanna West Africa.* Durham, NC: Duke University Press, 2022.

Delbourgo, James. "The Knowing World: A New Global History of Science." *History of Science* 57 (2019): 373–99.

Derksen, Maarten. "Turning Men into Machines? Scientific Management, Industrial Psychology, and the 'Human Factor.'" *Journal of the History of the Behavioral Sciences* 50 (2014): 148–65.

Doherty, Jacob, and Kate Brown. "Labor Laid Waste: An Introduction to the Special Issue on Waste Work." *International Labor and Working-Class History* 95 (2019): 1–17.

Felten, Sebastian. "The History of Science and the History of Bureaucratic Knowledge: Saxon Mining, circa 1770." *History of Science* 56 (2018): 403–31.

Fernando, Tamara. "Seeing like the Sea: A Multispecies History of the Ceylon Pearl Fisheries, 1800–1925." *Past and Present* 254 (2022): 127–60.

Fisher, James. *The Enclosure of Knowledge: Books, Power, and Agrarian Capitalism in Britain, 1660–1800*. Cambridge: Cambridge University Press, 2022.

Groeger, Christina Viviana. "In Higher Education, Neutrality Is Not an Option." *American Historian* (June 2023): 23–28.

Hellawell, Philippa. "'The Best and Most Practical Philosophers': Seamen and the Authority of Experience in Early Modern Science." *History of Science* 58 (2020): 28–50.

Herzig, Rebecca, and Banu Subramaniam. "Labor in the Age of 'Bio-Everything.'" *Radical History Review* 127 (2017): 103–24.

Hogarth, Rana. *Medicalizing Blackness: Making Racial Difference in the Atlantic World, 1780–1840*. Chapel Hill: University of North Carolina Press, 2017.

Hui, Alexandra, Lissa Roberts, and Seth Rockman. "Let's Get to Work: Bringing Labor History and the History of Science Together." *Isis* 114 (2023): 817–26.

Jones, Elin. "Stratifying Seamanship: Sailors' Knowledge and the Mechanical Arts in Eighteenth-Century Britain." *British Journal for the History of Science* (2022): 1–19.

Jones-Imhotep, Edward. "The Ghost Factories: Histories of Automata and Artificial Life." *History and Technology* 36 (2020): 3–29.

Klein, Ursula. "Depersonalizing the Arcanum." *Technology and Culture* 55 (July 2014): 591–621.

Kumar, Prakash. "Plantation Science: Improving Natural Indigo in Colonial India, 1860–1913." *British Journal for the History of Science* 40 (2007): 537–65.

Laemmli, Whitney. "Taylorism Transfigured: Industrial Rhythm and the British Factory." *Grey Room* 88 (2022): 102–26.

Latour, Bruno. *Reassembling the Social: An Introduction to Actor-Network Theory*. New York: Oxford University Press, 2005.

Leong, Elaine. *Recipes and Everyday Knowledge: Medicine, Science, and the Household in Early Modern England*. Chicago: University of Chicago Press, 2018.

Long, Pamela O. *Artisan/Practitioners and the Rise of the New Sciences, 1400–1600*. Corvallis: Oregon State University Press, 2011.

Montgomery, David. *The Fall of the House of Labor: The Workplace, the State, and American Labor Activism, 1865–1925*. New York: Cambridge University Press, 1989.

Murphy, Kathleen S. "Translating the Vernacular: Indigenous and African Knowledge in the Eighteenth-Century British Atlantic." *Atlantic Studies* 8 (2011): 29–48.

Resnikoff, Jason. "The Myth of Black Obsolescence." *International Labor and Working-Class History* 102 (2022): 124–45.

Roberts, Lissa, Seth Rockman, and Alexandra Hui. "Science and/as Work: An Introduction to this Special Issue." *History of Science* 61 (2023): 439–47.

Roberts, Lissa, Simon Schaffer, and Peter Dear, eds. *The Mindful Hand: Inquiry and Invention from the Late-Renaissance to the Industrial Revolution*. Amsterdam: Koninkliijke Nederlandse Akademie van Wetenschappen, 2007.

Robinson, Leslie-William T. "Military Medicine, Morale, and the Affective Management of Men in the Early Twentieth-Century United States." PhD diss., Brown University, 2022.

Roediger, David R., and Elizabeth D. Esch. *The Production of Difference: Race and the Management of Labor in U.S. History*. New York: Oxford University Press, 2012.

Rood, Daniel. "Toward a Global Labor History of Science." In *Global Scientific Practice in an Age of Revolutions, 1750–1850*, edited by Patrick Manning and Daniel Rood, 255–74. Pittsburgh: University of Pittsburgh Press, 2016.

Rosenthal, G. Samantha. *Beyond Hawai'i: Native Labor in the Pacific World*. Berkeley: University of California Press, 2015.

Russell, Andrew L., and Lee Vinsel. "After Innovation, Turn to Maintenance." *Technology and Culture* 59 (2018): 1–25.

Scheffler, Robin Wolfe. "The Power of Exercise and the Exercise of Power: The Harvard Fatigue Laboratory, Distance Running, and the Disappearance of Work, 1919–1947." *Journal of the History of Biology* 48 (2015): 391–423.

Scott, Joan Wallach. *Gender and the Politics of History*. New York: Columbia University Press, 1988.

Seow, Victor. "Psychology as Technology: Industrial Psychology for an Industrializing China." *History and Technology* 38 (2022): 257–73.

Shapin, Steven. "Invisible Science." *Hedgehog Review* (Fall 2016): 34–46.

Shapin, Steven. "The Invisible Technician." *American Scientist* 77 (November–December 1989): 554–63.

Shermer, Elizabeth Tandy. "What's Really New about the Neoliberal University? The Business of American Education Has Always Been Business." *Labor* 18, no. 4 (2021): 62–86.

Smith, Pamela. *The Body of the Artisan: Art and Experience in the Scientific Revolution*. Chicago: University of Chicago Press, 2004.

Smith, Pamela. *From Lived Experience to the Written Word: Reconstructing Practical Knowledge in the Early Modern World*. Chicago: University of Chicago Press, 2022.

Uekötter, Frank. "Introduction to Roundtable: Should Agricultural Historians Care about the New Materialism?" *Agricultural History* 96 (2022): 223–24.

Werrett, Simon. "Voyages of Maintenance: Exploration, Infrastructure, and Modernity on the Krusenstern–Lisianskii Circumnavigation between Russia and Japan from 1803 to 1806." *History of Science* 61 (2023): 338–59.

Williams, J'Nese. "Plantation Botany: Slavery and the Infrastructure of Government Science in the St. Vincent Botanic Garden, 1765–1820s." *Berichte zur Wissenschaftsgeschichte* 44 (2021): 137–58.

Examination
(for Phillis Wheatley)

Charles Coe

How strange the moment must have seemed
sitting before eighteen august gentlemen
under their coolly appraising gazes
fielding their questions about the Bible
and the classics, and waiting to be assessed.

They stared, but no one touched you
the way they touched you down on the docks
the day you arrived in Boston as a child.
When they squeezed your arm, and opened your mouth
to check your teeth. When they calmly examined you,
the little girl whose true name
had been tossed over the ship's rail,
and now bobbed on the waves of that endless sea.

CHARLES COE has written four books of poetry: *Picnic on the Moon, All Sins Forgiven: Poems for My Parents, Memento Mori*, and *Purgatory Road*, all published by Leapfrog Press. He is also author of the novella *Spin Cycles*, published by Gemma Media. Charles is adjunct professor of English and teaches in the MFA programs at Salve Regina University in Newport, Rhode Island, and at Bay Path University in Longmeadow, Massachusetts. He serves on the board of directors of Revolutionary Spaces, Inc. (an organization devoted to promoting the history of Boston), the advisory board of the New England Poetry Club, and the *Unitarian Universalist Magazine* editorial board. Charles is also a member of the Steering Committee of the Boston chapter of the National Writers Union, a labor union for freelance writers and editors.

Labor: Studies in Working-Class History, Volume 21, Issue 1
DOI 10.1215/15476715-10948881 © 2024 by Charles Coe

Entanglements of Coerced Labor and Colonial Science in the Atlantic World and Beyond

Zachary Dorner, Patrick Anthony, Jody Benjamin, Nicholas B. Miller, and Kate Luce Mulry

The five participants in this conversation have followed different paths to the intersection of labor history and the history of science but share common research questions regarding the relationship of coercion, colonialism, and scientific knowledge production. Collectively their scholarship is global in scope and offers the opportunity to think comparatively across a range of colonial regimes, populations, scientific disciplines, and modes of labor mobilization. Their inquiries emphasize the importance of the seventeenth, eighteenth, and nineteenth centuries to the structures of knowledge and power that continue to organize the modern world, while also suggesting that historians of more recent periods might gain theoretical insights from studies of a more distant past. This conversation began in Philadelphia in June 2022, unfolded diachronically in early 2023, and has been edited for clarity. An appendix contains citations for scholarship mentioned in the text.

1. How—or even when—did you find yourselves, as historians interested in science, addressing coerced labor as a research topic? In other words, what makes the history of labor important to your history of science?

Jody Benjamin: I come to this conversation as a historian of West Africa whose research on the history of textiles and dress led me to explore questions of labor, craft, and specialized knowledge. A central concern has been to contend with the ways African knowledge practices have been both appropriated within and excluded from narratives of Western science-making. This is not simply a matter of historical recovery for me but rather a gesture toward thinking beyond epistemologies and practices of knowledge production attached to colonial extraction.

Nicholas B. Miller: I first came to the history of science through the global and comparative history of indentured labor during the long nineteenth century. Having trained as a social and intellectual historian, I wanted to identify actors who left sub-

Labor: Studies in Working-Class History, Volume 21, Issue 1
DOI 10.1215/15476715-10948894   © 2024 by Labor and Working-Class History Association

stantial written testimony about the operative political and social ideas in emergent plantation settings. This brought me to a cohort of globe-trotting European botanists who participated in the propagation of indentured labor in contexts like Hawai'i and the Malay Sultanate of Johor prior to formal imperial overrule. These botanists drew on their scientific networks to share knowledge relating to plantation production, including draft indentured labor contracts. Ultimately, I found that to understand the history of plantation labor, I needed to know more about the history of plantation science.

Zachary Dorner: Tracing the business of medicine across the eighteenth-century Anglo-Atlantic world brought me to science and labor's intersection. The ways medicines were produced, moved, sold, and consumed and who did the producing, moving, selling, and consuming are fundamentally considerations of labor from across the spectrum of coercion and dependency. Approaching the history of medicine in this way frames the laboratory and pharmacy as sites akin to the cotton mill or plantation, where globally distributed labor enabled the production and distribution of scientific and medicinal goods, such as new pharmaceuticals. The early modern world is an essential setting for this story because it featured the hardening of ideologies, such as racial difference, empire, or even empiricism, before the legal regimes of the nation-state and industrialized society. Understanding how science as an economic arena of labor, profit, and trade contributed to these transformations drives my work.

Kate Mulry: My attention to labor history emerged from my research into early modern medical practitioners and colonizers' interests in examining and controlling laboring and productive bodies. My current project tracks a series of exploitative claims made by English colonial physicians about how to sustain physical labor and boost reproductive labor in plantation economies. They sought new colonial drugs and distillations that would power the daily work of servants and the enslaved and that would cure sterility and enhance fertility. Their bioprospecting activities were linked to their investigations into the human body and were framed as a means of securing and extracting labor.

Patrick Anthony: The spatial field of coercion drew me here. I study a set of environmental sciences that performed a double act of displacement around the turn of the nineteenth century: the practices by which Europeans delocalized observations as "universal" matters of fact were viciously linked to the practices by which they evacuated Indigenous lands for expropriation by white settlers. Scientific itineraries were also routed into the forced migrations of enslaved and exiled populations. In particular, I trace the movements of central European agents who served foreign empires as mercenaries of a kind by surveying mineral resources and climatic conditions. At stake here is an understanding of how science as mercenary-craft not only intensified particular forms of coercion—from Ibero-American slavery to penal colonization in Siberia—but also advanced global capitalism through techniques meant to quantify, compare, and coordinate disparate commodity frontiers.

2. Two hallmarks of historical eras prior to, say, 1900 were the ubiquity of regimes of coerced labor—such as slavery, peonage, and penal transportation—alongside the rise of new ways of understanding the world and acquiring knowledge. What might be gained by examining sites of coerced labor as spaces where knowledge production took place?

NBM: I think the plantation is a good place to start, given its character as perhaps the paradigmatic site of early modern coerced labor. A focus on how plantations served as places where knowledge was gathered, deployed, and negotiated—and how plantations served to instigate the collection and development of knowledge—can help historicize the field of concerns and insights that have lately coalesced around the Plantationocene. Coined about a decade ago by Donna Haraway, the concept posits "that large-scale, export-oriented agriculture dependent on forced labor has played a dominant role in structuring modern life since the insertion of European power in the Americas, Asia and Africa," to use Wendy Wolford's recent definition. Proponents of the concept have expanded the notion of forced labor, extending it beyond humans to encompass animals, insects, and plants. Building on this insight through the prism of knowledge production, we could study the dynamic process by which human actors pursued new tactics for squeezing maximum yields from these most diverse forms of laborers in the spaces and places of the plantation. I term this field of inquiry "plantation knowledge," or the types of expertise, experience, and information processing that have made and continue to make plantations possible.

KM: The production of scientific knowledge about the natural world relied on various forms of coercion in many sites around the early modern Atlantic, and the desire for that knowledge shaped the kinds of labor myriad individuals were forced to perform for colonizers' financial and political gain. Through threats and violence, colonizers exploited the intellectual and physical labor of Indigenous, African, and African-descended people. Colonial naturalists' letters and travel accounts are full of anecdotes about their reliance on knowledgeable Native and enslaved guides and healers when conducting bioprospecting activities. The naturalist John Lawson urged Carolina's proprietors to encourage colonizers of a "lower rank" to "Marr[y]" Native residents as a "Method" of extracting "Indians Skill in Medicine and Surgery" from them and for gleaning information about "the Situation of our Rivers, Lakes, and Tracts of Land." Lawson's proposal echoed those of other colonial scientists who encouraged white men to form intimate connections with Indigenous women to compel them to reveal botanical and medical knowledge. Attention to racial and gendered power dynamics highlight the coercive nature of such relationships. The pursuit of science was laced with violence and sexual exploitation. Scholars such as Judith Carney also reveal how planters sought to enslave West African people who could transfer entire "African knowledge systems" about rice cultivation to help develop colonial plantation economies in the Carolinas. In other words, Indigenous and African knowledges, often held by women, were mobilized by colonizers and slaveholders to develop colonies and plantation economies.

ZD: Kate's point about the exploitation of physical and intellectual labor in colonial spaces is important, and one I would like to extend by adding that Caribbean plantations (and South Asian trading company outposts, for that matter) were also sites of medical knowledge production through human testing. Information generated under such conditions, as Londa Schiebinger has shown, informed standards of experimentation at the turn of the nineteenth century and shaped the bulk purchasing of medicines in those places. The medical care provided in response to the institutionalized violence and deprivation of plantation slavery also generated more quotidian observations about medicines, anatomy, and the human body's capacity for work. From this vantage, not only is the plantation or trading company outpost a site of knowledge production, but so too is the human body itself. As I am exploring in a new project, health care was routinely provided in exchange for work that had damaged the body, often beyond repair. This exchange had significant implications not only for labor and science but also for state power and political economy.

JB: In my work on early nineteenth-century Senegal, I am attentive to the presence of multiple sites of knowledge production, from the French colonial plantation to the mosque or Quranic school, the blacksmith's shed, the indigo dyers' compound, and the spaces where village potters fired their clay vessels. In each of these, a different type of person held authoritative knowledge, and the modes of transmission were also distinct. We are confronted with multiple regimes of coerced labor at play, not all of which are tied to Euro-Atlantic commerce. But when we focus on the production of knowledge that underpinned colonial society, we see that this involved not only the invisibilizing of the labor and labor struggles that produced its findings but also the dismissal and erasure of sites and forms of knowledge production outside colonial control.

The hierarchies of social status and knowledge active on plantations become evident when considering how work was organized and data recorded. Botanists enjoyed a place of privilege on the colonial farms, most notably Baron Roger, who even served as governor of the Saint Louis colony (1822–27) while overseeing agricultural projects in the interior floodplains of Waalo. His role makes evident the function of power over laborers in producing scientific knowledge in this period, indicating how agricultural experiments initially conceived as an alternative to Caribbean slavery in some ways reproduced the social logics of the slave plantation, as Kate and Zack have described them.

PA: It is also worth considering tensions and connections between different sites and modalities of coerced labor, since knowledge was not only produced *in* but also *across* geographies of dependence. As Kate notes above, forced migration was itself a "site" in which colonizers violently reassembled and recirculated horticultural and medical sciences. One site where colonial agents "reproduced the social logics of the slave plantation," as Jody notes, were the alluvial gold and diamond mines of Brazil. In the eighteenth and nineteenth centuries, technicians came from the silver-mining hubs of central Europe to manage enslaved Afro-Brazilian miners. Yet as these agents also worked across mineral empires, they attempted to render Atlantic World slavery commensurable with, for instance, the Russo-Siberian system of serf- and convict-based mining. Their dehumanizing calculations of labor power across hemispheres were underpinned by a global geological survey of precious metals, which one Prussian, Alexander von Humboldt, described as a "universal chain-linkage." This example suggests how the institutionalization of violence and deprivation that Zack has described at the plantation could be exported and intensified through mediation or translation. In attempting to translate across different coerced labor regimes, there was also an attempt to bind and "link" the world into a single, commensurable economy of dependent labor.

3. The history of coerced labor is also a history of mobility: of forced migrations, resettlement, or convict transportation. Similarly, travel and circulation are major themes in the history of colonial and globalized sciences. What can we learn by bringing these histories into a common frame? How can we theorize the intersection of free and forced itineraries?
PA: This brings to mind James Clifford's prompt to rethink travel in a capacious sense, as a comparative concept that allows for "(problematic) translation" between people compelled by indenture, enslavement, or exile and the apparently unencumbered travels of colonial scientists. More recently, Linda Andersson Burnett urges attention to the "multiple mobilities of colonization," recognizing how European naturalists moved through the same circuits as pressed sailors and enslaved laborers. Indeed, colonial scientists frequently depended on unequal exchanges with Indigenous actors whom colonizers aggressively targeted with removal or sedentarization policies. Yet by attending to these frictional crossings and encounters we see that traveling savants and settler-scientists were themselves subject to controlled migratory channels, moving through what Clifford calls "highly determined circuits."

NBM: Like Pat, I think that, for the mid- to late nineteenth century at least, bringing the "free" itineraries of colonial scientists into a common frame with "forced" itineraries of laborers and convicts suggests that we understand mobility along a spectrum. Colonial scientists in this period certainly experienced "freer" itineraries than indentured migrants, but their movements could be constrained and compelled by political factors. It is unclear whether the German botanist, medic, and immigration commissioner that I have studied for the Kingdom of Hawai'i, Wilhelm Hillebrand, was forced to leave Germany in 1848 due to liberal political convictions. However, it is clear that many of his early botanical associates—including in Australia, the Philippines, and Hawai'i—were '48ers who had left for precisely that reason. In its prevailing legal sense today, political persecution is included in the category of forced migration along with enslavement and convict transportation. However, as these nineteenth-century scientific refugees show, there is no necessary conjuncture between forced migration and forced labor.

ZD: Early modern mobilities generated new "problems"—for example, high mortality and morbidity—in search of scientific "solutions," which in turn facilitated yet more mobility and new ideas about all sorts of things. As I argue in *Merchants of Medicines*, transoceanic movement hastened a turn toward viewing individuals as interchangeable patients who could benefit from similar remedies. Within such an ontological framework, a particular medicine could have the same effect on anybody in any location suffering the same affliction, regardless of age, sex, skin color, or rank. Consider how much simpler it would be for a ship's surgeon to identify an ailment across a crew and prescribe a remedy rather than individually assess the balance of each sailor's humors. European physicians could hardly comprehend treating alike the scores of people who found themselves moving about the Atlantic world along free and forced itineraries. That an enslaved person on a Caribbean plantation could receive a similar preparation of cinchona bark for a fever as a merchant in London or trading company employee in South Asia represented a radical idea at the time for the vision of human uniformity it implied. To put it another way, the scale of human mobility across the early modern European empires opened new overseas markets for medicines, prompting adjustments to preexisting therapeutic approaches.

KM: The "highly determined circuits" Pat mentions above prompt me to think about how many early English scientific endeavors relied on the network of slave ships crisscrossing the Atlantic to transport people, specimens, and knowledge. Quite simply, English imperial science was made possible by the infrastructure of the slave trade. In the seventeenth century the Royal Society did not have the resources to fund research trips, so, for instance, they sent collectors as passengers on slave ships. They depended on ship captains, sailors, and vessels involved in the slave trade, as well as on planters, to amass cabinets of curiosity and botanical gardens. Kathleen S. Murphy has followed natural philosophers' passage aboard slave ships, while James Delbourgo's work on Royal Society president Hans Sloane demonstrates the indebtedness of mobile seeds, specimens, and books that traversed the Atlantic from Jamaica to London to slavery. In these histories, the labor of enslaved people made transatlantic scientific mobility possible.

PA: Picking up on infrastructures of coerced labor, I have found that German savants deployed to Russian Siberia in the earlier nineteenth century moved through the circuits of the imperial exile system, following the footsteps of the three hundred thousand people banished beyond the Urals between 1823 and 1861. They geologized in mines barred with iron gates to lock convicts in the earth, surveyed from mountaintop prisons, and networked meteorology through the *katorga* system of penal labor. Critical here is the multiplicity of sites of coerced labor: the penal fortress in Omsk was penitentiary to some, an observatory to others.

The Siberian system of exile and inquiry exhibits a complex history of dependence: a history not only of the dependent labor of Russian convicts, serfs, and coerced settlers and enslaved or assimilated Indigenous groups but also of the way in which sciences depended on coercive labor and their routinized migrations. Here, then, is a problematic translation, as James Clifford urged. Of course, there is no equivalence between the savant and the Siberian convict. But recognizing the essential dependence of scientists afoot in geographies of unfreedom goes some ways toward understanding their vital role in the expansion and intensification of such systems.

JB: Mobility could also contribute to the status of naturalists, as in the context of a plantation colony in West Africa. The authority of their knowledge was derived not only from their education in Europe but was also, importantly, enhanced by their travel between colonial outposts in Asia, Africa, and the Americas. Traveling along "highly determined circuits" of commerce, slave trading, and empire, they made comparisons in pursuit of "universal" findings. Accumulated knowledge from travel also functioned as a form of accumulated social capital. The movements of naturalists defined the reach and viability of imperial networks from which they sourced the seeds of plants for their experiments. Before his time in Senegal from 1824 to 1829, the botanist George Perrottet had already traveled to Reunion, Java, and the Philippines, where he collected varieties of plants that he later experimented with growing in French Guyana. In Senegal, he planted indigo seeds imported from Guatemala and introduced the nopal cactus there in a bid to cultivate the cochineal insects that produced a bright red dye. French Caribbean planters sent enslaved or formerly enslaved workers with experience growing indigo in the Caribbean to Senegal to aid work on French plantations in Senegal.

Perrottet's mobility-fueled knowledge, backed by the power and reach of imperial networks, was to be contrasted with that of the "native" African farmer, whether free or enslaved, whose knowledge was presumably limited and inferior. Colonial records transformed the farmers into "laborers" whose value was to be measured in their "productivity." Findings from the experimental farms in Senegal were included in reports sent to the Académie des Sciences in Paris. Although abstracted without reference to the labor and material conditions of the farms, the links between commerce and labor in the production of scientific knowledge are clear. There was also, however, a larger history of indigo dyeing in West Africa beyond the colonial farms that remained opaque to early colonial naturalists. This artisanal history was shaped by the migration, settlement, and commercial histories of groups with specialist knowledge, such as Soninke and Fuulbe women dyers. Also, Africans and Afro-descendants on the move around the Atlantic and Indian Ocean as sailors, migrants, or enslaved people were also knowledge producers, although their archival footprint is generally less visible.

ZD: Our discussion of mobility reflects the ways each of us emphasize the significance of experiences outside European centers to the histories of science and medicine—though, as Jody notes, imperial power often shaped what was possible or visible beyond those centers. The encounters and itineraries of mobile people across the premodern world placed new demands on infrastructures designed to manage their labor and extract knowledge from their bodies.

4. In what ways, then, did the work of practitioners of science and medicine bolster coercive labor regimes by crafting racist claims about health and bodily differences? What were the implications for governance and populations more broadly?

KM: One reason I hope labor historians might be interested in these questions is that the English medical writers I examine were explicit about their search for foods and medicines that might sustain labor, enhance reproduction, and secure English claims to Jamaica. As I outlined in *An Empire Transformed*, colonial officials and promoters sought to remake the island's environment to suit colonizers' health and to plant sweet-smelling gardens of efficacious medicines to bolster the population. Now, I'm focused on the claims colonizers and medical writers made about which commodities could fuel more labor. In these instances, laboring bodies were themselves sites of medical and scientific experimentation. Stephanie E. Smallwood has explained how ship surgeons on slave trading vessels often experimented with supplying the minimal amount of food required to sustain a human life on the Middle Passage. Practitioners of science and medicine also made claims about racial differences that they sought to embed in bodies. Katherine Johnston has shown how Caribbean planters began to allege that Black bodies were better able to labor in hot climates than white bodies only to deflect calls for the end of the slave trade and to "justify" their proslavery stances with racist medical claims. In other words, colonial scientists and planters aimed to secure a steady supply of labor for the plantations by engaging in dehumanizing experimentation and fabricating myths.

Early modern English colonizers were interested in which Atlantic cultivars might be used as food and medicine to stimulate laboring bodies and enhance reproductive labor. I have been tracking Jamaican colonizers' claims that consuming cacao prepared as a chocolate drink could both boost women's fertility and power the daily labor of servants and the enslaved on the island, even if they were offered little other sustenance. My work suggests that colonizers' claims about chocolate should be read alongside pronatalist policies promoted by an increasingly vocal coterie of English officials who collected data on population size and women's reproductive health and invested in the slave trade. They sought to secure more labor and the birth of future laboring bodies, in service of an expanding empire. Physicians and planters imagined chocolate as a means to increase the population and to bolster the slave plantation regime on Jamaica.

ZD: Racial difference is such a powerful example of what is produced at the intersection of labor and science in early modernity. Understanding the racist claims about bodily difference that emerged from very specific medical and scientific contexts in the early modern world offers an opportunity for historians of twentieth-century labor to historicize the claims used to support coercive work regimes. For example, European medical practitioners attributed health outcomes they witnessed among enslaved people in the Caribbean to a higher tolerance for pain and heat inherent to people of African descent rather than, say, to coerced labor practices or a lack of adequate food or clothing. In this context, white bodies were seen to be more susceptible to fevers than those of Black folk, who were also believed to tolerate high doses of strong medicines, such as those prepared from mercury and antimony, for common plantation ailments like tapeworm or ulcers. Such observations were published in plantation manuals and health guides and eventually entered the European medical canon, where they provided evidence for theories of innate physiological differences. As Kate discusses as well, ideas (and anxieties) about health, labor, and authority often ran together in this period. The production of race in the context of early modern coercion still structures the present day, such as in the racial segmentation of labor markets, differential access to and outcomes from health care, and "race-norming" in US professional sports.

JB: By the early nineteenth century, Euro-Atlantic notions of race had already been shaped by centuries of Atlantic slave trading and, for the French, the loss of the important Saint-Domingue slave colony in 1804. In coastal Senegal, this discourse took the form of value-laden ethnographic descriptions by Europeans that categorized distinct African groups as alternately "an intelligent race," or "wildly deceitful" or "lazy." After European sailors and soldiers experienced high levels of mortality on the Senegal River, a commonsense notion emerged among French officials that Africans were better suited to labor in the local climate and also "closer" to nature. Botanists articulated these notions as much as other European observers, supporting a logic of racial othering at a period in which the cause of malaria was not yet understood. Their assessments had additional weight as comparative claims based on their experiences in parts of Asia and the Americas before arriving in Senegal.

PA: These responses point to a process by which claims about racial difference in the context of labor are then weaponized in the service of a broader biopolitics directed toward the management of "populations." One critical question here is how biopolitics rooted in plantations were adapted to settler-colonial projects, some of which repurposed claims about the alleged suitability of Black and brown people to particular forms of labor into schemes about the removal or ethnic cleansing of Indigenous and African-descended populations. In Brazil's mineral plantations, for instance, a Hessian mercenary-geologist inscribed Indigenous and West African nomenclature into a telling stratigraphy of annihilation that consigned Amerindian and Afro-Brazilian workers to prehistory. This by the same agent (the director of mines in Minas Gerais) who rigorously tabulated population statistics to argue for the replacement of Black Brazilians by government-subsidized European settlers.

A related process played out above ground, as other colonial agents mapped Indigenous labor into discrete elevational zones, in upland mines and farms of the Andes and the central Mexican plateau. Not only early modern slavers, then, but also anticolonial activists built climatic theories of race into their designs for new nation-states in Latin America. The Prussian Alexander von Humboldt worked closely with members of the Creole elite in viceregal Colombia and Mexico to map the vertical arrangement of climatic bands in the Americas, from tropical lowlands up to frigid Andean heights. These mappings also enrolled climatic theories of race to demarcate the supposed suitability of Indigenous labor at high elevations, clearing more "temperate" slopes for white settlement. Naturalizing colonial histories of Indigenous removal and forced labor, these cartographies fixed notions of climatic "fitness" into political economy at a decisive moment of Creole-dominated state formation. Taken together, both episodes show how early modern logics of racial difference were remapped onto apparently novel arrangements of social order around 1800. White and Creole actors who claimed European heritage repurposed the logic of plantation enslavement into settler regimes of evacuation.

NBM: Here I think it is important to consider what labor historians—particularly those focused on the colonial politics of labor—might add to accounts of the production of social and racial differences couched within the history of medical thought. As Kate was pointing to earlier, tropical plantation colonies throughout the seventeenth, eighteenth, and nineteenth centuries were sites of nearly obsessive debates about population and labor migration. In these discussions, naturalized bodily differences, including the putative "fitness" (or not) for agricultural work noted earlier by Jody and Zack, were prominent though often contested. The German botanist I have studied for Hawai'i, Wilhelm Hillebrand, advocated repeatedly for German homesteaders, who he thought could grow sugar on an independent model despite the climate (this experiment was never tried, though several hundred Germans did migrate to Hawaiian plantations in the late nineteenth century on indentured modalities). Cristiana Bastos has studied how Portuguese laborers—namely from the Atlantic islands of Madeira and the Azores—constituted a type of liminal category, as European but not quite white, whose putative ancestral connection to sugar cultivation (imagined in the case of the Azores, several centuries antedated in the case of Madeira) qualified them for fieldwork in the colonial plantations of British Guiana and Trinidad in the mid-nineteenth century, followed by Hawai'i in the late nineteenth century. As the self-serving racist conceits of New World planters and plantation statesmen became embedded within medical science during the eighteenth and nineteenth centuries, coethnic and eventually coracial settler-colonial aspirations dovetailed with ever adaptive forms of labor exploitation to result in local variations on-site.

5. It is clear that coercion and dependence are an intersection where labor and science meet, but recent scholarship has also underscored that coercion is multimodal and dependence is a spectrum. Given this variety, how do distinctive modes of coercion or dependence shape the histories you write? Can we move from the specifics of these histories to more theoretical perspectives?

NBM: In studying what I term the grafting of plantation complexes across the globe after the early nineteenth century, indentured labor serves as the reference mode of coercion and domination in my historical contexts. Following the abolition of the Atlantic slave trade and then ultimately of slavery across European empires and independent, Creole-dominated American states during the nineteenth century, new tactics for bonded labor migration known as indenture emerged wherein laborers bound themselves to work at a specific plantation or plantation colony for a defined period of time, thus satisfying a legal criterion of "free" labor. Actual practices on the ground—including forced contract renewals, deceit, and the misrendering of contractual provisions—belie this distinction. A great volume of work has pursued the commensurability—or not—of indentured labor in the nineteenth and early twentieth centuries with slavery and earlier forms of contract labor. Building on the work of Alessandro Stanziani and Richard Allen, my approach instead understands what might be termed postabolition indenture as itself produced by the entanglement of labor and science. As I show in my work situated in the Kingdom of Hawaiʻi, the scientific networks forged by individual scientists—particularly botanists—provided a primary avenue through which evolving tactics for labor bondage circulated across and beyond imperial space during the long nineteenth century. As implied by the term *colonial science*, scientists operating in colonial spaces—and dependent on the employment or patronage of contemporary governments and planter societies—were inextricably entangled with the labor systems of their time.

KM: The early modern period was when some of the dichotomies (mind/body, science/labor) that we've discussed and have been crucial to justifying coercive labor regimes were amplified, for a variety of reasons. Many of the scientists from this period disavowed the hands-on, dangerous, and difficult work of knowledge production. Authors of gardening treatises such as John Evelyn were quick to point out that they were philosophical gardeners, not "cabbage planters" doing the actual labor of gardening. They did not risk their bodies, but they were willing to risk the bodies of others. They often defined what counted as science as antithetical to labor. They created hierarchies of knowledge that privileged mental labor over physical labor and integrated them alongside other kinds of racial, class, and gender hierarchies. A false divergence between bodies and minds was made to seem real in plantations, mines, and other sites of coerced labor when there were myriad incentives to claim and harden these distinctions and to disparage material, hands-on knowledge. Terms like *knowledge work* remind us of the labor involved in scientific endeavors and encourage us to consider the many individuals involved in creating science, often under dangerous, unhealthy, and coercive circumstances, akin to conditions Zack writes about.

 Colonial knowledge often emerged out of the processes and practices of physical work in regimes of coerced labor. Terms like *embodied science* further encourage scholars to think about how knowledge work takes place in conversation with material things. English medical writers were often explicit about the usefulness of the senses to their work. They smelled, touched, tasted, listened to, and examined materials and bodies. Those who made claims about the power of chocolate to enhance reproductive labor in Jamaica were embedded in medical traditions that emphasized the ways the human senses shaped women's reproductive health and pregnant bodies. They made claims about controlling the functioning of the womb through scents that ranged from "sweet" to "stinking," and they understood women's humoral bodies as particularly porous and open to environmental conditions. Attention to women's bodies, particularly their reproductive labor, was an important aspect of colonial science.

ZD: The study of work processes—core to labor history—directs attention to the embodied experience of toiling in the sweltering heat of a pharmaceutical manufactory boiling aromatic roots for an antimalarial tincture or breathing the toxic fumes from a distillation of vitriol (sulfuric acid). At every scale, from kitchen to pharmacy, preparing medicines was a corporeal process and largely continues to be. Reading laboratory notes, medical texts, and business records has led me to think about the entanglement of labor, medicine, and empire in terms of the physical toll of that work—chemical burns, for instance, but also the more mundane risks of smoke inhalation and fatigue.

Impairment and disablement are both by-products and tactics, as Nic uses the term, of coercion that we have not yet mentioned in our conversation. I have been thinking about the physical and mental impairment that occurred in care-related spaces, in part inspired by Stefanie Hunt-Kennedy's *Between Fitness and Death* that details the ways enslavers sought to keep the enslaved in a state "where their bodies were too broken to rebel but fit enough for forced labor." I've found that in the British Royal Navy, medical evaluators gave monetary values to injuries sustained during service, selectively marking some impairments as disabilities that carried legal, and labor, implications. Some of these impairments could be quite visible, such as the loss of an arm or leg, or, in the case of damage to one's reproductive organs, largely invisible. Either way, work reshaped one's relationship to one's own body and the world around it in ways that often intensified under coercive or scientific modes of labor organization.

JB: Multiple and overlapping modes of coercion and dominance organized nineteenth-century colonial plantations in Senegal that the French envisioned as an alternative to Caribbean slave plantations. One in particular for the French was of course language, specifically the modality of written words and figures used for accounting, recordkeeping, contracts, and treaties. This method of attempting to fix social relations and secure access to land through commitments on paper had limited effect. There were thus contrasting modes of domination being exercised between the French and African states that remained in tension—until later in the nineteenth century, when the accumulated European technological and economic advantages allowed them to break this pattern.

I'm struck by how the published accounts by the botanist Perrottet gloss over labor tensions, although the archival records reveal more. Perrottet's premise seemed to be that he could make the constraints of the local landscape of Senegal irrelevant by bringing seeds, tools, and "expertise" from elsewhere to produce a crop for export out of West Africa. Yet the agricultural farms weren't able ultimately to overcome the constraints of either the environment or labor, nor did they effectively engage local "expertise." This brings us back to the quest of many naturalists for "the universal" or findings that were generalizable across space and populations, which has come up a few times in this roundtable thus far and which has some problematic implications. My approach has been to focus on how local "knowledge workers" (to use the phrase

Kate is suggesting) practiced their specialized crafts, even transferring knowledge to others while working within volatile environmental and political constraints.

6. Final thoughts! What remains unanswered for you? What new directions do you see at the intersection of coerced labor and colonial science?

PA: This conversation works toward a history of the dependent epistemologies that endure in racial capitalism and other forms of inequality: ways of knowing based in colonizers' extraction of value from unfree humans. Kate shows, for instance, how British slavers judged medical and natural knowledge by its capacity to manipulate the bodies of enslaved Africans and maximize their labor. Here was a theory of knowledge that shows how natural and medical sciences were coproduced with the Plantationocene, as Nic explored at the outset of our discussion. This history should also account for the perverse mechanisms by which some of those same sciences became associated, like capitalism itself, with liberation. Consider anecdotal accounts of the manumission of enslaved and enserfed actors for deeds of scientific servitude (as collectors, guides, or cartographers). In Brazilian diamond mines, said one slaving geologist, the price of freedom was 17.5 carats. In Russian Siberia, an enserfed cartographer was freed for mapping gold and platinum alluviations at the behest of mercenary-geologists. These scientific customs are telling, as J'Nese Williams writes of botany in Caribbean context, precisely because they are the exceptions that prove the rule: the conditional freedom of some dependent laborers shows the essential unfreedom on which sciences depended. They can be read, like our conversation, as prompts to pursue a more capacious study of the many forms of peonage and precarity on which modern configurations of knowledge and power still depend.

ZD: What a great point with which to end, Pat. Rather than reiterate your nudge to pursue a more capacious study of precarity, I'll close by mentioning that the methodologies of doing this work can be fraught. As current discussions about the politics of the archive and, frankly, the politics of the profession have demonstrated—the responses to Judith Carney's *Black Rice* come to mind—there remains a lack of consensus about how to engage in recovery work. This is especially true of a labor history of science where who is permitted to "do" science has been carefully guarded for centuries and archival evidence that might expand that group has been obscured, intentionally and not. Nevertheless, this work is crucial to understanding the hierarchies that continue to underlie, and get reinforced by, knowledge work.

KM: As Zack and Jody have noted, histories of scientific labor have often been silenced. While the records may hide their stories, many individuals have toiled in knowledge-making enterprises, and this conversation underscores the importance of thinking about science and labor as entangled. While historians are increasingly attentive, say, to the "invisible" and uncredited labor of household members in the production of early modern medicine, or to the role of enslaved or Native people in histories of "colonial science," there is much work to be done to excavate specific actors, sites, processes, and modes of labor.

NBM: One takeaway I have from our discussion is the importance of interweaving consideration of systems and actors in histories of labor and science. The longstanding historiographical separation of labor and science perhaps stemmed from insufficient consideration of the porousness of both domains. Our discussion has provided many examples of interactions between "scientists" and "laborers" in various colonial contexts around the globe since the seventeenth century. We have all noted how various types of Western "scientists"—botanists in the case of Jody and me; medical practitioners with Kate and Zack; and even "mercenary" mining technicians by Pat—drew on the knowledge of coerced laborers—enslaved, indentured, and convict—to perform their knowledge work. This was a case not just of extraction or collection but, rather, of negotiation, translation, and even dependence on laboring actors who were traditionally perceived as beyond the pale of science but had distinctive routes to realms of knowledge that eluded these scientists. Future work might explore these actor relationships and tensions processually, revealing the coproduced character of colonial science and coerced labor.

JB: I think that is right, Nic. Work that pays careful attention to relational process and the coproduced nature of colonial science—while also holding on to the way inequalities of social and economic power shaped that "coproduction"—would be illuminating. What also stays with me from this roundtable discussion is the importance of continuing to question and historicize not only *how* scientific knowledge has been produced in particular instances but also under what conditions and *by whom*. Future work could pay more attention to knowledge produced *through* labor and to the voices and perspectives of laborers whose inputs have largely been invisibilized. It is important in my view to continue to carefully study the historical processes of extraction or of invisibilizing coercive relations because they allow us to theorize not only how such relations may continually reproduce themselves but also, more critically, how they might be reimagined.

PATRICK ANTHONY is an Irish Research Council Fellow at University College Dublin and a research partner of the project "Instructing Natural History: Nature, People, Empire" at Uppsala University. He is currently writing a history of extractive industries and environmental sciences that linked central Europe to Ibero-America and northern Eurasia in the long nineteenth century.

JODY BENJAMIN is assistant professor of history at the University of California, Riverside, and lead PI of the Mellon Sawyer Seminar 2022–23, "Unarchiving Blackness." His book *The Texture of Change: Dress, Self-Fashioning, and History in Western Africa, 1700–1850* is forthcoming.

ZACHARY DORNER is assistant professor of history at the University of Maryland, College Park, and is the author of *Merchants of Medicines: The Commerce and Coercion of Health in Britain's Long Eighteenth Century* (2020).

NICHOLAS B. MILLER is assistant professor of history at Flagler College and coeditor of the forthcoming volume *Plantation Knowledge*. His research was advanced through a project funded by the European Union's Horizon 2020 research and innovation program under the Marie Skłodowska-Curie Grant No. 889078.

KATE LUCE MULRY is associate professor of history at California State University, Bakersfield, and is the author of *An Empire Transformed: Remolding Bodies and Landscapes in the Restoration Atlantic* (2021).

References

Allen, Richard B. "Slaves, Convicts, Abolitionism and the Global Origins of the Post-emancipation Indentured Labor System." *Slavery and Abolition* 35, no. 2 (2014): 328–48.

Bastos, Cristiana, Andrea Novoa, and Noel B. Salazar. "Mobile Labour: An Introduction." *Mobilities* 16, no. 2 (2021): 155–63.

Burnett, Linda Andersson. "Collecting Humanity in the Age of Enlightenment: The Hudson's Bay Company and Edinburgh University's Natural History Museum." *Global Intellectual History*, June 14, 2022. https://doi.org/10.1080/23801883.2022.2074502.

Carney, Judith. *Black Rice: The African Origins of Rice Cultivation in the Americas*. Cambridge, MA: Harvard University Press, 2001.

Clifford, James. *Routes: Travel and Translation in the Late Twentieth Century*. Cambridge, MA: Harvard University Press, 1997.

Delbourgo, James. *Collecting the World: Hans Sloane and the Origins of the British Museum*. Cambridge, MA: Belknap Press of Harvard University Press, 2017.

Dorner, Zachary. *Merchants of Medicines: The Commerce and Coercion of Health in Britain's Long Eighteenth Century*. Chicago: University of Chicago Press, 2020.

Haraway, Donna. "Anthropocene, Capitalocene, Plantationocene, Chthulucene: Making Kin." *Environmental Humanities* 6, no. 1 (2015): 159–65.

Hunt-Kennedy, Stefanie. *Between Fitness and Death: Disability and Slavery in the Caribbean*. Urbana: University of Illinois Press, 2020.

Johnston, Katherine. *The Nature of Slavery: Environment and Plantation Labor in the Anglo-Atlantic World*. Oxford: Oxford University Press, 2022.

Lawson, James. *A New Voyage to Carolina*. London, 1709.

Mulry, Kate Luce. *An Empire Transformed: Remolding Bodies and Landscapes in the Restoration Atlantic*. New York: New York University Press, 2021.

Murphy, Kathleen S. "Collecting Slave Traders: James Petiver, Natural History, and the British Slave Trade." *William and Mary Quarterly* 70, no. 4 (2013): 637–70.

Schär, Bernhard. "Switzerland, Borneo and the Dutch Indies: Towards a New Imperial History of Europe, c. 1770–1850." *Past and Present* 257 (November 2022): 134–67.

Schiebinger, Londa. *Secret Cures of Slaves: People, Plants, and Medicine in the Eighteenth-Century Atlantic World*. Stanford, CA: Stanford University Press, 2017.

Smallwood, Stephanie E. *Saltwater Slavery: A Middle Passage from Africa to American Diaspora*. Cambridge, MA: Harvard University Press, 2007.

Stanziani, Alessandro. *Bondage: Labor and Rights in Eurasia from the Sixteenth to the Early Twentieth Centuries*. New York: Berghahn, 2014.

von Humboldt, Alexander. *Kosmos: Entwurf einer physischen Weltbeschreibung*. Vol. 1. Stuttgart: Cotta, 1845.

Williams, J'Nese. "Plantation Botany: Slavery and the Infrastructure of Government Science in the St. Vincent Botanic Garden, 1765–1820s." *Berichte zur Wissenschaftsgeschichte* 44, no. 2 (2021): 137–58.

Wolford, Wendy. "The Plantationocene: A Lusotropical Contribution to the Theory." *Annals of the American Association of Geographers* 111, no. 6 (2021): 1622–39.

Whence Automation? The History (and Possible Futures) of a Concept

Salem Elzway and Jason Resnikoff

ChatGPT burst onto the scene at the end of 2022, and with it came yet another over-heated discussion in the press about the supposedly imminent end of work. In the months that followed, artificial intelligence (AI) gained renewed media attention as the latest in automation, now poised to become a decisive historical force that would unilaterally destroy jobs and change the face of work. To get a sense of the tone, *Time* magazine referred to it by turns as both a "revolution" and "the end of humanity."[1]

The past decade has witnessed a renewed interest in the history—and possible futures—of automation. For about a generation after World War II, automation was a ubiquitous concern across the industrialized world and particularly in the United States. While the fervor over automation began to wane in the 1970s, the mass unemployment following the Great Recession, the accelerating precarity of working people, and the considerable economic and political power of Big Tech, led to a renaissance in the fortunes of automation in the early twenty-first century.[2]

As one might expect, automation's big splash in the 2010s led to a wave of scholarly attention. The first and most obvious conclusion to come out of the new scholarship is that automation has not, in fact, meant a revolution in the social relations of production. Human beings continue to labor, often quite hard, and often in workplaces that employers and outside observers have nevertheless called automated. Recent studies have demonstrated the persistence of human labor throughout the global economy and in some of the most spectacularly "automated" labor processes, from service work, to online platforms, to the very operations of AI itself.[3] This dis-

We would like to thank Seth Rockman for stewarding this essay along as well as Joshua Freeman and Julie Greene for their helpful comments.

1. Cover story, *Time*, June 12, 2023.

2. Frey and Osborne, "Future of Employment"; *Transformative Impact of Robots and Automation*.

3. Benanav, *Automation and the Future of Work*; Smith, *Smart Machines and Service Work*; Crawford, *Atlas of AI*.

Labor: Studies in Working-Class History, Volume 21, Issue 1
DOI 10.1215/15476715-10948907   © 2024 by Labor and Working-Class History Association

covery has troubled the waters for historians of both labor and science and technology, who as recently as just a few years ago took "automation" to be a clear-cut technical phenomenon, a hard-and-fast element of capital, what David Noble famously called one of the "forces of production."[4] While automation functions as a synonym for "labor-saving" technologies that will accelerate productive output, the reality is that work organized under the umbrella of "automation" has only saved some people's labor while intensifying, devaluing, and degrading others'. Productivity has been extracted, therefore, not through the magic of technology but through intensified modes of making the laboring body conform to the machine in the service of lowering production costs and generating corporate profits.

Automation discourse nonetheless continues to hold a great deal of explanatory authority if not power, offering a seductive and ready-to-hand teleological narrative about history, work, and technological change. The word *automation*, like the term *science*, functions to obscure political choice and contingency behind seemingly incontestable and objective realities. Science, Technology, and Society (STS) offers several analytical tools that can enable labor historians to break out of these narrative traps by stripping terms like *automation* of their explanatory authority, and to get an idea just how much of the labor process remains contingent and open to political negotiation. Using this framework, we can recognize how the automation discourse fails to explain changes to the workplace over the better part of the past century and can see more clearly what automation really has been: a powerful discursive mechanism within the political economy of capitalism to shroud class domination, labor exploitation, and work degradation in the language of "progress." The frameworks provided by STS allow us to see how "automation" was, in fact, the codification of class domination in the American technopolitical regime of the postwar period.

Technopolitics and the Origins of the Automation Discourse

The term *automation* is of relatively recent vintage. Coined by then–General Motors (GM) factory manager Delmar "Del" Harder in 1936, the term gained public life after Harder established an Automation Department at the rival Ford Motor Company in 1947. The first print appearance of *automation* came in the October 1948 issue of *American Machinist*, while the term entered the broader public conversation in an April 1950 *New York Times* article that described it as "the newest production science in industry." As is common with such designations, determining what made automation "scientific" was not itself a scientific process, although the article was happy to call automation the "science" of "automatically handling a product to and from a machine or assembly operation without physical effort."[5] By the time John Diebold published his book *Automation: The Advent of the Automation Factory* in 1952, making *automation* a household term, the word's status had far outstripped whatever tech-

4. Noble, *Forces of Production*; Hounshell, "Automation, Transfer Machinery, and Mass Production"; Bix, *Inventing Ourselves out of Jobs?*
5. "Automatic Devices Sweeping Industry," *New York Times*, April 16, 1950, F1.

nical rigor it had once possessed, becoming instead the postwar period's watchword for technological progress itself.[6]

The emergence of this automation discourse in mid-twentieth-century America serves as a potent example of what scholars in the interdisciplinary field of STS call *sociotechnical imaginaries.* According to Sheila Jasanoff and Sang-Hyun Kim, sociotechnical imaginaries are "collectively held, institutionally stabilized, and publicly performed visions of desirable futures, animated by shared understandings of forms of social life and social order attainable through, and supportive of, advances in science and technology."[7] Beyond any particular technical innovation, the automation discourse arose when it did as a result of exigencies of postwar American politics and its technological enthusiasm, which held out the promise that the United States had the power not only to split atoms and construct electronic brains (that is, computers) but to fundamentally revise the industrial order itself.[8] Scientific advance, in the sociotechnical imaginary of the automation discourse, appeared on the verge of abolishing the industrial proletariat, replacing the semiskilled and unskilled physical labor of blue-collar workers with the brain work of white-collar professionals and effecting a nationwide upgrade of all Americans into the middle class. "The scientist and the engineer," said UAW president Walter Reuther in 1957, "are providing us with the physical means by which our material problems can be solved."[9] Rather than socially situated actors embedded in the broader sociotechnical systems of capitalism, these technical workers were mystified agents of "progress," ideologically shielded from their role in putting automation to work. "Automation," therefore, did not mean merely more mechanization nor even any specific scientific or technological innovation. Instead, contemporaries used the term to describe all manner of sociotechnical capabilities, some new and some old, to describe an ostensibly unprecedented historical era.[10]

The discourse and practice of automation quickly evolved into powerful exemplars of what STS scholars call *technopolitics*—the practice of conceptualizing, developing, and using technologies to accomplish political goals that would otherwise be more difficult or impossible to achieve, as well as the concomitant process of shaping politics to facilitate the development of these technologies.[11] For instance, in the automobile industry, where "Detroit automation" became a synecdoche of the phenomenon more broadly, the most important innovation spurring automation was

6. Bright, *Automation and Management*, 4–5; Diebold, *Automation.*

7. Jasanoff and Kim, *Dreamscapes of Modernity*, 4.

8. Resnikoff, *Labor's End.*

9. "Automation and the Second Industrial Revolution," resolution adopted by the UAW Sixteenth Constitutional Convention, 1957, Atlantic City, NJ, file 47, box 26, Ted F. Silvey Collection, accession no. 625, Walter P. Reuther Library.

10. D. S. Harder, "Address before the Quad-City Conference on Automation at the Davenport Masonic Temple, Davenport, Iowa, on August 27, 1954," file 24, box 45, UAW President's Office, Walter P. Reuther Collection, Accession No. 261, Walter P. Reuther Library.

11. Hecht, *Entangled Geographies*; Mitchell, *Rule of Experts*; Noble, *Forces of Production.*

not technological but political: the rise of a militant industrial labor movement in the 1930s that had entrenched the country's most powerful union, the UAW, on the shop floor. But whereas the Big Three auto corporations could maintain an openly anti-union position in the 1930s, outright hostility to the principle of organized labor had become politically untenable in the years following the war and the rise of an apparent liberal consensus. The widespread technological optimism of automation offered the Ford Motor Company, which only recognized the UAW in 1941, a way to square the circle. When the company's engineers designed new machines, time-studied the motions of workers to further the division of labor, reorganized the layout of the factory floor, degraded job classifications through deskilling, or fired workers who were deemed extraneous to the productive process, it was not, they claimed, to be understood as an attempt to weaken the union but merely management's reaction to the iron dictates of technological development. The contingencies of capital accumulation, the dynamics of managerial discretion, and the naturalization of social processes were all occluded by and sublimated in "automation." That *people* made choices about the who, what, where, when, why, and how of automation was essentially (and conveniently for some) absent from popular conversation about what was almost invariably conceptualized as a purely technical phenomenon. A key dimension of technopolitics, therefore, is the displacement of power onto the artifacts, systems, and practices commonly called "technology," a process that often camouflages power rather than illuminating it.

Union leaders found themselves hard-pressed to articulate alternate visions of an ideal world in which working people might exercise a measure of democratic control over the means of production, for the automation discourse served to depict the divorce of working people from any claim to ownership they might have over their jobs as the very definition of scientific advance. In addition to the perennial conflict between labor and management, with the rise of the automation discourse the labor movement now had to weave the story of scientific development into its political program and was hard-pressed to criticize the very forces that were, potentially, endangering the working conditions of union members. As one official for the Communications Workers of America warned union leadership that same year, they did not want "the labor movement becoming identified as 'weepers' on this subject" of scientific advance. Officials should instead "use our influence to get AFL-CIO spokesmen to point not only to the problems and difficulties of automation but to acknowledge the tremendous benefits it provides."[12]

This was especially unfortunate considering that most of the changes inaugurated under the aegis of "automation" did not eliminate human labor but, rather, degraded it. Throughout the postwar period, workers laboring in supposedly automated workplaces complained of mandatory overtime, dangerous conditions, a relentless pace of production, and the degradation of jobs so that one person was made to

12. Sylvia Gottlieb to J. A. Beirne, Subject: Automation Sub-Committee—AFL-CIO Economic Policy Committee, January 16, 1957, folder 8, box 100: Communications Workers of America Records, Wag. 124, Tamiment Library and Robert F. Wagner Labor Archive, New York University.

do the work of many. Across the board, job degradation became a hallmark of post-war automation, from meatpacking to coal mining to office work.[13]

From Productivity to Technoscience

Looking at the grand sweep of human history, increasing labor productivity won through technological and scientific development has, paradoxically, not meant the reduction in the amount of work people generally do. Quite the opposite: innovation and development have led to both increased productivity *and* more work under unvaryingly hierarchical conditions.[14] Astounding breakthroughs in agriculture and manufacturing have not translated into the long-predicted era of leisure. Undoubtedly, industrial civilization gained new powers and new capacities for abundance as new technologies made it more productive. But these achievements occurred within the framework of capitalist social relations where increases in productivity have resulted in not an end of work but, instead, a further intensification of work, a search for new resources, and the endless pursuit of profit and power.[15]

The story of the automation discourse in the postwar period provides one example of this phenomenon. Workers themselves described "automation" at Ford—its ostensible birthplace—as a speedup. Between 1947 and 1957, Ford witnessed a 0.5 percent increase in employment and a 50 percent increase in production. During the same period, the automobile corporations' before-tax profits increased by approximately 300 percent, while average wages increased by 70 percent.[16] And indeed, these productive increases spelled enormous changes at Ford. For example, the company hailed its Brook Park plant as a showpiece of "automation" when it was completed in 1951. But back at the more antiquated River Rouge facility (described only a few decades earlier as the epitome of mass production), Black workers were assigned the worst jobs and experienced discrimination in discipline, pay, and treatment. Local 600 at the Rouge was one of the most militant in the industry and a continual headache for both Ford's management and the UAW's leadership. The primary products at the Rouge included engines, the exact product Ford's Automation Department designed the Brook Park plant to produce. The shift of engine production from Detroit to Cleveland caused employment at the Rouge to drop off a cliff from a post–World War II high of eighty-five thousand workers to thirty thousand by 1960, which in turn significantly weakened Local 600. Workers at the Rouge, and Black workers in particular, therefore had not only their jobs but also their political power within the industry "automated" away—away to the Brook Park plant, that is.

Such an outcome had less to do with the technical changes to the labor process and more to do with the technical language of collective bargaining. In 1950, Reuther famously negotiated the "Treaty of Detroit" with GM that gave management exclusive rights to decide what to produce, where to produce, and how to produce—

---

13. Resnikoff, *Labor's End.*
14. Schor, *Overworked American*, chap. 3; Scott, *Against the Grain*, chap. 5.
15. Fressoz, "Pour une histoire désorientée de l'énergie."
16. *Administered Prices*, vii, 2207.

technically called "production standards" and pithily captured in the phrase "[management's] right to manage"—while the UAW was given exclusive rights to bargain for higher wages and better benefits. In other words, management could make at-will changes to the means of production, while the union was left to fight over labor's share of income. Five years after the treaty was signed, Jack Conway, administrative assistant to Walter Reuther and chair of the UAW's Committee on Automation, described the broad mechanics of the arrangement: "When management makes decisions to 'automate' production, it becomes necessary for workers through their union to 'automate' the wage, classification and seniority structures in the plants. Just as old machinery becomes obsolete in the new technology, so do wage rates, job classifications, seniority groupings, and wage payment methods."[17] But there was a catch: the UAW's income gains were tied to the industry's productivity (itself yoked to economic growth more generally), which incentivized more "automation"—that is, more capital investment. Furthermore, the UAW's rank and file were left to bargain at the local level with management over production standards and worker discipline, the two key dimensions of the automation discourse on the shop floor. Union leadership thus made a devil's bargain: increasing productivity could raise labor's share of income, and it could also defang the union's primary source of power, its membership, through weakened shop-floor control.

Automation, in addition to its sociotechnical imaginaries and technopolitics, was also a signal example of *technoscience*, a bricolage category describing the increasingly inseparable domains of engineering, science (both physical and social), and technology that emerged during and after World War II.[18] Like other technosciences, such as aerospace engineering, microbiology, and nuclear physics, management's mechanization project ushered in under the aegis of "automation" was capital intensive, required highly skilled practitioners for its design and implementation, and was intended to dominate the physical world rather than simply "discover" how it worked. The Cold War setting of automation's emergence in the late 1940s and early 1950s imbued the phenomenon with geopolitical significance, as the fight against communism was imagined not just as an existential war of ideology and military might but as a demonstration of capitalism's capacity for generating the technoscience that would strengthen the economy and thereby national security. As a result, the development of automation was deeply embedded in the "military-industrial complex"—perhaps the most powerful technopolitical assemblage in human history—and envisioned as a weapon in the nation's Cold War arsenal.[19]

The automation discourse quickly metabolized the language of the Cold War and national security more broadly. John Diebold, the most prominent "evangelist for

17. Jack Conway, "Labor Looks at Automation," 8, April 13, 1955, folder: Automation Committee, 1954–1964, box 45: UAW President's Office, Walter P. Reuther Records, Walter P. Reuther Library, Wayne State University, Detroit.

18. Haraway, *Modest_Witness@Second_Millennium*; Latour, *Science in Action*; Mackenzie, *Inventing Accuracy*.

19. Elzway, "Arms of the State."

automation," argued, "It is only by increasing output per manhour worked [i.e., productivity] that we will be able to build effective defense against the aggressive powers of communism. And it is only by this means that we will be able to enlist the effective support of the people of the free world in this cause."[20] In similar Dieboldian language, John I. Snyder Jr.—president of an industrial conglomerate with sizable military contracts that manufactured automation machinery and commercialized the first industrial robot—testified at the 1955 congressional hearings on automation that "it [could] prove dangerous to limit automation in face of the present international political situation." As a result, he continued, America's "dominance" abroad could be assured only by its "preponderance in productivity" at home.[21] Testifying at the same hearing, Walter Reuther concurred, calling for the United States to "take advantage of the rising productivity that automation makes possible to increase our national strength and improve living standards at the same time."[22] "I believe," he elaborated, "that this developing technology [automation] is going to put in the hands of freemen the tools with which they can prove that the Communists are wrong."[23]

To realize the sociotechnical imaginary of a "preponderance of productivity" was exceedingly expensive and remarkably risky, which disincentivized private actors from individually investing in the forces of production that purportedly grounded such power. Corporate executives, government bureaucrats, labor leaders, politicians, and prominent scientists, therefore, tasked the federal government and the military specifically as the financier of first resort with underwriting the computers, industrial robots, and numerically controlled machine tools, as well as the suite of managerial practices and theories such as operations research, rational choice theory, and systems analysis that made up "automation." Whether in isolation or in concert, many of these practices and technologies would make their way to the shop floor, and by the early 1960s the American state's support for the underlying principles of automation—high productivity at the expense of the working class—was undeniable. As autoworker and radical activist James Boggs observed in 1963,

> The great bulk of the capital invested in automation today comes from the government and is paid for by every member of the American population, whether he is a worker, a member of the middle class, or rich. This is all done in the name of research and defense, but, whatever it is called, the benefits are as great to the capitalists as if they had put out the capital themselves. Thus the capitalists have found a way to get around the high cost of automation.[24]

In other words, while the automation discourse sold technological innovation and the promises of progress it entailed as products of "free enterprise" and "the market," in reality the "Invisible Hand" of automation was attached to the "Invisible Arm" of the

20. Diebold, *Automation*, 170; Burgin, "Market Politics in an Age of Automation," 147, 163.
21. *Automation and Technological Change*, 565.
22. *Automation and Technological Change*, 112.
23. *Automation and Technological Change*, 117.
24. Boggs, *American Revolution*, 103–4.

Pentagon, and the technopolitics of socializing the costs of developing automation to fight "socialism" was an irony seemingly (or conveniently) lost on the power elite who supported such processes.

Automation, State Technopolitics, and the Civil Rights Movement

As the technoscience emerging from these developments diffused more broadly throughout the economy, policymakers and their allies inside and outside the Kennedy and Johnson administrations began directly referring to "automation" in their shaping of the state's reaction to unemployment. Nonetheless, legislation such as the Area Redevelopment Act (1961) and the Manpower Development and Training Act (1962), both of which were designed to assist technologically displaced workers through targeted community investment, unemployment insurance extensions, and vocational retraining programs, proved ineffectual. Additionally, a lack of consensus within the administration stalled any significant action on the issues beyond creating momentum for an official congressional commission on automation. Furthermore, officials in the Bureau of the Budget, the Council of Economic Advisers (CEA), and the Department of Commerce were skeptical that the unemployment accompanying automation was a problem and held that even if it was, the dislocations were natural, temporary, and solvable through Keynesian-induced economic growth—the imagined panacea to all social problems during the period. Walter Heller, for example, Kennedy's CEA chairman, argued that while the "human fallout" of technological displacement had to be addressed, automation was "the key to faster growth and our ability to compete in world markets."[25]

A policy document accompanying Heller's statement declared, "We have accepted the costs [of automation] as part of the price of progress."[26] But the "human fallout" who bore the cost of the "price of progress" was not a secret then and it will definitely not surprise historians now: African American workers were disproportionately the victims of automation and made up an increasingly larger proportion of the unemployed. The "science" of industrial relations still entailed discriminatory practices that relegated Black workers to the worst jobs, while the political economy of military-funded technoscience channeled resources and technical capacities to the managers of automation, who only exacerbated the issue. In the auto industry, the degradation of work accompanying "automation" overwhelmingly fell, literally, on the backs of Black workers. Jobs that had previously occupied two, three, or even

25. Walter Heller to President Kennedy, "Automation: Menace or Millennium?," November 20, 1963, folder: Automation: Menace or Millennium? [November 6–December 13, 1963], Files of Walter W. Heller: Subject Files, Council of Economic Advisers under President Johnson, Proquest History Vault, https://hv-proquest-com.proxy.lib.umich.edu/pdfs/100371/100371_001_1201/100371_001_1201_From_1_to_10.pdf, 1.

26. Council of Economic Advisors, "Suggested Conceptual Framework for LMAC Inquiry into Technological Change and Unemployment," November 6, 1963, folder: Automation: Menace or Millennium? [November 6–December 13, 1963], Files of Walter W. Heller: Subject Files, Council of Economic Advisers under President Johnson, https://hv-proquest-com.proxy.lib.umich.edu/pdfs/100371/100371_001_1201/100371_001_1201_From_1_to_10.pdf, 1.

four white workers were now being done by a single Black worker.[27] Black workers often referred to the automation speedup as "n*****mation," or "the process of forcing humans to work harder and faster under increasingly unsafe and unhealthy conditions."[28] Simon Owens, autoworker and editor of the Detroit-based radical labor journal *News and Letters* (better known by his pen name, Charles Denby), described the physical effects of automation on workers with headlines like "We Don't Use the Machine; the Machine Uses Us," "The Loneliness of It," "2c More Wages; 19% Rise in Blue Cross Rates," "Urine as Red as Blood," and "Death by Automation."[29]

The automation discourse also played an important role in how the state chose to understand both the civil rights and broader social movements of the 1950s and 1960s. When a group of academics, intellectuals, and political activists styling itself the "Ad Hoc Committee on the Triple Revolution" sent a report to President Johnson urging radical action to alleviate what it saw as the ills produced by the three interdependent revolutions of automation, nuclear weapons, and racist discrimination, economists George P. Shultz and Arnold R. Weber academically confirmed the report's analysis during their investigation into automation for the Johnson administration.[30] As Schultz and Weber described it, "When technical change alters the occupational composition of the demand for labor, they ["Negroes"] lack the versatility to adjust to the new economic circumstances and are frequently left stranded in the labor market. In this respect, automation probably has done as much to ignite the civil rights revolution as Martin Luther King."[31] The utility of the sociotechnical imaginary could even help good liberals explain away the civil rights movement as itself a by-product of technological progress, rather than a response to centuries of injustice and a global anticolonial movement.

In 1964, Johnson established a commission on automation, and fifteen months later, the National Commission on Technology, Automation, and Economic Progress, published their final multivolume report, which situated automation as a positive force whose negative externalities were temporary, manageable, and a necessary evil.[32] The report stated explicitly that its investigation took "special cognizance of the civil rights 'revolution,'" and one study it commissioned put the situation bluntly: "When we place automation in its proper context within the total employment structure and examine the status of the Negro worker within that structure, the information is

27. "To the Point of Production—An Interview with John Watson of the League of Revolutionary Black Workers," *Movement*, July 1969, https://riseupdetroit.org/wp-content/uploads/2018/07/To-the-Point-of-Production-An-Interview-with-John-Watson-1969.pdf, 2.

28. Georgakas and Surkin, *Detroit, I Do Mind Dying*, 101–2; Bloice, "Black Worker's Future under American Capitalism," 17.

29. Denby, "Workers Battle Automation."

30. Ad Hoc Committee on the Triple Revolution, "Triple Revolution."

31. Shultz and Weber, "Variety in Adaptation to Technological Change," C-8.

32. Lyndon B. Johnson, "Remarks upon Signing Bill Creating the National Commission on Technology, Automation, and Economic Progress," August 19, 1964, in Gerhard Peters and John T. Woolley, *American Presidency Project*, https://www.presidency.ucsb.edu/node/241917.

ample to make a crystal clear picture—and dismal it is."[33] Shortly after the commission's findings were published in February 1966, Labor Secretary Willard Wirtz, echoing Shultz and Weber's sentiments from two years earlier, passed along worrying numbers regarding unemployment in "urban ghettos" to the president "with the ominous warning that unless something were done to change the situation, 'there would be a revolution.'"[34] For a variety of reasons, the revolution never came. Perhaps the most powerful reason, according to Boggs, was that "when workers fight the introduction of automation, they are taking on not only private capitalism but the federal government itself," and that was a fight against the technopolity itself.[35]

Lordstown

No event better captures the power of the technopolitical phenomenon called automation than the Lordstown strike of 1972. Originally built by General Motors in Lordstown, Ohio, in 1964, the Lordstown plant underwent significant redesign and retooling in the late 1960s to incorporate the newest and most advanced technoscience, what the *Wall Street Journal* described as a $100 million bet "on a new package of robot-operated assembly techniques, fast-paced manufacturing processes and pioneering designs."[36] All of this "automation" was to produce GM's response to the encroaching Japanese small-car market, the Chevrolet Vega. As a 1970 profile in *Popular Mechanics* touted, Lordstown was meant to be "the most modern, automated, robotized car-making complex in the world," with the capacity to raise GM's maximum production volume from fifty or sixty cars an hour to one hundred or more.[37]

To double production, engineers used IBM mainframe computers originally designed for the nation's air defense system and industrial robots first developed by defense contractor Unimation to combine old-school Taylorism with new-age technology into what GM called "Total Systems Engineering." Management broke work tasks down to the second and reengineered the plant accordingly to make jobs simpler, as well as to develop a suite of systems to manage the new, more detailed division of labor. Whereas average cycle time per job at other auto assembly plants averaged fifty-five seconds, "automation" at Lordstown reduced it to thirty-six seconds, making it the fastest-moving assembly line in the industry.[38] The deeper *technopolitical* nature of Lordstown's "automation" remained obscure to the public (and perhaps even industry observers): GM's management designed "Total Systems Engineering" specifically to limit the number of "Paragraph 78" grievances—an attempt to cir-

33. Puryear, "Technology and the Negro."

34. Mucciaroni, *Political Failure of Employment Policy*, 740.

35. Boggs, *American Revolution*, 103–4.

36. Charles B. Camp, "Stomping the Beetle? GM Resorts to Aggressive Automation to Pare Construction Costs of Mini-Car," *Wall Street Journal*, July 2, 1970.

37. Lund, "Made in Ohio by Robots."

38. Hak-Chong Lee, "The Lordstown Plant of General Motors," 1974, folder: Histories—1974—1975—Lordstown Historical Documents, box 3, Lordstown Collection, General Motors Heritage Center (GMHC), 5.

cumvent a clause in the collectively bargained contract that gave workers legal standing to strike once they had filed enough '78s.[39] Taylorism-on-technoscience, therefore, created a digital "drive system" that degraded and deskilled work to facilitate the speedup while inoculating GM from union power, the symbolic function of which, in sociotechnical imaginary fashion, was identified by *Business Week* as the "very model of automation."[40]

When the sociotechnical system proved less productive than desired, GM brought in a new management team, the General Motors Assembly Division (GMAD), an outfit notorious for its harsh approach to labor discipline under the leadership of its "tough-minded general manager," Joseph Godfrey.[41] When GMAD took over the plant in October 1971, it laid off hundreds of workers, instituted twelve-hour shifts and mandatory overtime, and deployed new disciplinary measures from verbal harassment (including racial slurs and targeting) to timing bathroom breaks.[42] Foremen specifically targeted "militant" workers for discipline and dismissals. Not surprisingly, Black workers bore the brunt of layoffs, particularly in the militant body shop, where industrial robots almost entirely took over spot welding, a job disproportionately performed by Black workers.[43]

From the workers' perspective, GMAD functioned like a totalitarian institution. One worker, a Vietnam veteran, compared Lordstown to his experience in the army: "If the foreman gives you a direct order, you do it, or you're out."[44] Other workers described GMAD managers as the "Gestapo" or "concentration camp guards" who demanded that "when you come in the plant leave your brain at the door, just bring your body in here, because we don't need any other part."[45] GMAD also brought in time-study experts to eliminate or reassign jobs considered too easy—meaning job classifications were assigned more tasks (and extra penalties when they weren't completed)—which made already mind-numbing, over-specialized, physically taxing, and repetitive jobs "excruciating."[46]

Local 1112's response to GMAD's attempt at turning them into "robots" was not surprising.[47] Beginning in November 1971, workers began a multimonth cam-

39. A. O'Keefe, "History of the GM Assembly Division," GMHC, 150.

40. *Business Week*, "GM's Mini."

41. *Business Week*, "The GM Efficiency Move That Backfired," 46, 47, 49.

42. Moberg, "Rattling the Golden Chains," 184, 216, 244, 453; Rubenstein, *Changing US Auto Industry*, 233.

43. Moberg, "Rattling the Golden Chains," 216–17; "UAW Chief Visits at Lordstown," *Warren Tribune-Chronicle*, August 24, 1970.

44. Moberg, "Rattling the Golden Chains," 424; Garson, "Luddites in Lordstown."

45. Monica Mastran-Czopor, "Jim Graham Interview," April 3, 2002, Youngstown State University Oral History Program: GM Lordstown (OH 2061), 7.

46. Rubenstein, *Changing US Auto Industry*, 233.

47. Moberg, "Rattling the Golden Chains," 557; Terkel, *Working*, 261; Erin Timms, "Norman J. Parry Interview," March 20, 2002, Youngstown State University Oral History Program: GM Lordstown (OH 2049), 7; and "Unionism Means Identity," *See Here*, May 1971, folder: UAW Local 1112 "See Here" 1971, box 1 (1971–1980), Walter P. Reuther Library, Wayne State University, 6.

paign of "working to rule," filing "78" grievances as well as not finishing jobs or leaving jobs undone altogether in order to "ship junk" or "ship shit," what in concert they called the "schmozzle." By the end of 1971, GMAD responded with five hundred short-term disciplinary actions and the elimination of over five hundred jobs, while workers filed more than three thousand grievances.[48] The combination of layoffs, harsh discipline, increasingly monotonous work, and the speedup meant it was only a matter of time before the "robots" who remained "manacled to the line" revolted.[49] On March 1, 1972, perhaps the most famous strike of the 1970s began—the very thing Lordstown's high-tech Taylorism and digital "drive system" of computer-augmented management was designed to prevent. Whether called mechanization, automation, or robotization, technological change in the capitalist idiom meant that, for workers, *plus ça change, plus c'est la même chose.*

Conclusion

The application of insights from STS, particularly the idea of technopolitics, has proven immensely useful to us in returning labor to the history of automation. Stripping technological innovation of its "objective" character has allowed us to find the worker behind the machine, still present and still sweating. But much research remains to be done. It falls to historians to locate the ways that capital seeks both to enclose and create new forms of labor through novel technological means. The owners of capital have proven themselves extremely adept at creating new mechanisms to hide human labor: Amazon Web Services' Mechanical Turk, which brings the principles of Taylorism to the crowdsourcing of human intelligence, seeks to fill in the gaps of artificial intelligence with some of the most degraded digital work imaginable.[50] At the same time, Big Tech, always hungry for data, has found ways to "scientifically enclose" modes of human life and expression that formerly could not be monetized—friendship, love, play—so that formerly unalienated activities become a form of labor, often unpaid.[51]

As the history of automation reveals its contingency, we can also get a better look at the ways that race and gender have from the beginning played a constituent role in the development of the idea of the technological obsolescence of labor.[52] But there is still more to do along these lines. While the term *automation* arose from very specific historical circumstances in the immediate postwar period, ideas of human obsolescence certainly have their roots in earlier phases of industrialization, if not in preindustrial times. Mechanization and technological transformation have served practically as givens in labor history. But if the messy history of the automation discourse shows us anything, it is that labor historians must also become historians of

48. Moberg, "Rattling the Golden Chains," 171, 187, 209.

49. Widick, "Men Won't Toe the Vega Line."

50. Dzieza, "AI Is a Lot of Work"; Schneider, "Intellectual Piecework,"; Schwartz, "Untold History of AI."

51. Zuboff, *Age of Surveillance Capitalism*; Bulut, *Precarious Game*.

52. Resnikoff, "Myth of Black Obsolescence."

science and technology if we wish to have a fuller understanding of the way capital has deployed technology to enclose and exploit labor.

SALEM ELZWAY is a postdoctoral fellow at the University of Southern California's Society of Fellows in the Humanities. His work investigates the intersections of labor, race, security policy, and technology in the twentieth-century United States. He is currently working on the first scholarly history of the industrial robot in postwar America.

JASON RESNIKOFF is assistant professor of contemporary history at the Rijksuniversiteit Groningen in the Netherlands. He is the author of *Labor's End: How the Promise of Automation Degraded Work*.

References

Ad Hoc Committee on the Triple Revolution. "The Triple Revolution." March 22, 1964. Accessed July 5, 2023. http://pinguet.free.fr/triplefac.pdf.

Administered Prices, part 6: *Automobiles*. Hearings before the Subcommittee on Antitrust and Monopoly, 85th Cong., 2nd sess. Washington, DC: Government Printing Office, 1958.

Automation and Technological Change: Hearings before the Subcommittee on Economic Stabilization of the Joint Committee on the Economic Report. 84th Congress, 1st sess. Washington, DC: Government Printing Office, 1955.

Benanav, Aaron. *Automation and the Future of Work*. London: Verso, 2020.

Bix, Amy Sue. *Inventing Ourselves out of Jobs? America's Debate over Technological Unemployment, 1929–1981*. Baltimore: Johns Hopkins University Press, 2000.

Bloice, Carl. "The Black Worker's Future under American Capitalism." *Black Scholar* 3, no. 9 (May 1972): 14–22.

Boggs, James. *The American Revolution: Pages from a Negro Worker's Notebook*. In *Pages from a Black Radical's Notebook: A James Boggs Reader*, edited by Stephen M. Ward, 77–143. Detroit: Wayne State University Press, 2011.

Bright, James R. *Automation and Management*. Boston: Division of Research, Graduate School of Business Administration, Harvard University, 1958.

Bulut, Ergin. *A Precarious Game: The Illusion of Dream Jobs in the Video Game Industry*. Ithaca, NY: ILR Press, Cornell University Press, 2020.

Burgin, Angus. "Market Politics in an Age of Automation." In *Beyond the New Deal Order: U.S. Politics from the Great Depression to the Great Recession*, edited by Gary Gerstle, Nelson Lichtenstein, and Alice O'Connor, 143–67. Philadelphia: University of Pennsylvania Press, 2019.

Business Week. "GM's Mini: The Very Model of Automation." *Business Week*, August 8, 1970.

Business Week. "The GM Efficiency Move That Backfired." *Business Week*, March 25, 1972, 46–49.

Crawford, Kate. *Atlas of AI: Power, Politics, and the Planetary Costs of Artificial Intelligence*. New Haven, CT: Yale University Press, 2021.

Denby, Charles. "Workers Battle Automation." *News and Letters* pamphlet, November 1960.

Diebold, John. *Automation: The Advent of the Automatic Factory*. New York: Van Nostrand, 1952.

Dzieza, Joshua, "AI Is a Lot of Work." *Intelligencer*, June 20, 2023. https://nymag.com /intelligencer/article/ai-artificial-intelligence-humans-technology-business-factory.html.

Elzway, Salem. "Armed Algorithms: Hacking the Real World in Cold War America." *Osiris* 38 (July 2023): 147–64.

Elzway, Salem. "Arms of the State: A History of the Industrial Robot in Postwar America." PhD diss., University of Michigan, August 2023.

Fressoz, Jean-Baptiste. "Pour une histoire désorientée de l'énergie." Paper presented at the 25th edition of the Journées Scientifiques de l'Environnement—L'économie verte en question, Créteil, France, February 18–20, 2014.

Frey, Carl Benedikt, and Michael A. Osborne. "The Future of Employment: How Susceptible Are Jobs to Computerisation?" Oxford Martin School Working Paper, September 17, 2013. https://www.oxfordmartin.ox.ac.uk/downloads/academic/future-of -employment.pdf.

Garson, Barbara. "Luddites in Lordstown." *Harper's*, June 1, 1972, 69.

Georgakas, Dan, and Marvin Surkin. *Detroit, I Do Mind Dying: A Study in Urban Revolution.* New York: St. Martin's, 1975.

Haraway, Donna J. *Modest_Witness@Second_Millennium: FemaleMan_Meets_OncoMouse: Feminism and Technoscience.* 2nd ed. New York: Routledge, 2018.

Hecht, Gabrielle, ed. *Entangled Geographies: Empire and Technopolitics in the Global Cold War.* Cambridge, MA: MIT Press, 2011.

Hounshell, David A. "Automation, Transfer Machinery, and Mass Production in the U.S. Automobile Industry in the Post–World War II Era." *Enterprise and Society* 1 (March 2000): 100–138.

Jasanoff, Sheila, and Sang-Hyun Kim. *Dreamscapes of Modernity: Sociotechnical Imaginaries and the Fabrication of Power.* Chicago: University of Chicago Press, 2015.

Latour, Bruno. *Science in Action: How to Follow Scientists and Engineers through Society.* Cambridge, MA: Harvard University Press, 1987.

Lund, Robert. "Made in Ohio by Robots." *Popular Mechanics*, September 1970, 81.

Mackenzie, Donald. *Inventing Accuracy: A Historical Sociology of Nuclear Missile Guidance.* Cambridge, MA: MIT Press, 1993.

Mitchell, Timothy. *Rule of Experts: Egypt, Techno-Politics, Modernity.* Berkeley: University of California Press, 2002.

Moberg, David. "Rattling the Golden Chains: Conflict and Consciousness of Autoworkers." PhD diss., University of Chicago, March 1978.

Mucciaroni, Gary. *The Political Failure of Employment Policy, 1945–1982.* Pittsburgh: University of Pittsburgh Press, 1990.

Noble, David F. *Forces of Production: A Social History of Industrial Automation.* New York: Oxford University Press, 1984.

Puryear, M. T. "Technology and the Negro." In National Commission on Technology, Automation, and Economic Progress, *Technology and the American Economy, Appendices 1–3,* III-131–43. Washington, DC: Government Printing Office, February 1966.

Resnikoff, Jason. *Labor's End: How the Promise of Automation Degraded Work.* Urbana: University of Illinois Press, 2021.

Resnikoff, Jason. "The Myth of Black Obsolescence." *International Labor and Working-Class History* 102 (2022): 124–45.

Rubenstein, James. *The Changing US Auto Industry: A Geographic Analysis.* New York: Routledge, 1992.

Schneider, Nathan. "Intellectual Piecework." *Chronicle of Higher Education*, February 16, 2015. https://www.chronicle.com/article/intellectual-piecework/.

Schor, Juliet B. *The Overworked American: The Unexpected Decline of Leisure.* New York: Basic Books, 1991.

Schwartz, Oscar. "Untold History of AI: How Amazon's Mechanical Turkers Got Squeezed inside the Machine." *IEEE Spectrum: Technology, Engineering, and Science News*, April 22, 2019. https://spectrum.ieee.org/untold-history-of-ai-mechanical-turk-revisited-tktkt.

Scott, James C. *Against the Grain: A Deep History of the Earliest States.* New Haven, CT: Yale University Press, 2017.

Shultz, George C., and Arnold R. Weber. "Variety in Adaptation to Technological Change: The Midwestern Experience." *Seminars on Private Adjustments to Automation and Technological Change*, May–June 1964, C2–C45.

Smith, Jason E. *Smart Machines and Service Work: Automation in an Age of Stagnation.* London: Reaktion Books, 2020.

Terkel, Studs. *Working: People Talk about What They Do All Day and How They Feel about What They Do.* New York: Ballantine Books, 1990.

The Transformative Impact of Robots and Automation: Hearing before the Joint Economic Committee, Congress of the United States. 114th Cong., 2nd sess. Washington, DC: Government Publishing Office, 2016.

Widick, B. J. "The Men Won't Toe the Vega Line." *The Nation*, March 27, 1972, 403.

Zuboff, Shoshana. *The Age of Surveillance Capitalism: The Fight for a Human Future at the New Frontier of Power.* New York: Public Affairs, 2019.

Cocoa at Work: Materials and Labor in the Making of Global Chocolate

Marta Macedo

On the last day of April 1901, the board members of the British chocolate firm Cadbury assembled to discuss an offer of a plantation for sale in São Tomé, a small Portuguese colonial island in the African Gulf of Guinea and one of the world's major cocoa producers.[1] Almost half the cocoa that entered Cadbury's factory already came from that colony.[2] The proposal on the table described the plantation's area, current and potential cocoa yields, and operating costs (labor and supervision, materials, taxes, transport) and predicted a 30 percent profit rate to justify the £200,000 purchase price. Among the avalanche of numbers, the document had a troubling but not totally surprising figure. The property was worked by "200 negro hands," described as "fed principally on bananas." These "hands" appeared as an asset, just after cattle valued at £3,500. Balking at the equation of people and property, the directors concluded that "this seems to confirm other indirect reports that slavery, either total or partial, exists on these cocoa estates" and determined to consult the Anti-Slavery Society.

Eight long years later, in 1909, Cadbury joined with other major chocolate firms to boycott cocoa from São Tomé. Many historians have examined this episode as a test of the Christian business ethics of this Quaker family company.[3] The labor sourcing of Cadbury's cocoa stood in scandalous contrast to the company's marketing of their chocolates as embodying the virtues of wholesomeness, fairness, and

Research for this article received funding from the European Research Council Project, *The Colour of Labour*, PI Cristiana Bastos.

1. Cadbury Brothers Board Minutes, 1901, April 30, Cadbury Archive, Mondelez International, Bourneville, Birmingham, UK (hereafter cited as CA).

2. Although it is sometimes the case that cocoa beans are referred to as *cacao* and the powdered version of roasted cacao as cocoa, in this article the word *cocoa* is used in both contexts, as historical actors tended to apply that terminology.

3. Dellheim, "Creation of a Company Culture." On the various interpretations of the maneuvers of the chocolate industry, antislavery groups, and the Foreign Office, together with the responses of the Portuguese government and colonial planters, see Grant, *Civilised Savagery*; Higgs, *Chocolate Islands*; Satre, *Chocolate on Trial*; Jerónimo, *"Civilizing Mission" of Portuguese Colonialism*.

Labor: Studies in Working-Class History, Volume 21, Issue 1
DOI 10.1215/15476715-10948920   © 2024 by Labor and Working-Class History Association

social betterment. However, little scholarly attention has been paid to the relationship between the Cadburys' moral concerns and the materiality of the items that sustained their business: both the cocoa shipped from São Tomé and the chocolates that came out of their factory in Bourneville near Birmingham. Closer attention to cocoa and chocolate production *as a material process* fulfills labor history's imperative to study diverse forms of labor mobilization along lengthy global supply chains, while also raising new questions about expertise, knowledge production, and nonhuman agency that have not usually figured in this historiography.

Since the pioneering work of Sidney Mintz's *Sweetness and Power*, up to Sven Beckert's more recent *Empire of Cotton*, following commodities on the move has revealed the connected geographies and unequal power structures of the modern world. These studies make clear that there is no history of mass-produced goods without a concurrent labor history of the plantation and the factory.[4] The histories of labor that unfold from such global engagement have stressed the diversity of labor systems, with different levels of coercion, working simultaneously to make sugar, cotton, coffee, or cocoa available to consumers in the industrial cities of Europe and North America.[5] Showing that slave, indenture, or contract labor were as essential as wage labor to produce the agricultural commodities that fed (literally and figuratively) modern capitalism, these histories have also placed imperial and racial politics at the heart of economic and social histories. The lingering presence of racialized and colonized African workers inside a modern British factory, and the conflict that emerged around "slave cocoa," is an eloquent example of how different sites of labor and different political regimes came together around concrete stuff.

But the majority of commodity histories, while bringing labor and their fruits to the forefront, have been rather dismissive of the material properties of the commodities being produced and the ways they molded the laboring lives of the people producing them. Shifting that premise, in this article I examine the distant workspaces of cocoa—the plantation and the factory—by sorting the beans exported from São Tomé, by unpacking the chocolate boxes and tin cans that came out of Bourneville, by concentrating on the very substances they were made of, and by questioning how these substances came into being.

This approach is inspired by an important body of scholarship that has called for a stronger engagement with matter and for the acknowledgment of materials' crucial role in shaping social worlds.[6] Historians of technology recognize power, and the strategies of differentiation and hierarchization that sustain it, as embedded in material forms and embodied practices.[7] As such, cocoa here is understood not as an inert "object" but as a "thick thing" whose physical attributes allowed or restricted different operations and uses and whose specific characteristics promoted or obstructed

4. Mintz, *Sweetness and Power*; Beckert, *Empire of Cotton*. For global commodity chains, see, for instance, Clarence-Smith and Topik, *Global Coffee Economy*; Clarence-Smith, *Cocoa and Chocolate*.

5. Van der Linden, *Workers of the World*.

6. Ingold, "Materials against Materiality"; LeCain, *Matter of History*.

7. Bray, *Technology and Gender*; Slaton, *Reinforced Concrete*.

particular labor forms and allowed for the stabilization of different modes of rule.[8] While advocating for more-than-human histories of labor, I am not suggesting that there is an agential symmetry of humans and nonhumans but that the two are deeply interrelated. I do recognize, following Seth Rockman, the explanatory power of locating "work processes in the relationship of the maker and the material, in the tacit and bodily knowledges that governs human activity, and in the sensory and haptic encounter of the human and the non-human."[9] Bringing the material to the forefront shines new light on the various labor practices and political configurations that supported the capitalist world of chocolate.

An equally useful theoretical framework has emerged from the efforts of historians of technology to recognize the physical and symbolic elements assembled around a given crop: the plants and pests, cultivation techniques and markets, tastes and values that converge to constitute a "cropscape."[10] This creative concept provides a means to see the broader assemblage of the social and material elements that cohere in mass-produced and standardized consumer goods and to cast new light on their historical consequences. Indian teascapes, for instance, are a good example of the different kinds of labor, human and nonhuman, involved in transplanting Chinese tea plants and skilled Chinese workers, integrating them into new plantation environments, "domesticating" wild Assam tea trees and indentured laborers, and creating an appetite for strong black Assamese teas across the British Empire.[11] The same can be said about the attention paid to fermentation's subtle chemical processes, to the collective work of microbial elements and scientists in producing new soy sauces, and their impacts on both the modern Japanese diet and modern Japanese nation.[12] For the purpose of this article, the term *cropscape* will help to draw attention to ways that cocoa plants and cocoa beans affected human actions, impacting the labor, expertise, and knowledge necessary to grow a specific cocoa and transform it into a very distinct chocolate. I argue that when we take the material properties of cocoa seriously, it is possible to see how mass chocolate production was a technological and scientific enterprise conceived to cope with the constraints of cocoa itself—an enterprise with profound consequences for the labor forms on the plantation and the factory. Materials bound plantation laborers and chocolate scientists to specific technological, economic, and political relations and demanded huge investments and much labor to create alternative ones.

"The Cocoa Knows Them, They Know Cocoa"

Creating São Tomé's intense and lucrative plantation monoculture depended on coupling coerced Angolan laborers with the cocoa plant. São Tomé "cocoascape"

8. Alder, "Thick Things"; K. Smith, "Amidst Things." On plants and animals treated as "thick things," see Saraiva, *Fascist Pigs*.

9. Rockman, *Der alte und der neue Materialismus*. I thank the author for access to the English translation of this text.

10. Bray et al., *Moving Crops and the Scales of History*.

11. Sharma, "British Science, Chinese Skill and Assam Tea"; Bray, "Translating the Art of Tea."

12. Lee, *Arts of the Microbial World*.

emerged from exactly that interaction. Between 1880 and 1908, more than seventy thousand men and women were brought to São Tomé from Angola, supposedly "rescued" and "redeemed" from local servitude. Supporting the Cadburys' concerns, countless contemporary records document how modern "recruiters" adopted earlier practices of the slave trade on behalf of São Tomé planters.[13] Caravans from the interior of Angola marched people supposedly "freed" from local chiefs on a lengthy journey to the coast, and from there they were sent to São Tomé.[14]

When cocoa plantations developed in the 1880s, slavery had been legally abolished in Portuguese imperial territories, and planters had to reinvent new forms of coerced labor relations and new racial discourses that allowed them to maintain the flux of peoples from Angola. Around those years, the colonial government created five-year indenture contracts that "protected" Africans from local forms of exploitation and introduced these inherently "lazy" subjects to the "virtues" of wage labor.[15] The success of the São Tomé plantation system, in contrast to other postabolition plantation contexts, was based on a lifetime indentureship system: workers were forced to endlessly renew their contracts on expiry.

Records from several plantations reveal the many tasks that transformed the cocoa plant into a crop and Angolan subjects into black plantation workers: felling trees, digging holes, fertilizing, planting banana trees and erythrinas for shading, planting cocoa trees, pruning, weeding, harvesting, breaking pods, bringing cocoa to the warehouses to ferment and to the patios to dry, selecting and grading cocoa beans, packing cocoa for export, and transporting it to the port. A profitable crop required each of these tasks to be performed correctly at a precise time of the year. Other operations sustained plantation infrastructure: opening roads, building or maintaining houses, loading and unloading provisions, and keeping the machinery in order. And work didn't stop there. Plantations also demanded the reproductive labor of cooks, washerwomen, and domestic servants to support the quarters, the main house, the plantation hospital, and the stables. In the highly regimented São Tomé plantations, work varied seasonally, but it was relentless all through the year and performed with military precision. In fact, army officers (retired or on leave) occupied leading administrative roles on these estates, enforcing a martial coercive regime of space and time. In 1904, the French botanist Auguste Chevalier openly affirmed that "the discipline to which all workers are subjected, is much more rigorous than the rules imposed in the French colonies, not only for workers in our railway construction sites, but even for the militias in Senegal."[16] Regulations did not police work exclusively, but they were "exhaustive upon every feature of the laborer's life."[17]

But the history of São Tomé plantation labor practices in the early 1900s is unintelligible without the natural history of the *Theobroma cacao* tree, a species native

13. See, for instance, Nevinson, *Modern Slavery*.
14. Miller, *Way of Death*; Candido, *African Slaving Port*.
15. Direcção Geral do Ultramar, *Collecção official da legislação portugueza*.
16. Chevalier, *Le cacaoyer dans L'Ouest Africain*, 64.
17. Harris, *Dawn in Darkest Africa*, 190.

to the Amazon basin. Cocoa reached São Tomé from Brazil in the early nineteenth century, following the geography of empire and slavery, and found a perfect habitat an ocean away from its origin.[18] Of the three main varieties of cultivated cocoa—Criollo, Forastero, and Trinitario—São Tomé plantations grew the Forastero type, especially the Amelonado subvariety. Forastero trees were more resistant to disease, more productive, and earlier bearers than Criollo or Trinitario, but their beans, rather flatter and less aromatic, were of an ordinary kind and priced accordingly. Besides the specific features of different varieties, the plant itself has unique characteristics that can help us understand the relations between laboring bodies and cocoa. Cocoa's reproductive system, for example, contrasts with common features of other fruit trees. Its tiny flowers do not sprout from branches but emerge directly from the trunk, and unlike other flowers, they have a lifespan of just twenty-four hours. They are also unscented, attracting only a distinct family of microscopic rainforest insects. Of an average of sixty thousand flowers that grow every year in a single tree, only about 5 percent are pollinated, and fewer than 1 percent of those will become fruit. It is also rather common to see cocoa trees simultaneously bearing flowers and fruits at different stages of maturity.

However, producing a crop out of raw cocoa involved not just biology but also chemistry and mechanics. Before being shipped to chocolate factories, beans had to be fermented and dried on-site. The chemical process that occurred during fermentation and drying was of the utmost importance. Besides the influence on color, fermentation determined cocoa's flavor, texture, and aroma and consequently its price. And fermentation, like pollination, was a very uncontrolled process. Microorganisms were rather wild, and unlike in other industries that involve fermentation, no starter cultures were used to assure consistency from batch to batch.

In São Tomé, a rewarding crop was possible only when the harvest contained fruits of even ripeness, because the effects of ripeness in fermentation were clear: only beans from ripe pods fermented properly. While cocoa trees bore flowers and fruits year round, harvest and ripeness were concentrated in the two different periods. The main harvest took place from March to May, and a second one from October to December. Harvest time, however, was not fully compatible with the island's two climatic seasons, coinciding with a lengthy rainy season that lasted from October to May. Thus, rainfall always hampered this operation. Taking into account that all fruits on a tree did not mature at the same rate, challenges of coordination were obvious. During harvest, overseers made men work quickly and precisely, moving them tree by tree in the course of a ten-hour working day in multiple waves of picking.

When we look at what plantation workers actually did at work, at the relation between cocoa and laboring bodies, at the actual tasks those bodies performed, and at the things that emerged from that process, it is possible to bring forward unexpected dimensions of the laborers' experiences (fig. 1).[19] Growing cocoa was not like

18. Norton, *Sacred Gifts, Profane Pleasures.*

19. For a reflection on the relation between technology and labor practices from inside the field of labor history, see Womack, "Doing Labor History."

Figure 1. Plantation laborers and plantation cocoa were part of the visual repertoire of São Tomé, as shown in this picture collected by William Cadbury. Photograph album. Views taken during a visit to S.Thome and Angola, Portuguese West Africa in 1908–9, Cadbury Research Library: Special Collections, University of Birmingham.

growing sugar or cotton: it created specific relations between peoples, plants, and technologies.

For example, there was a specific body discipline involved in managing the cutting tools during harvest. Plantation administrators assigned certain male workers to the task of picking ripe pods. Those "men must cut the peduncle of the fruit in a very precise way, not to tear off the bark, or bend, even slightly, the smallest branch."[20] Precision was needed to preserve the remaining fruits and flowers and to leave the trunks intact, thus preventing the attack of insects and fungi. Speed was also mandatory; as such, disciplines were always learned and performed under the "vigilant eye of the overseer."[21] Agronomists concluded that to execute this task, "the worker must be pretty skilled."[22] The embodied dimension of these disciplines led experts to use the word *dressage* to describe workers' instruction.[23] Evoking the French term used to designate the art of training and riding horses for obedience and choreographed movements was not a mere metaphor reflecting unequal power structures and racial

20. Montet, "Une plantation de cacaoyers," 51.
21. Montet, "Une plantation de cacaoyers," 51.
22. Montet, "Une plantation de cacaoyers," 51.
23. Blochouse, "La colonie portugaise," 256.

discourses but a description of the specific physical training men were subjected to. Like the supple and precise movement of trained horses, workers' motions during harvest should also be exact, restrained, and fast. The importance of practical knowledge and skills acquired on the job and learned on-site helps us unsettle a series of categorizations that frame our understanding of technology and labor, specifically the idea that plantation labor was unskilled and fungible. In São Tomé, labor was as carefully cultivated as cocoa, and laborers were not easily interchangeable.

Harvest was followed by fermentation, by far the most important operation in the creation of value. If "in the fresh state the seeds have a raw, bitter and astringent flavor," explained one observer, with "fermentation and drying the bitter and disagreeable taste has entirely disappeared."[24] Critical as it was, there were some perils in this procedure, as over-fermented cocoa acquired what brokers described as a "hammy smell." Fermentation also implied speedy and strenuous labor, because it needed to be performed during a small window of time. For optimal results, harvested and opened cocoa pods had to be transported from the fields to wooden fermentation boxes on the same day. These boxes were specially designed to facilitate the drainage of the liquid that resulted from the fermentation process and to guarantee proper oxygenation. Over the course of a week, workers had to shovel beans between boxes either daily or every other day. Considering that during fermentation the temperature of the pulp would rise from 25°C to 50°C, it is easy to imagine the harshness of the working conditions inside the warehouses.

Drying was the next step in the transformation of cocoa seeds into marketable cocoa beans. Removing the moisture from beans continued the chemical process that began with fermentation; as such, it contributed to reducing the levels of astringency and bitterness, which would impact cocoa's final quality. In São Tomé, drying operations were particularly troublesome because, as mentioned earlier, harvest coincided with the rainy season. Even if some planters had invested large sums of money in drying machinery, artificially dried beans were more prone to mold, and chocolate producers preferred the taste, smell, aroma, and flavor of beans dried by the sun. Attaining uniformity in the drying process required speeding up and regularizing it. That task was entirely dependent on women: they performed the meticulous and painful labor of manually turning each cocoa bean in the drying terraces. Violence and control made these operations not only possible but also profitable. Women were also the major actors in the last cocoa operation that impacted quality: selecting and grading. The removal of flat, unfermented, or broken beans was done entirely by women's hands. "Fine São Tomé" cocoa, the sorts of cocoa that supplied major chocolate manufacturers, could now be placed in jute sacks and shipped to Lisbon. From Lisbon a large percentage of those sacks would reach London.[25]

At the turn of the century, São Tomé accounted for around one-sixth of the world cocoa production, some twenty-five thousand tons. The seven largest planta-

24. H. H. Smith, *Fermentation of Cacao*, 49.
25. On the labor history of jute fibers and the making of a global commodity see Ali, *Local History of Global Capital.*

tions on the island, owned by Portuguese capitalist consortia, were responsible for half of that amount.[26] São Tomé cocoa became a global commodity, but it was not a generic one. To understand how its specific characteristics came into being, I have looked at the particular relationship between laborers and plants. Under a plantation coercive labor regime, the needs of the Amelonado variety and the labor routines of people from Angola (harvesting, fermenting, and drying) joined to create a "standard cocoa" that would fit the needs of the British chocolate manufacturers.[27]

"Factory in the Garden"

São Tomé beans arrived in Britain to find that country's chocolate industry experiencing significant growth within the context of an industrializing factory food regime that brought margarine, condensed milk, and affordable chocolate into the diets of the laboring classes.[28] But in the 1900s United Kingdom, industrialized food, very much like food in general, relied on imported supplies. São Tomé beans are a clear example of the way foodstuffs connected British households to the far corners of the world, drawing a gigantic organic network that expanded beyond the confines of the British Empire. Considering Britain's dependance on imported food commodities, the social, political, and economic impacts of foodstuffs were immense.

Cocoa emerged in this cosmopolitan gastro-landscape as a drink, competing with coffee and tea for the taste of the British public. While the latter stood out as the national drink, taken by everyone at all times, cocoa soon supplanted coffee as an energy beverage, also claiming nourishing and medical properties. The numbers are impressive: from a per capita consumption of cocoa of a mere 0.2 pounds per year in 1870 to 1.18 pounds in 1910, there was a sixfold increase in forty years. In the early twentieth century, the English consumed almost twice as much cocoa as coffee. And just as with São Tomé cocoa production, chocolate manufacturing in early 1900s Britain also became concentrated in a small number of large companies.[29]

Several factors contributed to these developments. While increasing cocoa production in the tropics led to a decline in the price of that raw material, industrial economies of scale and changing technologies also cheapened chocolate production in big and highly capitalized factories. In Europe, specialized engineering firms such as the German Lehmann of Dresden started to make processing machinery exclusively for cocoa and chocolate. Those mechanisms allowed for the emergence of new products that in turn were supported by modern distribution and marketing strategies.[30] Newspaper ads and other forms of publicity were crucial in the integration of chocolate into the diet and culture of the British middle and laboring classes.[31]

Cadbury exemplified that great transformation in cocoa and chocolate manufacturing at the turn of the century. The firm, founded in the early 1830s, initially

26. Chevalier, *Le cacaoyer dans L'Ouest Africain.*
27. Macedo, "Standard Cocoa."
28. Edgerton, *Rise and Fall of the British Nation*; Otter, *Diet for a Large Planet.*
29. Othick, "Cocoa and Chocolate Industry in the Nineteenth Century."
30. Fitzgerald, "Products, Firms and Consumption."
31. Doyle, "Cocoa and Class in British Popular Press Advertising."

traded cocoa, tea, and coffee but soon began specializing in cocoa and adopted new processing technologies. The actual and prospective growth in production, revenues, and laborers influenced the decision to move the factory from the crowded and polluted inner city to an idyllic spot on the outskirts of Birmingham, close to the river Bourn. In the late 1870s, when "French chocolates were then looked upon as the best," the Cadburys tapped into the popular imagination of glamour and fine taste and named the new site, comprising the works and a model garden city, Bourneville.[32]

Bourneville's new buildings allowed for the expansion of Cadbury's operations. Cadbury's consumption of cocoa grew from 598 tons in 1880 to more than 6,000 tons in 1910.[33] At that time the spacious and fully mechanized factory employed more than three thousand laborers, making it larger than major Birmingham plants such as Dunlop or Wolseley Motor Company.[34] While this reminds us that mundane and trivial food items such as chocolate can be as relevant and disruptive as mobility technologies in histories of modernity, Cadbury also prompts us to acknowledge women's factory labor. This firm had always employed a disproportionally larger number of women, or, to be more precise, unmarried women. While "women were thought to be especially suited for the labor intensive and often tedious work involved in confectionery production, such as hand dipping centers in chocolate," their presence on the shop floor was greatly motivated by economic reasoning: they were paid less than men.[35]

Edward Cadbury's 1912 book, *Experiments in Industrial Organization*, summarized the transformation of labor management by the founders' grandsons.[36] Their paternalistic approach, aimed at overcoming the antagonism and conflicting goals of employers and employees, translated into factory canteens with food at fixed prices, medical care, and a pension scheme for male workers, thus providing a minimum of social welfare. However, the vast majority of female factory laborers were still bound to a penalizing piece rate system coupled with strict surveillance by forewomen. "Bad work" and "bad conduct," ranging from "careless affixing of labels, leaving finger marks on goods and incorrect weighting" to "noisiness, imprudence to superiors and moral delinquencies," placed women workers in a precarious position.[37] Discipline, which the Cadburys imagined as "reformative and not merely punitive," intruded on workers' personal hygiene (e.g., mandatory nail clipping) and involved a number of measurements to monitor the daily pace of work.[38] Even under a piece-rate system, "slow girls" were a major concern of the firm. Ultimately, disciplinary procedures revolved around production savings: as a report of work output stated, "1 grain improvement on 20 million packages is more than 1½ tons saved in the year."[39]

32. Williams, *Firm of Cadbury*, 58.

33. Cocoa reports, Various 1911–1835, Raw cocoa: Cadbury consumption based on the quantity cleared through customs each year, CA.

34. Hopkins, "Industrial Change and Life at Work in Birmingham."

35. Smith, Child, and Rowlinson, *Reshaping Work*, 70.

36. Cadbury, *Experiments in Industrial Organisation*.

37. Cadbury, *Experiments in Industrial Organisation*, 74, 76.

38. Cadbury, *Experiments in Industrial Organisation*, 71.

39. Cadbury Brothers Board Minutes, March 26, 1901, CA.

Bourneville labor relations must be understood in connection with a specific production process happening inside the factory walls. The Cadburys aimed at a model factory for chocolate-making, and as such, they were responding to the very physical properties of cocoa.[40] In fact, as contemporaries put it, a "factory in which foodstuffs are prepared for the consumption of the million" demanded special attention in the planning and construction of the workspace.[41] Chocolate was, above many others, a very sensitive foodstuff, so the "trinity of atmospheric environment—light, heat and air" needed to be kept under strict control.[42] Although good natural lighting was essential throughout the manufacturing process, architects also had to cope with the troublesome melting relationship between cocoa and direct sunlight. In the old factory in Birmingham it was impossible to overcome the difficulties posed by south-facing windows, but in Bourneville "in most of the shops the windows are arranged as sky lights so that well diffused overheard illumination is possible and direct glare avoided."[43] Chocolate production sometimes needed to begin before dawn: as there were seasons for cocoa, there was also a season for chocolate, coinciding with Christmas festivities. For nine months, the factory ran from 8:35 a.m. to 5:30 p.m., but from September to December work began at 6 a.m. For those early morning hours, sanitary electric bulbs, lit with energy produced on-site, illuminated the works as early as 1896.[44]

As with direct sunlight, chocolate also did not tolerate temperature imbalance, so "the work rooms [were] so arranged that the temperature [was] kept even, ventilators being freely used."[45] Foreign contaminants caused extra problems. "Floors of workshops and corridors" made of cement guaranteed "cleanliness by facilitating sweeping and washing, and rendering the accumulation of putrefiable substances impossible"; in addition, all disagreeable odors that could compromise the final taste of chocolate needed to be eliminated. Specialized magazines praised the innovative technologies experimented at Cadbury's for that specific purpose. For instance, in the box-making department "over each glue pot is a funnel shaped hood connected with the general system of exhaust piping. These dry away the disagreeable fumes from the glue directly without permitting them to escape into the room."[46] All these innovations are mentioned in contemporary journals and magazines as improvements in the laboring conditions of Cadbury workers. And while this was true, they resulted as much from the specific needs of cocoa and of the chocolate manufacturing process as from any overarching concern with worker welfare.

While it is hard to dispute that the particular qualities of chocolate structured the organization of the shop floor, when entering into the factory laboratories, occupied by a different kind of worker, it is possible to get yet a deeper sense of how cocoa's

40. On the design of Bourneville as a social landscape see Chance, *Factory in a Garden.*
41. "Sanitary Factories: 1. Bourneville (Cadbury Brothers)," 288.
42. Gentle, "Raising the Workman's Efficiency," 163.
43. Gentle, "Raising the Workman's Efficiency," 165.
44. "Sanitary Factories: 1. Bourneville (Cadbury Brothers)."
45. Thackray, "Employees' Welfare in England," 455.
46. Gentle, "Raising the Workman's Efficiency," 165.

properties shaped the chocolates being produced and the necessary labor to overcome cocoa's limitations.

"Cocoa: All About It"

Chocolatiness was not easy to achieve. As a German expert scornfully declared, "Recipes don't mean much. With the same recipe a very fine chocolate can be made and also one of moderate good."[47] Exemplary recipes had to be combined with good ingredients, perfected processes, and sensible human operators to obtain the best-tasting chocolate possible. Among the most vital operation in the entire production process of cocoa powders was roasting: like fermentation, roasting altered the chemistry of the cocoa bean, impacting its final flavor and aroma. While mechanical revolving drums were used to rotate and tumble cocoa beans, ensuring homogeneity, roasting in the 1900s was still a "delicate operation requiring experience and discretion."[48] Although "there have been attempts to replace the æsthetic judgment of man, as to the point at which to stop roasting," instrumentation could never establish failsafe parameters of duration and temperature.[49] As such, "a skilled workman, endowed with a keen sense of taste and smell, is always to be seen at the roasting machine" taking samples from the drum from time to time until the moment the desired aroma was attained, and the roasting process could be stopped immediately.[50] Chocolate was not different from other industries involving high heat procedures, where it was impossible to fully implement automation and standardization of procedures. For example, early twentieth-century steelmaking also depended on the sensibility of the workman at the forge.

Regardless of mechanization, roasting remained very much an art, but artists performed better with better materials. It was well-known among chocolate manufacturers that ripe, well-fermented dry beans could be roasted for shorter periods of time with moderate heat, thus maintaining their natural and mild chocolate taste. With "São Tome cocoa the danger of a slow deterioration is not so great . . . and attentive manufacturers will therefore easily be able to determine a smaller loss in roasting" when using that cocoa.[51] Even if this cocoa did not do away with the need for human judgment, by being more uniform and generally less bitter than other cocoas, it made roasting a less risky operation and allowed for more control over the final product. São Tomé roasted nibs transferred all their chocolatiness to the final products.

British manufacturers bought different cocoa to fulfill different needs and, as such, were reluctant to define what a "quality cocoa" was. But they unanimously acknowledged that "constancy or reliability of quality" was by far "the most highly

47. Cocoa reports Various 1911–1935, CA. "On the Quest for Mistakes," translation of an article at *Gordian*, 384, April 20, 1911.

48. Knapp, *Cocoa and Chocolate*, 126.

49. Knapp, *Cocoa and Chocolate*, 128.

50. Zipperer, *Manufacture of Chocolate*, 92.

51. Cocoa reports Various 1911–1935, CA. "On the Quest for Mistakes," translation of an article at *Gordian*, 384, April 20, 1911.

appreciated character."[52] Cocoa that varied from bag to bag and season to season was not appreciated. In São Tomé plantations, "not only have the cultivation, fermentation and drying of cacao . . . been brought to the highest state of perfection," but a norm of consistency had also been achieved.[53]

São Tomé beans were definitely less bitter and more homogeneous than other cocoas bought by Cadbury at similar prices. And they had that specific characteristic because of the cruel plantation labor regime used to produce them. But in the early 1900s this Quaker firm was dealing with a dilemma: how to keep feeding their production lines with "slave cocoa" without losing consumers' respect. Cadbury would turn to its technical departments to find a solution for that ethical and commercial problem.

It is important to note that as the firm grew, it transformed its internal organization, and in 1899 it became a limited liability company. Although control remained in the hands of the family, the new generation of Cadburys had received specialized training that allowed them to assume managerial roles in different areas of the firm. Just as important, the company hired experts to fill the positions of new technical departments: an Engineers' Department was founded in 1900, followed by a Chemists' Department in 1901, another devoted to advertising in 1905, and one centered on planning in 1913.

Norman Booth, the chief chemist running the Chemists' Department since 1901 and until the early 1920s, proved to be a decisive figure in solving the problem posed by "slave"-grown cocoa (fig. 2).[54] Booth worked to improve productivity but also to assure the consistency of the chocolate manufacturing processes. As with any mass-produced product, Cadbury's chocolates could not vary by batch; they would need consistent taste, smell, color, and mouthfeel. But Booth was also tasked with making cocoa behave in ways that would improve Cadbury's profits and allow the company to remain competitive when their rivals introduced an alkalized cocoa powder known as "Dutch cocoa" and Swiss manufacturers developed the "milk chocolate bar." Both of Cadbury's goals—keeping up with competitors and eliminating slavery from their supply chain—would have to be responsive to cocoa's material properties.

Until the 1910s, the most successful line at Cadburys was a specific chocolate powder named Cocoa Essence.[55] Essence, produced since the mid-1860s, was the outcome of an important technological innovation: hydraulic presses to extract large amounts of fat (cocoa butter) from cocoa beans. To fabricate Essence, beans were cleaned, roasted, husked, and ground, and the cocoa butter was pressed out, thus reducing by almost half their fat content. Essence was thus a cocoa "cake" that was then pulverized into cocoa powder. Considering that more than half of the cocoa "nib" is composed of butter, manufacturers had over the years mixed their cocoa with

52. Booth and Knapp, "Qualities in Cacao Desired by Manufacturers," 174.
53. Knapp, *Cocoa and Chocolate*, 102.
54. On the Chemists' Department at Cadbury see Horrocks, "Consuming Science."
55. Bradley, *Cadbury's Purple Reign*.

Figure 2. In modern factories, chemists rendered themselves both invisible and indispensable. This is a rare image of a scientist at work in the laboratory (Norman Booth, Cadbury). Image Collection, Cadbury Archive, Mondelez International, Bourneville, Birmingham, United Kingdom.

a variety of substances, from powdered lentils to arrowroot, but also potato starch and sago, to improve digestibility. Essence's "purity" seduced customers who were alarmed by campaigns on the perils of food adulteration, and it helped construct Cadbury's reputation as a brand. In 1899 Cadbury was placing on the market around two thousand tons of Cocoa Essence annually, packed into sixteen million packages and three million tins.[56]

Essence, however, was far from perfect. Even if it was more digestible than previous full-fat cocoa versions, its solubility was questionable, and regardless of the mild characteristics of São Tomé's beans and the acidity-reducing effects of roasting, this cocoa preparation was inherently bitter. Alkalized cocoa, obtained from treating cocoa nibs with an alkali solution, produced a darker, more soluble powder with stronger "chocolate" flavors.

In the factory laboratory, experimenting with new recipes and processes through the manipulation of materials, "chemists rendered themselves both invisible and indispensable," as the historian Sally Horrocks puts it.[57] The annual reports

56. Cadbury Brothers Board Minutes, January 9, 1900, CA.
57. Horrocks, "Consuming Science," 178.

of the Chemists' Department confirm the labor and time necessary to create the new chocolates lines that would expand Cadbury's business: Cadbury Dairy Milk (Cadbury's milk chocolate) launched in 1905, and Bourneville Cocoa (Cadbury's alkalized cocoa power) launched in 1906. In 1902, Booth devoted "as much time as possible to research work, the subject taken being flavors" working in close collaboration with the Engineering Department.[58] The following year, after hiring another chemist who was responsible for "90% of routine work," Booth could to take up research entirely and started investigations into the "new chocolates."[59] After three years of testing, in 1905 he concentrated on "completing the Cadbury Dairy Milk and Breakfast Chocolate" and doing "experimental work in connection with the new Bourneville Cocoa." Five years had passed since the first trials, but he could claim that "Bourneville cocoa is being steadily manufactured and will be ready to stand the test of public opinion when the firm desires to bring it out."[60] After its launch in the 1906 Christmas campaign, Bourneville cocoa remained a concern for the firm, and Booth remarked crudely that "although a passable flavor has been obtained, the product is not yet satisfactory and needs further attention."[61]

As both technologies and inert products, Bourneville Cocoa (regardless of its flavor defects) and Cadbury Dairy Milk allowed Cadbury to break its dependence on São Tomé cocoa. Laboratory processes made it possible for Cadbury to bring lower grades of cocoa into their production lines. The firm had been looking for other suppliers before Booth's trials and errors. Well-prepared and high-quality ordinary cocoa could be procured elsewhere, mainly in Brazil, but it was more expensive. In 1901, Edward Thackray, the firm's cocoa buyer, was sent to Trinidad and Tobago to evaluate its cocoa potential.[62] But it was in another African country, the British colony of Gold Coast (Ghana, after independence), that the firm found the solution for its cocoa problem. From the late nineteenth century onward, local farmers there had developed a burgeoning cocoa industry based on family labor, low capital inputs, and plenty of cheap land. However, the Gold Coast cocoas were described by experts as "the crudest imaginable."[63] Considering that "the bulk of Gold Coast cocoa was of a far lower quality than which they were accustomed to using," Cadbury "was reluctant to advertise the fact that it was using Gold Coast cocoa because it was feared that this intelligence might damage its reputation within the trade."[64] But this cocoa, even if poorly fermented, dried, and sorted, could be safely and rewardingly used in the new cocoa and chocolate recipes—when mixed with milk and sugar or alkalized.

In 1912 and 1913, after the incorporation of less-standardized cocoas into the factory lines following the boycott of cocoa from São Tomé, Cadbury's established a

58. Chemists' Department Annual Reports (1902–1925), Annual report July 1902–June 1903, CA.

59. Chemists' Department Annual Reports (1902–1925), Annual report July 1903–June 1904, CA.

60. Chemists' Department Annual Reports (1902–1925), Annual report July 1905–June 1906, CA.

61. Chemists' Department Annual Reports (1902–1925), Annual report July 1906–June 1907, CA.

62. Higgs, *Chocolate Islands*, 135.

63. Johnson, *Cocoa*, 147.

64. Southall, "Cadbury on the Gold Coast, 1907–1938," 55.

Research Committee, uniting the Chemistry and the Engineering Departments, and a Cocoa Control Committee. The latter brought together Barrow Cadbury, Edward Thackray, Norman Booth, Thomas Hackett, Thomas King, and Fanny Price. Cocoa was a matter of interest for, respectively, the company's secretary, the firm's cocoa buyer, the chemistry department head, the chief of the works foremen, the person responsible for the roasting and nibbing operations, and the head forewoman. This new committee was to oversee all "the matters connected with the manufacture and packing of cocoa" and to "be responsible for the maintenance of cocoas to the best standards possible of quality, flavor, color, texture, packing and other relative points."[65] Working in between the laboratory and the shop floor, these men (and one woman) carefully monitored the stocks of cocoas, controlled samples, and devised new processing methods, from pressing to grinding. Booth kept experimenting with every type of analytical control that might guarantee an economic advantage. For example, he began testing hundreds and then thousands of samples taken from individual pressers to evaluate the "uniformity of pressing."[66] Those men who revealed standard performances were paid a bonus. The strength of a human arm and the amount of cocoa butter extracted were two parts of a single equation intended to create the most rewarding final product. Uniting laborers and beans, the new lines in the Cadbury portfolio constituted a technical response at the intersection of the material and the social. The laboratory aligned the characteristics of cocoa beans with the competitive pressures, consumer desires, and ethical demands of the British marketplace.

Conclusion

This article joins other commodity-centered histories that discuss how the benefits of industrial growth and increased consumption in the Global North cannot be decoupled from processes of exploitation of peoples and places located far away in the Global South. Blurring the neat boundaries, postulations, and prejudices underlying the industrial-agricultural division of labor, I have used cocoa and chocolate to bring plantations in São Tomé and a factory in Birmingham, and their different labor regimes, together in a single history. But this article has also added to that literature by embracing the challenge of thinking with materials and the ways they produced specific social worlds. Doing so allows us to reexamine labor practices and their categorizations, specifically the value-laden attribution of "skill" to some work and not other work and the resulting inequalities of such hierarchization. In this history, the skilled labor of plantation workers is coupled with the expertise of technicians in the factory.

On São Tomé plantations, producing cocoas that were uniform in terms of size, ripeness, and fermentation and drying methods also created and then naturalized a particular plantation social order: if laborers made a standard cocoa, cocoa also made people, organizing them along the lines of class, race, and gender. When we

---

65. Cocoa Control Committee Minutes (July 1913 to December 1917), July 5, 1913, CA.
66. Chemists' Department Annual Reports (1902–1925), Annual Reports, CA.

look at the materiality of cocoa, it is also possible to reappreciate the embodied and tacit knowledge—the techniques, dexterity, and coordination—that men and women mobilized in harvesting and sorting those beans. As a product of colonial brutality, their labor under coercion and surveillance was not "unskilled," and their specific expertise was essential for transforming the Amelonado variety into a "standard."

In the factory in Bourneville, cocoa properties were also restructuring labor relations and impacting even the very design of the shop floor. But it is the laborious and tedious work of chemists, essential in the process of testing raw materials, stabilizing chocolate flavors, and creating new recipes, that helps to cast light on the material powers of the cocoa beans and the labor necessary to tame them. Chemists were also bound to cocoa, though in a very different way than plantation laborers were. By reexamining the technological work being performed on plantations and inside British chocolate factories, we can see that mass production was very much rooted in and shaped by concrete things. Looking at cocoa and chocolate as a material process expands our understanding of the different labor and social worlds those materials sustained.

MARTA MACEDO is a researcher at the Institute of Contemporary History, NOVA University of Lisbon, Portugal. Her current project examines the circulation of coffee and cocoa plantation systems (São Tomé, Brazil, Angola, Belgium Congo, and Cameroon), combining approaches from history of science and technology, labor history, environmental history, and the history of capitalism. Recently she coedited the volume *Global Plantations in the Modern World: Sovereignties, Ecologies, Afterlives* (2023).

References

Alder, Ken. "Thick Things: Introduction." *Isis* 98, no. 1 (2007): 80–83.

Ali, Tariq Omar. *A Local History of Global Capital: Jute and Peasant Life in the Bengal Delta*. Princeton, NJ: Princeton University Press, 2018.

Beckert, Sven. *Empire of Cotton: A Global History*. New York: Alfred A. Knopf, 2014.

Blochouse, Marcel de. "La colonie portugaise de l'Ile de San Thomé sous l'equateur." *Annales de Gembloux* 15 (1905): 250–59, 381–93.

Booth, Norman P., and Arthur W. Knapp. "The Qualities in Cacao Desired by Manufacturers." In *Transactions of the Third International Congress of Tropical Agriculture*, vol. 2, 169–75. London: John Bale, Sons & Danielsson, 1914.

Bradley, John. *Cadbury's Purple Reign: The Story behind Chocolate's Best-Loved Brand*. Chichester, UK: John Wiley, 2008.

Bray, Francesca. *Technology and Gender: Fabrics of Power in Late Imperial China*. Berkeley: University of California Press, 1997.

Bray, Francesca. "Translating the Art of Tea: Naturalizing Chinese Savoir Faire in British Assam." In *Entangled Itineraries: Materials, Practices, and Knowledges across Eurasia*, edited by Pamela H. Smith, 99–137. Pittsburgh: University of Pittsburgh Press, 2019.

Bray, Francesca, Barbara Hahn, John Lourdusamy, and Tiago Saraiva. *Moving Crops and the Scales of History*. New Haven, CT: Yale University Press, 2023.

Cadbury, Edward. *Experiments in Industrial Organisation*. London: Longmans, Green and Co., 1912.

Candido, Mariana. *An African Slaving Port and the Atlantic World: Benguela and Its Hinterland*. Cambridge: Cambridge University Press, 2013.

Chance, Helena. *The Factory in a Garden: A History of Corporate Landscapes from the Industrial to the Digital Age*. Manchester: Manchester University Press, 2017.

Chevalier, Auguste. *Le cacaoyer dans L'Ouest Africain*. Vol. 4: *Les végétaux utiles de L'Afrique tropicale française*. Paris: A. Challamel, 1908.

Clarence-Smith, William Gervase. *Cocoa and Chocolate, 1765–1914*. London: Routledge, 2000.

Clarence-Smith, William Gervase, and Steven Topik, eds. *The Global Coffee Economy in Africa, Asia and Latin America, 1500–1989*. Cambridge: Cambridge University Press, 2003.

Dellheim, Charles. "The Creation of a Company Culture: Cadburys, 1861–1931." *American Historical Review* 92, no. 1 (1987): 13–44.

Direcção Geral do Ultramar. *Collecção official da legislação portugueza*. Lisbon: Imprensa Nacional, 1878.

Doyle, Daniel J. "Cocoa and Class in British Popular Press Advertising: A Process of Cultural Agency." In *Illusive Identity: The Blurring of Working-Class Consciousness in Modern Western Culture*, edited by Thomas J. Edward Walker, 11–39. Lanham, MD: Lexington Books, 2002.

Edgerton, David. *The Rise and Fall of the British Nation: A Twentieth-Century History*. London: Penguin Books, 2019.

Fitzgerald, Robert. "Products, Firms and Consumption: Cadbury and the Development of Marketing, 1900–1939." *Business History* 47, no. 4 (2005): 511–31.

Gentle, Henry. "Raising the Workman's Efficiency: Methods of Lightening, Ventilation and Cleansing the Atmosphere of One Factory That Help to Insure the Best Services of Employees with a Resulting Excellence of Product." *System: The Magazine of Business* 14 (August 1908): 163–65.

Grant, Kevin. *A Civilised Savagery: Britain and the New Slaveries in Africa, 1884–1926*. London: Routledge, 2005.

Harris, John. *Dawn in Darkest Africa*. London: Smith, Elder & Co., 1912.

Higgs, Catherine. *Chocolate Islands: Cocoa, Slavery, and Colonial Africa*. Athens: Ohio University Press, 2012.

Hopkins, Eric. "Industrial Change and Life at Work in Birmingham 1850–1914." *Midland History* 27, no. 8 (2002): 112–29.

Horrocks, Sally M. "Consuming Science: Science, Technology and Food in Britain: 1870–1939." PhD diss., University of Manchester, 1993.

Ingold, Tim. "Materials against Materiality." *Archaeological Dialogues* 14, no. 1 (2007): 1–16.

Jerónimo, Miguel Bandeira. *The "Civilizing Mission" of Portuguese Colonialism, 1870–1930*. Basingstoke, UK: Palgrave Macmillan, 2015.

Johnson, William Henry. *Cocoa, Its Cultivation and Preparation*. London: John Murray, 1912.

Knapp, Arthur W. *Cocoa and Chocolate: Their History from Plantation to Consumer*. London: Chapman and Hall, 1920.

LeCain, Timothy J. *The Matter of History: How Things Create the Past*. Cambridge: Cambridge University Press, 2017.

Lee, Victoria. *The Arts of the Microbial World: Fermentation Science in Twentieth-Century Japan*. Chicago: University of Chicago Press, 2022.

Macedo, Marta. "Standard Cocoa: Transnational Networks and Technoscientific Regimes in West African Plantations." *Technology and Culture* 57, no. 3 (2016): 557–85.

Miller, Joseph Calder. *Way of Death: Merchant Capitalism and the Angolan Slave Trade, 1730–1830.* Madison: University of Wisconsin Press, 1988.

Mintz, Sidney. *Sweetness and Power: The Place of Sugar in Modern History.* New York: Penguin Books, 1985.

Montet, Maurice. "Une plantation de cacaoyers à Sao-Thome." *La dépêche coloniale illustrée* 7 (March 1907): 49–57.

Nevinson, Henry W. *A Modern Slavery.* London: Harper & Brothers, 1906.

Norton, Marcy. *Sacred Gifts, Profane Pleasures: A History of Tobacco and Chocolate in the Atlantic World.* Ithaca, NY: Cornell University Press, 2008.

Othick, J. "The Cocoa and Chocolate Industry in the Nineteenth Century." In *The Making of the Modern British Diet*, edited by Derek J. Oddy and Derek S. Miller, 77–90. London: Croom Helm, 1976.

Otter, Chris. *Diet for a Large Planet: Industrial Britain, Food Systems, and World Ecology.* Chicago: University of Chicago Press, 2020.

Rockman, Seth. *Der alte und der neue Materialismus in der Geschichte der Sklaverei.* Berlin: De Gruyter Oldenbourg, 2022.

"Sanitary Factories: 1. Bourneville (Cadbury Brothers)." *Sanitary Record: A Weekly Journal of Public Health* 18 (October 1896): 288–91.

Saraiva, Tiago. *Fascist Pigs: Technoscientific Organisms and the History of Fascism.* Cambridge, MA: MIT Press, 2016.

Satre, Lowell J. *Chocolate on Trial: Slavery, Politics, and the Ethics of Business.* Athens: Ohio University Press, 2005.

Sharma, Jayeeta. "British Science, Chinese Skill and Assam Tea: Making Empire's Garden." *Indian Economic Social History Review* 43, no. 4 (2006): 429–55.

Slaton, Amy. *Reinforced Concrete and the Modernization of American Building, 1900–1930.* Baltimore: Johns Hopkins University Press, 2001.

Smith, Christopher, John Child, and Michael Rowlinson. *Reshaping Work: The Cadbury Experience.* Cambridge: Cambridge University Press, 1991.

Smith, Harold Hamel. *The Fermentation of Cacao.* London: Bale and Danielsson, 1913.

Smith, Kate. "Amidst Things: New Histories of Commodities, Capital, and Consumption." *Historical Journal* 61, no. 3 (2018): 841–61.

Southall, Roger J. "Cadbury on the Gold Coast, 1907–1938: The Dilemma of the 'Model Firm' in a Colonial Economy." PhD diss., University of Birmingham, 1975.

Thackray, Edward S. "Employees' Welfare in England: Conditions of Four Thousand Employees in the Cadbury Cocoa Works." *The Commons* 10, no. 8 (August 1905): 455–62.

van der Linden, Marcel. *Workers of the World: Essays toward a Global Labor History.* Leiden: Brill, 2008.

Williams, Iolo Aneurin. *The Firm of Cadbury, 1831–1931.* London: Constable and Co., 1931.

Womack, John, Jr. "Doing Labor History: Feelings, Work, Material Power." *Journal of the Historical Society* 5, no. 3 (2005): 255–96.

Zipperer, Paul. *The Manufacture of Chocolate and Other Cacao Preparations.* Berlin: Verlag Von M. Krayn, 1915.

Science as Routine: Work and Labor in the Bureau of Science at Manila

Jonathan Victor Baldoza

At the beginning of the twentieth century, the Bureau of Science commanded the scientific endeavors of the American colonial government in the Philippines. Science at the bureau's Manila compound was work, involving various kinds of technical, manual, and clerical labor, and mobilizing varying skills and aptitudes from its "scientific force."[1] Though the bureau prioritized scientific research, conducting such scholarly workrequired the extensive support of clerical and manual personnel in everyday tasks such as filing documents, cataloging reference materials, arranging specimen collections, and cleaning laboratories (see fig. 1). The boundary between research and routine was blurry but essential to the bureau's operations.[2] While it recognized that doing scientific research involves repetitive and mundane labor, it also functioned to undervalue much of that work—and the workers who performed it—from what counted as science and who counted as a scientist in the American-

I am grateful to the organizers of the 2022 Gordon Cain Conference, especially Seth Rockman for his encouragement and feedback. I thank my colleagues in the "Labor Takes Place: Workscapes, Topographies, and Infrastructure" panel for helping me think through initial ideas and questions, particularly Trish Kahle. I also thank Michael Gordin, Eva Molina, Uyen Nguyen, and Patrick Anthony for reading and commenting on earlier drafts.

1. Freer, *Fifth Annual Report*, 14. I primarily examine the annual reports of the bureau, tools of "bureaucratic knowledge" generated every fiscal year of the colonial government. See Felten and von Oertzen, "Bureaucracy as Knowledge," 8.

2. Scientists classified the bureau's work across divisions and sections under two broad categories, "research" and "routine," without precise definitions. From my reading, routine work, whether in entomology, botany, or another, primarily referred to manual labor that provided regular assistance to laboratory investigation and fieldwork. It also included clerical support to the bureau's overall operation.

3. The exclusive devotion to general scientific research made the bureau distinctive. There were other domain-specific scientific agencies, such as the Philippine Weather Bureau. Led by Jesuit José Algue, it retained the structure and personnel of the Observatorio Meteorológico de Manila as it became part of the American colonial state. See Warren, "Scientific Superman." For a history of Philippine bureaucracy, see Corpuz, *Bureaucracy in the Philippines*.

Labor: Studies in Working-Class History, Volume 21, Issue 1
DOI 10.1215/15476715-10948933   © 2024 by Labor and Working-Class History Association

Figure 1. The Silk House, with two Filipino routine workers: a male and female silk attendant.

ruled archipelago.[3] Scientists acting as bureaucrats underscored the importance of routine to the workings of the bureau, yet they stressed that such class of work was perfunctory and menial, involving little or less significant scientific competence, and always second fiddle to research.[4] Negotiating the zone between research and routine labor, the bureau ascribed legitimacy to certain types of expertise and skills while denying such status and associated social power from other forms of labor that were equally indispensable to scientific work.

This article explores the labor history of science in the Philippines by examining the bureau's management and routinization of scientific knowledge production. Under the bureau, the management of scientific work resembled what Lukas Rieppel has described in the nineteenth-century United States as "a distinctly bureaucratic vision of the way that a large, capital-intensive, and organizationally complex institution ought to be managed."[5] American scientists, assigned bureaucratic roles by the colonial government, applied organizational acumen developed by business leaders during an "age of incorporation" to fuel the scientific bureau's productivity, efficiency, and growth.[6] These insights shaped how the bureau's divisions and hierarchies of labor were arranged, how the personnel, workspaces, and resources were managed, and how its institutional goals were planned.[7]

---

4. On "routine work" described as "essential but humble scientific work" in an African context, see Jacobs, *Birders of Africa*, 192.

5. Rieppel, *Assembling the Dinosaur*, 114.

6. Trachtenberg, *Incorporation of America*; Haber, *Efficiency and Uplift*; Hays, *Response to Industrialism*; Freeman, *Behemoth*.

7. Rieppel, "Organizing the Marketplace," 246.

Managing a bureau so complex in its range of work entailed some kind of "logic of organization."[8] This was supplied by the scientists who supervised the bureau's operations and managed the direction of its growth.[9] As managers and bureaucrats, scientists had to categorize and divide areas of work, quantify results and yields from investigations, and pen mandatory reports on the goods and services the bureau provided. They vigorously expanded the scope of scientific work, reorganizing divisions and sections, increasing lines of investigation, and opening both credentialed and noncredentialed positions. They led the scientific force in producing, testing, and analyzing the data that informed the administration of the colony.[10] Such data, meticulously recorded and published in reports and scientific journals, cultivated trust in state governance and enhanced the rationality of the colonial project as a whole.[11] Both American and Filipino scientists employed by the bureau served as managers and bureaucrats, assigned to lead and administer knowledge production under the state and provide governance with a scientific element.[12]

Despite its hierarchies, the bureau also promoted a coherent "ecology" within the Manila compound that kindled national and professional identities, becoming a place for Filipino men and women to develop a scientific career and reputation.[13] Angel Arguelles, the bureau's first Filipino director, appointed in 1934, started as assistant chemist in 1909, performing supervised routine labor in the chemistry division, and gradually advanced into expert and administrative work. In this way, the bureau's function as "training ground" for scientists reinforced the notion that in providing tutelage US imperialism was exceptional.[14] Arguelles would later praise and echo his American predecessors' advocacy for science as the basis for economic prog-

---

8. Rieppel, "Organizing the Marketplace," 233. These biological insights informed nineteenth-century industrial society in the United States, which, as Lukas Rieppel has argued, mirrored the growth of corporate firms "subject to managerial oversight, rational planning, and top-down control." See Rieppel, "Organizing the Marketplace," 251.

9. Chandler, *Visible Hand*; Kohler, "Management of Science."

10. Bayly, *Empire and Information*; Cohn, *Colonialism and Its Forms of Knowledge*, 5. All civil service positions were subject to colonial state regulations. Required qualifications varied according to the type of work needed. The Bureau of Science, for example, required technical and scientific knowledge for its higher-level positions.

11. Porter, *Trust in Numbers*.

12. On scientists as bureaucrats in the nineteenth-century Habsburg empire, see Coen, *Climate in Motion*.

13. Rosenberg, "Toward an Ecology of Knowledge"; Star and Griesemer, "Institutional Ecology, 'Translations' and Boundary Objects."

14. Bradley Brazzeal makes a similar point in his discussion of Mary Polk's mentorship of Filipino librarians in the Bureau of Science Library. See Brazzeal, "Science Librarianship in Colonial Philippines," 9–10. In the late nineteenth century, Kerby Alvarez has argued that the Observatorio Meterológico de Manila served as a scientific "training ground" for its male Filipino workers. Alvarez, "Instrumentation and Institutionalization," 405, 413. Furthermore, James Warren wrote that under Jesuit José Algué's supervision, Filipino laborers were "recruited, trained, and assigned to postings throughout the archipelago where they were authorized to make synchronous weather predictions for their areas and to telegraph local conditions to the Manila office." Warren, "Scientific Superman," 509.

ress and political modernity. Yet he spoke for the benefit of the forthcoming national republic rather than the US colonial state.[15]

The "Unity" of Scientific Work

The US colonial state in the Philippines required the work and labor of science—capaciously understood—in exploring the archipelago's natural resources and tropical environment.[16] Initial scientific work included installing laboratory facilities for the production of vaccines and employing the clinical expertise of physicians associated with pacification and disease eradication.[17] In 1901, as the US regime transitioned from military to civil rule, scientific work ranging from chemical and biological analyses to medical treatments became anchored in colonial social engineering, as well as commercialization and industrial development.[18]

Scientific knowledge production formed part of the developing colonial administrative state, first as the Bureau of Government Laboratories, and then consolidated in 1905 as the Bureau of Science.[19] Such centralization marshaled a variety of sciences, combining biological, chemical, and geological investigations.[20] Centralization also managed the resources furnished by the US colonial state more judiciously. The leading scientist-bureaucrat in the bureau's first decade, Paul Freer, a chemist and physician, argued that the "fusion of work" allowed for more efficient coordination of expertise and better allocation and use of resources and laboratory facilities. More so, it avoided the unnecessary duplication of scientific investigations (see fig. 2).[21]

The eagerness to unite all scientific work informed the managerial vision of Freer, a chemistry professor at the University of Michigan prior to his stint in the

15. On the bureau shaping ambivalent reception and interpretation of US imperialism among Filipino scientists, see Baldoza, "Under the Aegis of Science," 89–92. See also Anderson and Pols, "Scientific Patriotism."

16. Anderson, "Science in the Philippines"; Bankoff, "Science of Nature"; Baldoza, "Under the Aegis of Science"; Pagunsan, "Nature, Colonial Science and Nation-Building." On how the Spanish imperial bureaucracy shaped scientific work, see De Vos, "Research, Development, and Empire."

17. Ileto, "Cholera and the Origins of the American Sanitary Order in the Philippines"; Anderson, *Colonial Pathologies*.

18. May, *Social Engineering in the Philippines*. On how the colonial state devised scientific ways of addressing problems of food scarcity and hunger, see Ventura, "Medicalizing *Gutom*."

19. Act No. 156, "An Act Providing for the Establishment of Government Laboratories for the Philippine Islands," enacted on July 1, 1901. In *Public Laws and Resolutions Passed by the United States Philippine Commission*. The "Reorganization Act" of 1905 (Act No. 1407, enacted on October 26, 1905) established the Bureau of Science as the central scientific agency. In *Public Laws and Resolutions Passed by the United States Philippine Commission. Division of Insular Affairs, War Department*. Volume 5, Manila: Bureau of Printing, 1907.

20. Hays, *Response to Industrialism*, 48–49. The structure included components and divisions like the scientific library: the Biology Division, with sections for entomology, botany, and zoology; the Chemistry Division (which investigated the economic potential of materials like gums, resins, oils, and fibers); a Serums and Prophylactics Division; and a Mines Division (which worked on geological and topographical surveying and mapping).

21. Freer, *Fifth Annual Report*, 3.

Figure 2. Paul Freer, the first director of the Bureau of Science.

Philippines. This followed the "dream" of Dean Worcester, the colonial government's interior secretary and Freer's Michigan colleague and brother-in-law. Worcester later wrote that he had envisioned all Manila-based scientific institutions to operate "standing side by side and working in full and harmonious relationship," sharing laboratory facilities, equipment, and personnel.[22]

Like Worcester, Freer was keen to develop the general scientific work in the Philippines by coordinating the work of publicly funded institutions.[23] Requesting more funds, he argued that all colonial, science-related institutions needed to work together, with employees of equivalent rank paid equally, "in such a way that no danger of any rivalry between the two institutions would ever exist."[24] He preferred "close union" among scientists headquartered in Manila: "The entire body, clinical and laboratory, should form a united scientific unit."[25] When the General Hospital and Medical School opened in 1907, the first practitioners and instructors were from

22. Worcester, *The Philippines Past and Present*, 489. Worcester drew from his experience as a zoology professor at the University of Michigan where "questions of jurisdiction," he wrote, drove scientists to isolate and reject collaboration. Such "unscientific and ungenerous" working environment, Worcester contended, must be avoided in the Philippines. See Worcester, *The Philippines Past and Present*, 492–95.

23. For a background on Paul Freer written by his colleagues, see the *Philippine Journal of Science* 7 (1912). The facilities of the Bureau of Science were likewise enjoyed by scientist-bureaucrats from other agencies such as the Bureau of Agriculture. They also published research results in the bureau's *Philippine Journal of Science*. See Ventura, "Medicalizing *Gutom*," 50.

24. Freer, *Tenth Annual Report*, 11.

25. Freer, *Seventh Annual Report*, 11.

the bureau. The director was appointed dean, while other staff joined the faculty and engaged in instruction, clinical investigation, and affiliated laboratory work.[26] Freer wrote that the work of these new institutions felt "so inseparable that one can scarcely be considered without the other."[27] The following year, the state university was established, absorbing the medical school. The added teaching workload complicated the bureau's division of labor, as the staff of the bureau formed part of the initial faculty and even offered positions with better pay. Freer criticized the competing opportunities offered by this arrangement.[28]

As the government expanded, so did scientific work. From 1905, the bureau's primary divisions constantly shifted, requiring reclassification of resources, spaces, and personnel. Classifying divisions and sections hinged on the practical importance of particular lines of investigation, as well as the immediate availability of labor, facilities, and apparatus to pursue them.[29] But the most pressing factor in reorganization was how the bureau's scientists addressed the needs of the colonial administration. Scientific requests from different state agencies decided the priority level of particular research activities.

By 1913, the bureau's range of work had grown to seventy-eight specific lines of scientific investigation. Such growth highlighted the increase in public trust, credibility and prestige of the bureau. It became an essential source of scientific information for government agencies and the general public. It also needed more funding, more scientific workers, better conditions and salaries, and continued institutional development.[30]

Addressing various types of technical problems and questions presented by government agencies was classified as routine work. Chemist Alvin Cox, successor to Freer as director of the bureau, wrote that "in practically every branch of its activities the Bureau of Science needs more scientific employees to keep up with the regular work of the institution, to do the work requested, to be ready to supply desired information, and to answer questions when they arise."[31] Routine work in the chemistry division, for example, included multiple inquiries and consultations that could be answered by "referring to reports or publications covering the point in question" that the bureau already possessed.[32]

26. Freer, *Sixth Annual Report*, 7–8; Freer, *Seventh Annual Report*, 3–12. On public health initiatives and medical activities as components of the Bureau of Science, see Planta, *Traditional Medicine in the Colonial Philippines*, 104–9.

27. Freer, *Seventh Annual Report*, 9.

28. In Freer's critique, the colonial government "founded a new institution which can, by a greater advantage in funds, do damage to another established by the same government." Freer, *Tenth Annual Report*, 10. See also Alfonso and Bauzon, *University of the Philippines*.

29. For example, the section of ichthyology, already organized for the study of fish and fisheries, was envisioned to gradually include studies of other types of marine life (sponges, corals, and pearl oysters). Its anticipated expansion would elevate it to the "status of a division and ultimately [having] a permanent force, equipment, and laboratories." Freer, *Sixth Annual Report*, 25; Star, "This Is Not a Boundary Object."

30. Freer, *Ninth Annual Report*, 7.

31. Cox, *Fifteenth Annual Report*, 61.

32. Cox, *Eleventh Annual Report*, 24.

But the growing bureau was getting too many external requests from government agencies.[33] Cox complained that the increasing variety and amount of requested routine work, and the lack of space and manpower to fulfill those requests, made it almost impossible for credentialed force to conduct research.[34] Describing the activities of the botany section, Cox wrote that only two botanists, Elmer Merrill and William Brown, administered the specialized section, which made it "a manifestly impossible task to keep up the routine work of the herbarium, prepare and edit the manuscripts for the section of botany of the *Philippine Journal of Science*, teach from nine to eighteen hours per week at the University, and do anything else."[35] Thus, addressing routine requests required more workers to unburden scientists, who were already strategizing with "improved methods, overtime work, and neglect of important research."[36]

Science as routinized work demanded time and energy that scientists did not want to give entirely. It interfered with accomplishing research and developing new areas of investigation, which were regarded as the main tasks of the "scientific employees" of the bureau.[37] As later acting director Richard McGregor, an ornithologist and part of the zoology division, would write, "An institution that does only routine can present a pleasing annual report, but is as dead as a director who does nothing but sign the documents to his desk."[38]

For the botanist Merrill, also later director, the term *routine* was "unfortunate in the sense that it conveys to many individuals the idea of perfunctory daily tasks, perfunctorily accomplished; whereas, as a matter of fact, the enormous mass of routine work carried on by the institution demands on the part of its technical staff charged with the performance or supervision of these duties high technical training, wide experience, and distinct ability."[39] As such, routine-related issues could be resolved by the employment of more trained laborers from the local population to which routinized tasks could be delegated.[40] Hiring Filipinos as routine laborers would not be a problem, as many of them had already been working in the bureau when it began.[41]

33. Cox, *Twelfth Annual Report*, 104–5.

34. Cox, *Twelfth Annual Report*, 14.

35. Cox, *Thirteenth Annual Report*, 56.

36. McGregor, *Nineteenth Annual Report*, 4.

37. Cox, *Thirteenth Annual Report*, 55.

38. McGregor, *Nineteenth Annual Report*, 4.

39. Merrill added, "Not only the ability to perform the technical daily tasks efficiently and well, but also to initiate new work, to modify standard methods to meet local needs, and to apply locally the results obtained by modern research, whether carried on here or elsewhere." Merrill, *Twenty-First Annual Report*, 4.

40. Freer, *Fifth Annual Report*, 14.

41. Cox, *Thirteenth Annual Report*, 36; Freer, *Sixth Annual Report*, 37. A named routine worker of the bureau was Andres Celestino, "the only assistant in this division, [who had] made collections in northern Mindanao, in Siquijor, and in Bulacan Province, Luzon, securing 402 specimens of birds and a few insects, mollusks and mammals." Freer, *Seventh Annual Report*, 40.

Figure 3. The Bureau of Science grounds in Manila.

Routine labor, then, was essential work in the production of scientific knowledge, even if it was considered mundane and less significant. Nevertheless, while acknowledging routine as part of the bureau's regular work, Cox maintained, "Research work indicates the latent wealth of the nation, and bears the same relation to the commercial world that blocked-out ore does to a developed mine."[42]

"Under the Same Roof"

The expansion of the bureau compound in Manila mirrored both its institutional growth and the developing areas of scientific work in the Philippines, organized and reorganized according to equally diverse categories and branches of science. Having the workspaces centralized within the bureau's compound meant that scientific work followed analogous administrative procedures in the same location (see fig. 3).

Scientists arranged spaces to be near each other in the bureau building, which had laboratory facilities, collection and storage rooms, and lecture spaces. The physical "unity" was represented by spatial construction, designed by Freer "to promote the feeling of scientific unity among the members of the staff."[43] Freer argued that for "unity of work" the different constituent parts, "the working collections, together with the staff connected with them, should not be separated from the main structure" and that working "under the same roof" provided closer communication among the scientific workers.[44] The library, herbarium, and museum were important appendages

42. Cox, *Twelfth Annual Report*, 15.

43. Freer, *Fifth Annual Report*, 8. The aspiration to "scientific unity" among the Bureau's scientists would endure in justifying centralization. As later director Elmer Merrill would write in 1923, scientific work was centralized in the bureau "in order to avoid duplication of technical personnel, equipment, and literature by other units of the Government service; in other words, to gain economy and efficiency in administration." Merrill, *Twenty-First Annual Report*, 4.

44. Freer, *Sixth Annual Report*, 6.

to the central building, separate spaces but fundamentally part of scientific work. As a focal point, the library was in charge of cataloging and classifying materials and handling the general circulation of scientific literature, including references, publications, volumes of scientific journals, expedition reports, manuals, and maps.[45]

Every year, as the work grew, overcrowding and limited storage space prompted interest in expanding the compound.[46] The bureau's leading scientists proposed to build new wings, more shelves and rooms for the library, and more cases for the herbarium.[47] Aside from the need for a higher budget, the additions demonstrated how scientists understood scientific labor as shaped by the built environment.[48]

"Inadequate laboratory space" resurfaced as a yearly problem; scientists were always "working in crowded rooms."[49] By 1920, new spaces were still needed, like a new building for experiments involving plague rats, as "the sickening odor from the long-dead rats renders work in the library and the division of mines well-nigh impossible."[50] The following year, Elmer Merrill, then the director, reported that the bureau was "becoming badly cramped for space," the "library has reached maximum expansion," and the herbarium too has "reached its maximum development in its present quarters."[51] Again, Merrill emphasized "overcrowded" laboratories with little room for expansion.[52]

In addition, creating a space for workday interactions addressed other challenges facing the bureau. In the first place, American scientists complained of the climate, which made it challenging to recruit properly qualified personnel. Many perceived the tropical environment as having negative effects on the body and well-being of the preferred white, male scientists.[53] Freer reflected, "Scientific isolation is the greatest handicap we have to contend with in the Tropics, and this condition can only be ameliorated by the freest and most general contact among the members of the force."[54]

Thus, the centralized operation of the bureau encouraged "the mutual stimulus and enthusiasm which result by bringing all or most scientists together in one place for the performance of their various work."[55] Outside the office, scientists-bureaucrats would socialize together, swimming, playing golf, and gathering at the Manila Polo Club with other colonial officials.[56] Governor-General William Cameron

45. Freer, *Sixth Annual Report*, 12–15.

46. Freer, *Fifth Annual Report*, 4.

47. Freer, *Seventh Annual Report*, 28. In 1910, to promote the cultivation of silk for commerce, a silk house was constructed in nearby Singalong with "ant-proof" racks and appropriate lighting conditions.

48. Freer, *Fifth Annual Report*, 4.

49. Cox, *Fifteenth Annual Report*, 61.

50. McGregor, *Nineteenth Annual Report*, 45.

51. Merrill, *Twentieth Annual Report*, 61.

52. Merrill, *Twenty-First Annual Report*, 45.

53. Raby, *American Tropics*.

54. Freer, *Fifth Annual Report*, 8.

55. *Extract of Assembly Resolution No. 108*, November 9, 1915.

56. William Cameron Forbes, entry for Saturday, August 13, 1904, vol. 1 of Typewritten Transcript of Journals, p. 40, MSS20982, William Cameron Forbes Papers, Manuscript Division, Library of Congress, Washington, DC.

Forbes recalled meetings in early 1904 with different heads of bureaus, building rapport for officials who were part of the colonial infrastructure, arguing that "the institution of eating together once a week proved to be of the utmost administrative value [as it] made for esprit de corps and team play in the department."[57] Informal contact was good in cultivating mutual trust and sociability among the scientific staff.[58]

In the late 1900s, the bureau recruited more credentialed US-trained Filipinos to do routine work supervised by higher-ranked scientists, part of the "Filipinization of the force."[59] While the bureau relied on employees trained for scientific work under the Spanish empire, this new group consisted of those who had attended public schools and government *pensionados* sent abroad for graduate education and training.[60] Starting in 1909, Filipinos like José del Rosario, Timoteo Dar Juan, and Angel Arguelles worked as part of the scientific staff in the chemical laboratory, after having been assessed satisfactorily for their "capability" in performing tasks in "minor positions."[61] University-educated and laboratory-trained female scientists would also enter the bureau's workforce as junior specialists in their respective fields.[62]

Managing the Scientific Force

Leading the bureau required scientists to realize their own organizational plans and managerial visions.[63] For Freer, increasing the bureau's respectability and prestige demanded a system that could attract skilled personnel, with opportunities for promotion and intellectual advancement. A tenure mechanism, subject to the rules of

57. William Cameron Forbes, entry for Saturday, Saturday, September 10, 1904, vol. 1 of Typewritten Transcript of Journals, p. 66, MSS20982, William Cameron Forbes Papers, Manuscript Division, Library of Congress, Washington, DC.

58. Withers, "Place and the 'Spatial Turn' in Geography and in History"; Shapin, "Placing the View from Nowhere," 6; Livingstone, "Spaces of Knowledge."

59. Freer, *Ninth Annual Report*, 32–33. For a discussion on Filipinization, see Corpuz, *The Bureaucracy of the Philippines*, 195–213.

60. Hugo Navarro, formerly a draftsman for the Inspección General de Minas, was employed in the bureau's Division of Mines. Freer, *Seventh Annual Report*, 54. Discussing the labors of a forester in late nineteenth century Spanish Philippines, Greg Bankoff argues that state-sponsored forestry as scientific practice was both colonial and indigenous, because of the presence of assistants or *ayudantes*. In this regard, Filipino state foresters represented the Spanish imperial state in collecting duties, enforcing regulations, and surveying lands, and submitted log reports of their activities; see Bankoff, "Month in the Life of José Salud." See also Gutierrez, "Region of Imperial Strategy," 107–29. For the "native staff," see Alvarez, "Instrumentation and Institutionalization," 405–7.

61. Strong, *Eighth Annual Report*, 5.

62. On Filipino women entering the professional scientific fields, see Nery, "Feminine Invasion"; Baldoza, "Under the Aegis of Science." On women in the emergent nursing profession, see Catherine Ceniza Choy, *Empire of Care*, 31–38.

63. Karen Miller has drawn attention to a distinctive type of American masculinity that became valuable in empire building, one exhibited by men through the exercise of administrative work, rather than military aptitude. See Miller, "'Thin, Wistful, and White.'" On soldiers performing alternative labor for the US colonial state, specifically collecting specimens that required natural curiosity and environmental sensibility, see Kohout, *Taking the Field*.

Figure 4. The Scientific Staff in 1912, including Filipino scientists like Angel Arguelles.

the colonial civil service, would prevent "trained men" from finding another place to work while still employed, leaving their work in the bureau unfinished.[64] What the bureau needed, Freer argued, were "energetic and well-trained scientific men" who "[would] be willing to enter the Bureau in the lower positions with the hope and expectations of working their way to the top (see fig. 4)."[65]

Freer envisioned, "a thorough organization of high standing with ample facilities and an efficient means of bringing its work before the world" to attract more trained scientists to work in Manila.[66] He aspired to gather different specialists and to make the bureau the place for professional scientists to generate legitimate and authoritative science. As Freer wrote, "Places are always available in other parts of the world for good, scientific men, and to retain our own we must make conditions which are favorable to them."[67]

To create this, the bureau must be a stable working environment for local and foreign talent who could cultivate "epistemic values" and endow the bureau's scientific force with professional legitimacy and authority.[68] More than training, valued skills included initiative and enthusiasm.[69] Freer wrote that younger employees must act on their own and "should constantly be spurred on by the spirit of *work* and enthu-

---

64. Freer, *Seventh Annual Report*, 12.
65. Freer, *Fifth Annual Report*, 7.
66. Freer, *Fifth Annual Report*, 7.
67. Freer, *Seventh Annual Report*, 14.
68. Daston and Galison, *Objectivity*.
69. In 1909 Freer wrote, "Any member of the Biological Laboratory who hopes to continue his connection with the Bureau must continually be prepared to make the most of his opportunities and to spend his time when not engaged in routine work, in investigations which he makes an effort to find, and not simply in waiting for what may come to his hands." Freer, *Sixth Annual Report*, 19.

Figure 5. The Clerk Room.

siasm which alone builds up a scientific institution."[70] As the bureau grew, however, problems in salary and conditions for research and promotion challenged Freer's and his successors' vision to increase the bureau's international reputation in the scientific world.[71]

Likewise, scientific knowledge production operated through bureaucratic routine, deploying paperwork that facilitated managerial oversight, planning, and the accounting and tracking of work.[72] To handle the scientific bureaucracy's paperwork, a clerical division was established for filing, bookkeeping, and financial reporting.[73] Clerical work required workers skilled in the mechanisms and rules of information tracking, recording, reporting, and documentation (see fig. 5).[74]

As in other government agencies, clerks and stenographers were indispensable to the operation of the bureau.[75] At the beginning, scientists preferred American clerks. Freer wrote that the tasks needed "high order of clerical efficiency and a knowledge of English which few Filipino clerks have as yet acquired."[76] However,

---

70. Freer, *Seventh Annual Report*, 11.

71. Freer, *Sixth Annual Report*, 18.

72. Rieppel, *Assembling the Dinosaur*, 114, 130–35.

73. Freer, *Seventh Annual Report*, 71.

74. Rieppel, *Assembling the Dinosaur*, 136.

75. Then–acting director Richard Strong wrote that there was a "scientific character to routine work," which ranged from "recording examinations, analyses, tests" to the managing of the bureau's regular correspondence. Strong, *Eighth Annual Report*, 48.

76. Freer, *Tenth Annual Report*, 55.

starting in the 1910s, as American clerks departed, new duties and positions became available to Filipinos. By 1912, more Filipino stenographers were hired, including more women who became part of the bureau's routinized workforce.[77]

By 1913, the bureau employed 144 clerks and laborers, almost three times more than the 50 people working on the scientific, credentialed staff. The asymmetry between expert and routine laborers revealed an organization with constant growth but one where labor was being deliberately reorganized and reclassified.[78] In addition, the problems of overwork, insufficient staff, and lack of space and equipment frustrated the bureau's leadership, more keen to prioritize the scientific agency's research agenda. As Richard McGregor, who became acting head of the bureau in 1920, remarked, "A scientific institution is judged by its discoveries in the treatment of diseases, by its improvement of chemical processes, by its publications on the native plants, animals, and minerals, and by similar additions to knowledge that are useful to the world at large as well as to the country whose government is responsible for the work."[79] Accomplishing routine work did not amount to scientific contribution that the scientists valued, and must be delegated to lower-ranked laborers as much as possible.[80]

In addition, the changing landscape of work in the bureau was not without friction, especially in the wake of Filipinization in the 1910s, which affected the relations between Filipino and American employees. On July 19, 1913, a letter to the *Philippine Free Press*, signed by "Taga-Tansa," described a bureau that was unfair, with two separate pockets, one for Americans and one for Filipinos.[81] The pseudonymous author also attacked the "racial prejudice" in the bureau, made visible by the fact that highly capable Filipinos were paid less than their American counterparts because of the color of their skin.[82] The Filipinization of the scientific force was a "delusion," the letter lamented, an undelivered promise that Filipino workers at the bureau still anticipated.

77. Cox, *Eleventh Annual Report*, 46.

78. Cox wrote, "The growth of this [routine] phase of our work has seriously interfered with our research, and handicapped us in carrying on new lines of investigation as well as completing those already begun. We are in sore need of more employees and laboratory space to carry the additional work entailed by the normal growth of this Bureau. Unless our appropriation is increased, we cannot continue to develop. Our greatest usefulness is curtailed by lack of funds." Cox, *Eleventh Annual Report*, 49–50.

79. McGregor, *Nineteenth Annual Report*, 4.

80. In 1928, the bureau's director William Brown would write, "The most lasting benefits are obtained not from routine work, however important this may be, but by the establishment of new principles and improved practices which result from investigation." Brown, *Twenty-Seventh*, 6.

81. This particular conflict emerged from an incident during which certain Filipino scientists had been told that there were no funds for their requested salary raise. Yet, despite the supposed lack of money, additional Americans were hired as personnel, receiving good salaries even without proper qualifications. In *Typescript of Letter Sent to the Philippine Free Press, July 19, 1913*, signed by "Taga-Tansa." 4 pages in box 3, folder 11, Worcester Papers, Special Collections, Hatcher Library, University of Michigan, Ann Arbor.

82. On the issue of race in the intertwined history of US racial formation and empire building in the Philippines, see Kramer, *Blood of Government*.

83. Porter, "Revenge of the Humdrum," 2.

Conclusion

Scientific work in the early twentieth-century Philippines involved both specialized and mundane labor, which found coherence in the Bureau of Science's administrative management and routinization. Doing research was more valuable, as the publication of results drawn from these investigations validated and increased the legitimacy of scientific work.[83] In this way, a scientific contribution to publications like the *Philippine Journal of Science*, by way of authorship, indicated expert knowledge, a recorded visibility that marked the boundary between a scientist and a mere laborer.[84] On the other hand, devoting time to unremarkable routine work pushed scientists to invisibility. Menial work was anonymous, easily tabulated in the aggregate but never bringing prestige to any given scientific worker. If visibility meant being a named reference in scientific publications, invisibility implied the opposite—no authored publication, and no contribution to science.[85]

Negotiating the boundary between research and routine also worked another way. To Americans, Filipinos provided evidence of scientific potential when they labored *well* at routine tasks. If equipped with further education and training, such Filipinos could cultivate their scientific sensibility and ultimately become good scientists.[86] This arrangement reflected the US colonial agenda as a whole, in that it perceived supervised routine work as a potential avenue to more significant scientific work.

When Arguelles was appointed director in 1934, he had proved his stature as a scientist trained in both research and routine in his two-decade career at the bureau. By this decade, most of the bureau's staff already consisted of Filipinos, both routine laborers and credentialed scientists who formed part of a scientific community that had emerged.[87] Yet, certain Americans still believed that Filipinos, even a veteran like Arguelles, were incapable of leading a scientific agency as prestigious and well-known as the Bureau of Science.[88] They believed the bureau must remain in American hands, echoing an earlier opposition to Filipinization, on the grounds that it was premature and even risked the deterioration of the reputable bureau began by Freer and his colleagues.[89] This made the appointment of Arguelles questionable, if not

84. Shapin, "Invisible Technician"; Barnett, "Showing and Hiding," 253.

85. Shapin, "Invisible Technician," 556.

86. Catherine Ceniza Choy has argued that nursing education offered professional and social mobility to Filipino women, which also served to legitimate the US colonial agenda and confirm the racial and social hierarchies it engendered. In this context, only through supervision and training could Filipino nurses be seen as competent and professional equals. See Choy, *Empire of Care*, 31. On the category of "mechanical work" inscribed in hierarchies of scientific distinction, see especially Blair, "New Knowledge Makers," 168–70.

87. Anderson, "Science in the Philippines," 289, 306; Baldoza, "Under the Aegis of Science."

88. Anderson, "Science in the Philippines," 304–5.

89. Anderson, "Science in the Philippines," 304, 307. Vice Governor Joseph Hayden criticized the Filipino-dominated Bureau of Science of the 1930s: "Not only has the scientific work of these institutions lacked coordination, but professional, institutional, political, and even racial jealousies have at times caused

entirely objectionable, even if he had indeed established and cultivated his scientific career working with and under American scientists in the bureau.[90]

Meanwhile, as director, Arguelles followed his American predecessors in defending centralized scientific work. He supervised more than two hundred employees and confronted similar administrative problems.[91] Under his helm, science remained an integral component of state administration, and the bureau's scientists continued to grapple with competing objectives that determined which kinds of scientific work were more valuable and what they should achieve.[92]

As Filipinos negotiated for more autonomy toward the withdrawal of American sovereignty, scientists like Arguelles contributed their perspectives to national planning, insisting that the Bureau of Science needed continuous support and better funding. Independence, he argued, would require a strong scientific base for the economy and industry.[93] In this moment, though, the science that earlier justified and supported US occupation would no longer serve empire, as Filipino scientists reoriented its pursuit toward national development after independence. Arguelles provided the scientific element in this vision of a Philippine postcolonial future, bearing the authority of science as "the legitimating sign of rationality and progress," a view his fellow Filipino scientists shared into the succeeding years.[94]

JONATHAN VICTOR BALDOZA is a doctoral candidate in history from Princeton University. His research has appeared in *Philippine Studies* and *Archipel*.

---

a diffusion and overlapping of effort which has injured the public interest and reduced the effectiveness of the large body of well-trained Philippine scientists." See Hayden, *Philippines*, 543.

90. George Dunham, technical adviser to the Governor General on Public Health, assessed that the bureau in 1933 was "scarcely a scientific institution, in so far as research work is concerned" because of the deluge of routine work. Dunham believed that only an American could revive the institution, as he knew "no Filipino who would build up the bureau into a scientific institution approaching its former status." On the problem of the bureau's leadership, Dunham recommended that Arguelles be consulted, not appointed as director. See Memorandum for the Governor-General, titled "Reorganization of the Bureau of Science," dated July 25, 1933, in box 10, folder 23, Ralston Hayden Papers, Bentley Historical Library, Ann Arbor, Michigan.

91. Arguelles, *Thirty-Third Annual Report*, 3–5.

92. Ophir and Shapin, "Place of Knowledge: A Methodological Survey," 9.

93. Arguelles, "Progress of Science in the Philippines." Cox had already made a similar argument in a previous annual report: "Successful economic development of the Philippines must be preceded by adequate research, and economic independence must precede successful political independence." Cox, *Seventeenth Annual Report*, 61.

94. Prakash, *Another Reason*, 7.

References

Alfonso, Oscar M., and Leslie E. Bauzon. *University of the Philippines: The First 75 Years (1908–1983)*. Manila: University of the Philippines Press, 1985.

Alvarez, Kerby C. "Instrumentation and Institutionalization: Colonial Science and the Observatorio Meteorologico de Manila, 1865–1899." *Philippine Studies: Historical and Ethnographic Viewpoints* 64, nos. 3–4 (2016): 385–416.

Anderson, Warwick. *Colonial Pathologies: American Tropical Medicine, Race, and Hygiene in the Philippines*. Durham, NC: Duke University Press, 2006.

Anderson, Warwick. "Science in the Philippines." *Philippine Studies* 55, no. 3 (2007): 287–318.

Anderson, Warwick, and Hans Pols. "Scientific Patriotism: Medical Science and National Self-Fashioning in Southeast Asia." *Comparative Studies in Society and History* 54, no. 1 (January 2012): 93–113. https://doi.org/10.1017/S0010417511000600.

Arguelles, Angel S. "Progress of Science in the Philippines." In *Encyclopedia of the Philippines*, vol. 7: *Science*, edited by Zoilo Galang, 17–30. Manila: P. Vera and Sons, 1936.

Arguelles, Angel S. *Thirty-Third Annual Report of the Director of the Bureau of Science to the Honorable the Secretary of Agriculture and Commerce*. Manila: Bureau of Printing, 1905.

Baldoza, Jonathan Victor. "Under the Aegis of Science: The Philippine Scientific Community before the Second World War." *Philippine Studies: Historical and Ethnographic Viewpoints* 68, no. 1 (2020): 83–110.

Bankoff, Greg. "A Month in the Life of José Salud, Forester in the Spanish Philippines, July 1882." *Global Environment* 2, no. 3 (2009): 8–47.

Bankoff, Greg. "The Science of Nature and the Nature of Science in the Spanish and American Philippines." In *Cultivating the Colonies: Colonial States and Their Environmental Legacies*, edited by Christina Folke Ax, Karen Oslund, Niels Brimnes, and Niklas Thode Jensen, 78–108. Columbus: Ohio University Press, 2011.

Barnett, Lydia. "Showing and Hiding: The Flickering Visibility of Earth Workers in the Archives of Earth Science." *History of Science* 58, no. 3 (2020): 245–74.

Bayly, Christopher Alan. *Empire and Information: Intelligence Gathering and Social Communication in India, 1780–1870*. New York: Cambridge University Press, 1996.

Blair, Ann. "New Knowledge Makers." In *New Horizons for Early Modern European Scholarship*, edited by Ann Blair and Nicholas Popper, 167–82. Baltimore: Johns Hopkins University Press, 2021.

Brazzeal, Bradley. "Science Librarianship in Colonial Philippines: Mary Polk and the Philippine Bureau of Science Library, 1903–1924." *Science and Technology Libraries* 40, no. 2 (2021): 154–71.

Brown, William H. *Twenty-Seventh Annual Report of the Director of the Bureau of Science to the Honorable the Secretary of Agriculture and Natural Resources*. Manila: Bureau of Printing, 1929.

Chandler, Alfred D., Jr. *The Visible Hand: The Managerial Revolution in American Business*. Cambridge, MA: Harvard University Press, 1977.

Choy, Catherine Ceniza. *Empire of Care: Nursing and Migration in Filipino American History*. Durham, NC: Duke University Press, 2003.

Coen, Deborah R. *Climate in Motion: Science, Empire, and the Problem of Scale*. Chicago: University of Chicago Press, 2018.

Cohn, Bernard S. *Colonialism and Its Forms of Knowledge: The British in India*. Princeton, NJ: Princeton University Press, 1996.

Corpuz, Onofre S. *The Bureaucracy in the Philippines.* Manila: University of the Philippines Institute of Public Administration, 1957.

Cox, Alvin J. *Eleventh Annual Report of the Director of the Bureau of Science to the Honorable the Secretary of the Interior.* Manila: Bureau of Printing, 1912.

Cox, Alvin J. *Twelfth Annual Report of the Director of the Bureau of Science to the Honorable the Secretary of the Interior.* Manila: Bureau of Printing, 1913.

Cox, Alvin J. *Thirteenth Annual Report of the Director of the Bureau of Science to the Honorable the Secretary of the Interior.* Manila: Bureau of Printing, 1915.

Cox, Alvin J. *Fifteenth Annual Report of the Director of the Bureau of Science to the Honorable the Secretary of the Interior.* Manila: Bureau of Printing, 1917.

Cox, Alvin J. *Seventeenth Annual Report of the Director of the Bureau of Science to the Honorable the Secretary of the Interior.* Manila: Bureau of Printing, 1919.

Daston, Lorraine, and Peter Galison. *Objectivity.* New York: Zone Books, 2007.

De Vos, Paula S. "Research, Development, and Empire: State Support of Science in the Later Spanish Empire." *Colonial Latin American Review* 15, no. 1 (2006): 55–79.

Felten, Sebastian, and Christine von Oertzen. "Bureaucracy as Knowledge." *Journal for the History of Knowledge* 1, no. 1 (2020).

Freeman, Joshua B. *Behemoth: A History of the Factory and the Making of the Modern World.* New York: W. W. Norton & Company, 2018.

Freer, Paul. *Fifth Annual Report of the Director of the Bureau of Science to the Honorable the Secretary of the Interior.* Manila: Bureau of Printing, 1906.

Freer, Paul. *Sixth Annual Report of the Director of the Bureau of Science to the Honorable the Secretary of the Interior.* Manila: Bureau of Printing, 1907.

Freer, Paul. *Seventh Annual Report of the Director of the Bureau of Science to the Honorable the Secretary of the Interior.* Manila: Bureau of Printing, 1909.

Freer, Paul. *Ninth Annual Report of the Director of the Bureau of Science to the Honorable the Secretary of the Interior.* Manila: Bureau of Printing, 1911.

Freer, Paul. *Tenth Annual Report of the Director of the Bureau of Science to the Honorable the Secretary of the Interior.* Manila: Bureau of Printing, 1911.

Gutierrez, Kathleen C. "The Region of Imperial Strategy: Regino García, Sebastián Vidal, Mary Clemens, and the Consolidation of International Botany in the Philippines, 1858–1936." PhD diss., University of California, Berkeley, 2020.

Haber, Samuel. *Efficiency and Uplift: Scientific Management in the Progressive Era, 1899–1920.* Chicago: University of Chicago Press, 1964.

Hayden, Joseph. *The Philippines: A Study in National Development.* New York: Macmillan, 1942.

Hays, Samuel P. *The Response to Industrialism, 1885–1914.* Chicago: University of Chicago Press, 1957.

Ileto, Reynaldo C. "Cholera and the Origins of the American Sanitary Order in the Philippines." In *Imperial Medicine and Indigenous Societies,* edited by D. Arnold, 125–48. Manchester: Manchester University Press, 2017.

Jacobs, Nancy J. *Birders of Africa: History of a Network.* New Haven, CT: Yale University Press, 2016.

Kohler, Robert E. "The Management of Science: The Experience of Warren Weaver and the Rockefeller Foundation Programme in Molecular Biology." *Minerva* 14, no. 3 (1976): 279–306.

Kohout, Amy. *Taking the Field: Soldiers, Nature, and Empire on American Frontiers.* Lincoln: University of Nebraska Press, 2023.

Kramer, Paul A. *The Blood of Government: Race, Empire, the United States, and the Philippines*. Chapel Hill: University of North Carolina Press, 2006.

Livingstone, David N. "The Spaces of Knowledge: Contributions towards a Historical Geography of Science." *Environment and Planning D: Society and Space* 13, no. 1 (1995): 5–34.

May, Glenn Anthony. *Social Engineering in the Philippines: The Aims, Execution and Impact of American Colonial Policy, 1900–1913*. Westport, CT: Greenwood, 1980.

McGregor, Richard. *Nineteenth Annual Report of the Director of the Bureau of Science to the Honorable the Secretary of the Interior*. Manila: Bureau of Printing, 1921.

Merrill, Elmer. *Twentieth Annual Report of the Director of the Bureau of Science to the Honorable the Secretary of the Interior*. Manila: Bureau of Printing, 1922.

Merrill, Elmer. *Twenty-First Annual Report of the Director of the Bureau of Science to the Honorable the Secretary of the Interior*. Manila: Bureau of Printing, 1923.

Miller, Karen R. "'Thin, Wistful, and White': James Fugate and Colonial Bureaucratic Masculinity in the Philippines, 1900–1938." *American Quarterly* 71, no. 4 (2019): 921–44. https://doi.org/10.1353/aq.2019.0068.

Nery, Leo Angelo. "'Feminine Invasion': Women and Philippine Pharmacy in the Early Twentieth Century." *Philippine Studies: Historical and Ethnographic Viewpoints* 66, no. 2 (2018): 137–72.

Ophir, Adi, and Steven Shapin. "The Place of Knowledge: A Methodological Survey." *Science in Context* 4, no. 1 (1991): 3–22.

Pagunsan, Ruel V. "Nature, Colonial Science and Nation-Building in Twentieth-Century Philippines." *Journal of Southeast Asian Studies* 51, no. 4 (2020): 561–78.

[?] Philippine Commission. *Act 156. Public Laws and Resolutions Passed by the United States Philippine Commission. Division of Insular Affairs, War Department*. Washington: Government Printing Office, 1901.

[?] Philippine Commission. *Act 1407. Public Laws and Resolutions Passed by the United States Philippine Commission. Division of Insular Affairs, War Department*. Volume 5, Manila: Bureau of Printing, 1907.

Planta, Maria Mercedes G. *Traditional Medicine in the Colonial Philippines: 16th to the 19th Century*. Manila: University of the Philippines Press, 2017.

Porter, Theodore. "Revenge of the Humdrum: Bureaucracy as Profession and as a Site of Science." *Journal for the History of Knowledge* 1, no. 1 (2020): 1–5.

Porter, Theodore M. *Trust in Numbers: The Pursuit of Objectivity in Science and Public Life*. Princeton, NJ: Princeton University Press, 1996.

Prakash, Gyan. *Another Reason: Science and the Imagination of Modern India*. Princeton, NJ: Princeton University Press, 1999.

Raby, Megan. *American Tropics: The Caribbean Roots of Biodiversity Science*. Chapel Hill: University of North Carolina Press, 2017.

Raj, Kapil. "Go-Betweens, Travelers, and Cultural Translators." *A Companion to the History of Science*, edited by Bernard V. Lightman, 39–57. Chichester, UK: John Wiley & Sons, 2016.

Rieppel, Lukas. *Assembling the Dinosaur: Fossil Hunters, Tycoons, and the Making of a Spectacle*. Cambridge, MA: Harvard University Press, 2019.

Rieppel, Lukas. "Organizing the Marketplace." *Osiris* 33, no. 1 (October 2018): 232–52. https://doi.org/10.1086/699856.

Rosenberg, Charles. "Toward an Ecology of Knowledge: On Discipline, Context, and History." In *Rise of the Knowledge Worker*, edited by James W. Cortada, 221–32. London: Routledge, 2009.

Shapin, Steven. "The Invisible Technician." *American Scientist* 77, no. 6 (1989): 554–63.

Shapin, Steven. "Placing the View from Nowhere: Historical and Sociological Problems in the Location of Science." *Transactions of the Institute of British Geographers* 23, no. 1 (1998): 5–12.

Star, Susan Leigh. "This Is Not a Boundary Object: Reflections on the Origin of a Concept." *Science, Technology, and Human Values* 35, no. 5 (2010): 601–17.

Star, Susan Leigh, and James R. Griesemer. "Institutional Ecology, 'Translations' and Boundary Objects: Amateurs and Professionals in Berkeley's Museum of Vertebrate Zoology, 1907–39." *Social Studies of Science* 19, no. 3 (1989): 387–420.

Strong, Richard. *Eighth Annual Report of the Director of the Bureau of Science to the Honorable the Secretary of the Interior.* Manila: Bureau of Printing, 1910.

Todes, Daniel P. "Pavlov's Physiology Factory." *Isis* 88, no. 2 (1997): 205–46.

Trachtenberg, Alan. *The Incorporation of America: Culture and Society in the Gilded Age.* New York: Macmillan, 1982.

Ventura, Theresa. "Medicalizing *Gutom*: Hunger, Diet, and Beriberi during the American Period." *Philippine Studies: Historical and Ethnographic Viewpoints* 63, no. 1 (2015): 39–69.

Warren, James Francis. "Scientific Superman: Father José Algué, Jesuit Meteorology, and the Philippines under American Rule, 1897–1924." Madison: University of Wisconsin Press, 2009.

Withers, Charles W. J. "Place and the 'Spatial Turn' in Geography and in History." *Journal of the History of Ideas* 70, no. 4 (2009): 637–58.

Worcester, Dean. *The Philippines Past and Present.* Volume 1. New York: The Macmillan Company, 1921.

Electric Discipline: Gendering Power and Defining Work in Electric Power Systems

Trish Kahle

On May 20, 1974, more than five thousand employees of the Pennsylvania Power & Light Company (PP&L) walked off the job—the first system-wide strike by the Employees Independent Association (EIA) in the company's history. Only months earlier, a five-month oil embargo had stoked deep-seated anxieties among Americans about the stability of their energy system.[1] PP&L's executives insisted the company would do everything possible during the strike to maintain power supply in their service area, which stretched across central eastern Pennsylvania between Philadelphia and Harrisburg. But the impossibility of normal operations without a normal workforce soon became apparent. A much smaller group of supervisory employees simply couldn't run the system on anything more than an emergency basis.[2] The weather didn't help. That summer was hot and humid, and PP&L was part of a power-sharing agreement with other East Coast utilities, which meant they sometimes had to share electricity with nearby cities and states. But when these conditions forced PP&L to lower service area voltages, they were quick to assure the public that the cuts were "in no way" related to the strike. Equally, they went to great lengths to avoid telling customers they had to conserve power—an effort to give the impression that PP&L management had the situation under control.[3]

If the difficulty PP&L faced in maintaining normal operations made freshly visible the often-overlooked labor of connecting users to the grid and maintaining that connection, it also hinted at how electric power systems depended on predict-

In addition to the editors of *Labor* and the special issue editors, I would like to thank my fellow collaborators at the 2022 "Let's Get to Work" conference, especially Tamara Fernando, as well as Anna Andrzejewski, Roger Horowitz, and Angus McLeod for their feedback on earlier drafts of this article.

1. Storch, "First General Strike Hits PP&L—5,000 Out"; Zaretsky, *No Direction Home*, 71–103.

2. *Inside Out*, July 18, 1974, and July 16, 1974, box 48: Corporate Communications 604.03, EIA Strike, News Releases 1974, Pennsylvania Power and Light Company Records (Accession 1962), Hagley Museum and Library, Wilmington, Delaware, 19807 (hereafter cited as PP&L Records).

3. Lockwood, "Power Cut to Safeguard Reserves."

Labor: Studies in Working-Class History, Volume 21, Issue 1
DOI 10.1215/15476715-10948947 © 2024 by Labor and Working-Class History Association

able rhythms of electric power demand—what the utility industry refers to as "load." PP&L's load in the 1970s was composed of a varied group of users: a few large industrial customers, a growing number of light manufacturing plants and regional office buildings, a commercial sector of retailers who used electric power to light displays and refrigerate perishable items, and, of course, residential use, which had grown rapidly in the post–World War II decades. Americans in 1970 used 674 percent more electricity in their homes than they had in 1950, a faster growth rate than electrical intensification in the commercial sector (533 percent) or industrial sector (391 percent). In PP&L's service area, residential demand fluctuated from a third to a half of total demand.[4] Maintaining load balance—the ratio between generation and user demand—was critical. Imbalance between the electricity generated and the electricity pulled from the grid and applied elsewhere had to remain in sync at all times, or the whole service area, the country's twenty-seventh-largest private power system, would experience brownouts (decreased available voltage) or blackouts (total loss of electric power).[5]

These rhythms of power demand, typically framed as electricity "consumption" or "use," played a central role in PP&L's load management—and they also entailed work. Electricity, in no small part thanks to utility advertising, often evoked images of leisure and comfort, of electricity as a "servant."[6] But on closer examination, electric power was more like a coworker than a servant. Workers manufactured prefabricated homes on electrified assembly lines. Sales workers organized elaborately lit displays in department stores. Clerical workers made copies on electric Xerox machines. And perhaps most overlooked of all, people, usually women, applied electricity to their housework. The broader social organization of work—where and when work happens, the scale and energy intensity at which that work takes place—thus played an important role in the daily functioning of electric power systems. That meant the labor PP&L managed directly, by managing its employees, had to be understood in relation to practices of *indirect* management, even if utility managers conceived of themselves as managing load instead of disciplining work. The invisibility of indirect management was possible because it operated within a gendered division of labor that designated housework as women's work and devalued the labor of women who worked in the home without wages, especially married, otherwise unemployed homemakers.[7]

4. Energy Information Administration, "US electricity retail sales to major end-use sectors and electricity direct use by all sectors, 1950–2020," *Monthly Energy Review*, March 2021, table 7.6, https://www.eia.gov/energyexplained/electricity/use-of-electricity.php; Pennsylvania Electric Association Economic Questionnaire, 1972, PP&L Records, box 52: Pennsylvania Electric Association (PEA), 1972.

5. *Electric Light and Power, Transmission and Distribution Edition*, "Alphabetical Listing of Company Performances," 53.

6. Thompson, "Living Electrically with Reddy Kilowatt."

7. Bose, Bereano, and Malloy, "Household Technology and the Social Construction of Housework"; on unwaged work, waged/unwaged work, I am drawing on a wide body of feminist labor history and social reproduction theory, especially Gimenez and Collins, *Work without Wages*; Bhattacharya, *Social Reproduction Theory*.

New forms of electric discipline proceeded under the guise of "power conservation." Beginning in 1970, PP&L sought to teach customers to "use electricity more wisely" as the utility struggled to build generating capacity quickly enough to match growth in demand.[8] While calls for residential conservation often implied that savings would come from curtailing leisure use, it was the targeting of women's unpaid housework that transformed conservation into a project of labor discipline. By calling on women to rearrange their use of electric appliances, illumination, and climate control throughout the day to complete their socially reproductive tasks in private homes, this electric discipline countered decades of work by home economists that had focused on making housework more efficient and less physically demanding for homemakers.[9] It also obscured other household labor arrangements that existed alongside the dominant midcentury image of the wife as a homemaker—working women, women engaged in home production, or other kinds of families and living arrangements ignored or vilified by heterosexual norms.[10] As a result, by the time the EIA went on strike in 1974, the idea of discipline through conservation was already well developed.

Both sustained and short-term calls for conservation could upend the working lives of those laboring in the home. And critically, utility company efforts to restrain, reorganize, and redirect women's electricity use ultimately demonstrated that these women were not simply user-consumers. The distinctive nature of electric power systems, where the relationship between generation and demand had to be maintained in careful balance, integrated activities that *looked* like consumption into a broader fabric of work, which made it possible to operate the electrical grid reliably and safely. While women's unwaged labor in the home was treated as separate from the so-called productive economy even as the social reproduction of the workforce and social order depended on that unwaged labor, electric power systems could tolerate no such fiction. Within the broad landscape of electricity generation, infrastructure, and application that Diana Montaño has termed the "electricscape," homemakers constituted a targeted workforce that could be managed at the intersection of gender ideology and electric power technology to enhance the stability of the grid and, by extension, the broader political economy it undergirded.[11] The PP&L strike, and the broader energy crisis of the 1970s, lay bare this mode of electrical discipline by utilities as well as forms of transgression by electricity users. Together, electric discipline and its transgression revealed the social organization of labor that made the electric power system function.

Laboring the Electricscape between Work and Energy

Energy work, as I call the constellation of waged and unwaged labors necessary to the functioning of an energy system, offers a useful analytic lens for understanding how

8. W. D. Cobb, memo with proof, "How You Can Use Electricity More Wisely," 1972, PP&L Records, box 46: Corporate Communications 101.0, Newspaper Advertising Correspondence 1970–72.

9. Gilbreth, Thomas, and Clymer, *Management in the Home*.

10. Boris, *Home to Work*; Self, *All in the Family*, 10.

11. Montaño, *Electrifying Mexico*, 7.

other forms of social and economic power flow through the electric grid alongside the current. Although electric power systems require a lot of work to build, fuel, maintain, and repair, the images we associate with the grid are often unpeopled. Massive generating facilities tower above the surrounding town. Power lines draw our eyes to the vanishing point on the horizon. These images draw on a long visual tradition of the technological sublime while reinforcing a common trope about the relationship between energy and labor in popular narratives: that other forms of energy, especially electric power, have displaced human labor—or at least human muscle power—in modern energy systems. This story holds an apparent truth, as histories of automation and mechanization suggest.[12] Yet labor historians would be the first to recognize that it is also more complicated. Energy systems like the electric grid are ways of organizing, regulating, and relating different forms of labor, both waged and unwaged. Some are hypervisible, like a crew clustered around a downed line after a storm, while others are harder to see or even actively obscured. This duality of visibility and invisibility has a long history and has played a central role in externalizing the human, social, and ecological costs of energy systems.[13]

In that duality lies a conceptual tangle. PP&L's efforts at load management through energy conservation hint at how energy and work overlap in often unsettling ways. These are slippery categories, especially when they intersect, and even more where they constitute each other as distinct social, cultural, and political objects. A rich, multidecade literature in the history of science and science and technology studies emphasizes the link between these two concepts as they emerged and developed in the nineteenth and early twentieth centuries. Modern notions of work and the science of energy were coproduced through the categories of thermodynamics. While the science of thermodynamics was worked out in learned treatises and laboratories, that inquiry was inseparable from the broader context of industrialization in which it emerged.[14] As thermodynamic understandings of work rooted in physics and social understandings of work rooted in industrial capitalist political economy became intertwined in the category of energy, scientific knowledge was adapted into a vernacular ideological metaphor.[15]

The science of thermodynamics rested on a totalizing idea of energy, one that understood all matter as interrelated by a continuous and universal energy, conserved through every transformation (the first law of thermodynamics) and increasingly disorganized (the second law of thermodynamics).[16] The ideological metaphor of energy, rooted in a new industrial reality, further drew strength from this new scientific understanding by making different forms of energy directly comparable. In nineteenth-century Europe, Anson Rabinbach has shown, the working body became

12. Noble, *Forces of Production*; Dix, *What's a Coal Miner to Do?*

13. Zallen, *American Lucifers*; Harrison Moore and Sandwell, *In a New Light*.

14. Smith, *Science of Energy*, 151–69.

15. Daggett, *Birth of Energy*.

16. Smith, *Science of Energy*, 2.

the metaphor through which this totalizing framework of energy was understood and from which it was extrapolated to broader society. As a result, the answers to the tensions of modernity were sought in workers' bodies. The metaphorical links between work and energy also varied from place to place, from interpreter to interpreter. Americans, Ann Norton Greene reminds us, thought in horsepower as much as labor power.[17]

The science and ideology of energy reflected the social and scientific position of the people who developed it: scientists, capitalists, inventors, and social reformers. The scholarship that has worked from this metaphor has paid less attention to other perspectives and ways of knowing energy. For most people, the intersections between energy and work were far less metaphorical; indeed, they required distinctive sets of skills in navigating the relationship between nonhuman energies and physical, mental, and emotional work, the particulars of that skillset in part shaped by the position one filled in the wider energy system. The work of applying electric power to aid in the completion of domestic tasks, for example, was different from the work of hoisting wires onto utility poles and facilitating electric connectivity. At work, laboring bodies (both human and animal) and fuels produced power in relation to each other, creating dependencies, networks, and interrelation where industrial scientists saw commensurabilities and substitutability.

The scientists, inventors, capitalists, reformers, and workers who lived with these new ways to conceptualize total energy also inhabited a world where the distinctions between different forms of energy continued to matter quite a lot. As horses and steam power together fueled a new kind of urban life, fire departments used horses to move steam engines before shifting to steam power to spray the water to greater heights and at a greater intensity than previously had been possible.[18] Distinctions within individual sources of energy mattered too. Women and other domestic staff who tended coal stoves had to learn to work with different sizes and chemical compositions of coal or, if there was a shortage of coal, burn something else entirely. Variations in coal quality changed the way the stoves had to be tended.[19] At the very moment a totalizing idea of energy emerged in the sciences, ordinary people had to learn to coordinate the use of an increasing number of kinds of energy in their daily labors. These forms of energy had different ways of being stored and required different amounts of direct interaction, different kinds of knowledge about how to work with them. Homogenization of energy as an organizing concept for the sciences accompanied an incredible heterogeneity of the forms of energy that could potentially be available and that required a wide range of knowledge and skills to use safely and effectively.

The focus on the metaphorical and ideological power of the overlaps between energy and work has largely sidelined the work of producing, operating, and main-

17. Greenberg, "Energy, Power, and Perceptions of Social Change"; Rabinbach, *Human Motor*; Smith, *Science of Energy*; Jobson, "Dead Labor," 226; Greene, *Horses at Work*.

18. Greene, *Horses at Work*, 169.

19. Adams, "Making Coal Sharp."

taining energy systems. How was it possible that in histories of energy and work, the labor of producing and applying energy has largely been written out of the story? That absence is neither an aberration nor limited to the history of energy science. Indeed, histories of US electric utility workers are shockingly limited given the number of people who have been employed in the sector, their relatively uniform distribution throughout the United States, and their ubiquity in many of our lives.[20]

Scholarly inattention to that highly visible labor has rendered doubly invisible its relationship to those labors often categorized as energy consumption, particularly housework. Most scholarly accounts of domestic electricity use have framed this history within the practices and politics of consumption. Electrification created new forms of domestic dependence on what many referred to as "electric servants" or even as "energy slaves"—a term that hinted at the ways white supremacy and male domination shaped the application of electric power in homes. Terms such as "energy slaves" or "electric servants" suggested that housewives—white housewives in particular—had been "freed" from the drudgery of manual household labor. The power of that myth obscured the ways electricity actually intensified housework, as Ruth Schwartz Cowan demonstrated in her field-defining book *More Work for Mother*.[21] It also hid the way home-based electricity use continued to figure centrally in the broader electric power system's operation.[22]

Instead I have come to see the labors of the electric power system as different kinds of *energy work* that merit critical examination and historical narration as a single category. I define energy work as those labors—waged and unwaged—that facilitate energy transformations necessary to the functioning of a particular energy system. It is the work without which the energy system ceases to function. While such a definition has the capacity to become unwieldy, its use as a conscious, targeted framework can help us better understand the stakes of energy consumption practices within an electric power system, how the boundary between work and not-work is actively constructed and contested, and the extent to which social definitions of labor do not adequately describe the idiosyncrasies of how people live in energy systems. Energy work, as a category, can offer expanded insights into how we put energy to work, how energy systems operate, and how we govern the movement of energy through our societies. Energy work also allows us to critically engage the category of work anew, by examining the historical process by which energy practices get defined as work (production) and not-work (consumption), while also acknowledging that

20. See Palladino, *Dreams of Dignity, Workers of Vision*; Marsh, *Trade Unionism in the Electric Light and Power Industry*. More scholarship covers workers in electrical manufacturing or building trades. See Schatz, *Electrical Workers*; Moccio, *Live Wire*. Others have pointed to the work of computing and design in early electric power systems. See Tympas, "Perpetually Laborious"; Rosenberg, "Test Men, Experts, Brother Engineers, and Members of the Fraternity."

21. Cowan, *More Work for Mother*.

22. This means not that these scholars have separated this work from labor generally but that they have not integrated it into the day-to-day functioning of the energy system. For examples, see Nye, *Electrifying America*, 238–85; Johnson, "Energy Slaves."

the boundary between these two categories is often unclear. A fuller examination of energy work has much to offer to the study of energy systems that have largely explained their functioning from the perspective of engineers and scientists drawing on technical and scientific forms of knowledge, and to reveal the operation of industrial and state power (though the state lies outside my scope in this essay).[23] In other words, searching for energy work offers an epistemological exercise in how to conceive of the interrelationships between different forms of power.

To explore these problems, electric power systems form an ideal starting point. The image of a bounded "electric system" defined by the utility service area is problematic for a variety of reasons, not least that it often obscures its own "externalities"— the processes of resource extraction, waste dumping, and pollution integral to its operation. Indeed, a fuller examination should incorporate such externalities into thinking about the kinds of work that make electric systems possible. At the same time, and despite all that the fiction of the service area has the power to conceal, it is also *revealing* in the moments when human labor and electric power come into conflict and mold each other. The externalities of electrical power systems also reveal how utility companies use the distinctive character of those systems, where electricity must be generated and applied in balance simultaneously to preserve system function, as a disciplinary tool on a wider workforce than is typically associated with the utilities themselves. A closer reading of PP&L's archive shows how the company consciously leveraged gendered ideas about work to discipline unwaged workers. PP&L kept their grid functional—particularly in times of energy or capital shortages—by disciplining the labors of people throughout the service area, some of whom they employed, most of whom they did not.

Disciplined Conservation

When PP&L asked their customers to conserve power, what were they really asking them to do? Certainly, these public messages were not directed at their industrial customers. PP&L consultants *did* help individual industrial customers find ways to conserve power but did not intervene in the work process. Instead, they framed these changes as promoting profitability and market competitiveness, publicizing them only after they had succeeded. Public mention of power conservation in industry meant layoffs, and that was the last thing that PP&L's service area needed. Their service area almost perfectly overlapped with the Pennsylvania anthracite region, which had been devastated by precipitous decline in hard coal mining in the decades after World War II. And even though PP&L still cast their service area as the nation's "industrial heartland," home to the mighty Bethlehem Steel, harbingers of decline and plant closings loomed by the early 1970s.[24] Commercial customers, like department stores, could

23. See Cohn, *Grid*; Hirsh, *Technology and Transformation in the American Electric Utility Industry*; Hughes, *Networks of Power*.

24. On anthracite's decline, Dublin and Licht, *Face of Decline*; on shifts in steel, Stein, *Running Steel, Running America*, 197–228; Taft, *From Steel to Slots*, 15–56.

adopt the kinds of cost-saving measures they had during the energy crunch the previous winter, like reducing store hours to conserve energy used to light displays, but those changes too, portended further upset to the regional economy.[25]

Instead, PP&L's appeals for conservation relied on an appeal to *residential* users. That appeal was deeply gendered and tapped into the idea that energy conservation tempered consumption that took place in the home. PP&L's appeal rested on a wider understanding about the character of American economic life in this period—the gendered political economy organized around atomized nuclear families and supported by a single wage earner, what Robert Self has termed "breadwinner liberalism."[26] That perspective placed both the locus of economic life and the energy system outside the home. Indeed, from PP&L's perspective, its core was the generating station, the place where the utility took fuel and turned it into electric power that coursed out to the wider world through a system of power lines, substations, and transformers. By the time it reached women doing laundry, running vacuums, or cooking meals, it was a product they could use by turning a switch (fig. 1). Utilities promised women electricity would ease their labors, make them clean and gentle and comfortable.[27]

For the women putting electricity to use in their home, this system looked different. From the perspective of the home and those who labored within it, the so-called productive economy depended on the socially reproductive labors of the home, and the women who overwhelmingly performed that labor were connected to the electric power system by the industrialized practices of electrified housework. While household appliances *promised* to ease the burden of domestic labor and offer greater leisure time for the women who incorporated them into their daily lives, the reality was that those same technologies raised expectations for what constituted a well-kept house. They eased some of the physical burden of specific chores, like laundering clothes, but also placed women under incredible pressure to meet new, higher standards, as both appliances and the energy to power them became accessible to greater numbers of Americans in the union-dense postwar decades. Behind the veil of electricity consumption was in effect a classic speedup. Whether it was done by full-time homemakers, by working women on what feminists described as the "second shift" of housework, or (less often) by men and children, unwaged housework became more productive. But those same women were then expected to complete a greater number of tasks and to complete them to higher standards.[28]

The labors of housework and the extent to which they were electrified were not uniform, even by the 1970s, when almost every US household had access to elec-

25. Frederick and Zimmerman, "Clearfield County Taking Steps to Conserve Energy."

26. Self, *All in the Family*, 17–46.

27. Promotional advertisements, 1970, PP&L Records, box 46: Corporate Communications 101.0, Newspaper Advertising Correspondence 1970–72.

28. Cowan, *More Work for Mother*, 192; this same speedup almost certainly affected waged domestic laborers in the home, but they do not appear in the sources I have found so far and thus lie outside my scope here; Hochschild, *Second Shift*.

Figure 1. Overhead view of home appliances, Carolina Power & Light Company, ca. 1950s. Carolina Power and Light Photograph Collection, Audio Visual Materials, State Archives of North Carolina.

tricity and increased incomes and access to credit made it possible for many more people to purchase appliances like dishwashers, frost-free refrigerators, and in-home washing machines. The balance of muscle energy and electric power (and in some cases, like drying clothes, solar and wind energy) was shaped by one's social class. The texture of women's household labor reflected whether their family owned its home, whether they had access to credit and disposable income, and where their home was located, among other factors. Fewer than half of low-income families had automatic washing machines in 1975, whereas almost 90 percent of middle-class homes did. Having a washing machine at home required much less work than using a hand-wringing washer, which at least 15 percent of low-income households still used. It also took less human energy to operate a machine at home than to carry clothes to a communal washing room or a laundromat. But, as Cowan has shown, having a washing machine tended to increase how *often* clothes were washed, and social standards of cleanliness quickly adapted to those new middle-class laundering practices. This was a point at which electrical discipline could be introduced: where the social pressures, daily energy practices, and needs of the broader electric power system could overlap and thus, in moments of shortage or during peak periods, could come into conflict.[29]

Although PP&L addressed residential users as leisurely consumers in public facing statements, they were certainly aware of the ways electrifying housework had changed women's unwaged labor. Indeed, they had helped to make this new way of working a reality. For years, utilities like PP&L had employed a division of home economists to teach women how to intensify their use of electric power. They ran demonstration kitchens and completed home visits.[30] These interventions were

29. Greer, "Energy Consumption in American Households," 23; Cowan, *More Work for Mother*, 217–19.

30. Goldstein, *Creating Consumers*, 240–41; Dreilinger, *Secret History of Home Economics*, 67.

conceived of explicitly as part of the utility's load management, balancing residential use against the peak load demands of industrial and commercial sectors, as well as figuring into load-building plans more generally. By diversifying the electric power systems' users, a utility balanced their load structure, as the rhythms of housework, industrial production, and commercial use were all distinct yet interrelated.[31] While utilities had their reasons for expanding the ranks of their home economists, however, the home economists also had their own understanding of the importance of their work.

By applying electricity to housework, home economists hoped to make housework more efficient. Indeed, the American obsession with Taylorism had profoundly shaped the work of home economists in earlier decades, after Lillian Moller Gilbreth, who along with her husband Frank had used Taylorist motion studies to "optimize" work processes in industrial settings, also applied the technique to the home.[32] The amount of muscular energy women expended by walking around, performing repetitive motions like kneading bread, vacuuming, or scrubbing changed over the course of the twentieth century and became more or less efficient in direct relation to women's application of electricity in the course of their work. And the utility company home economists were central to that project as they showed women how to operate these new appliances. They also demonstrated how women could use electric appliances to reduce the muscular energy required by a particular task, meet the increasing standards for housework, and gain the less tangible benefits that labors in the home could accrue—such as the social status that came with being able to repeatedly produce a distinctive and difficult-to-achieve dessert.

It was therefore no accident that women's labor in the home became the target of PP&L's conservation campaign when the utility explicitly adopted conservation as a goal at the end of 1970. Instead, the campaign revealed which forms of energy work were valued and how. Residential use, even where it included substantial amounts of labor, was seen both as integral to load management and as marginal to the region's production-focused economy, lacking in economic value. The hidden abode of social reproduction didn't lay housewives off when electricity ran short, but electricity cuts to factories might stymie area development efforts—critical to PP&L's strategy to maintain, or even rebuild, industrial load in the face of ongoing deindustrialization of their service area.[33] The energy conservation campaign PP&L designed assumed that a nuclear, heterosexual household supported by a single income in an industrial economy was the norm, though that assumption certainly would not have mapped cleanly onto the lived reality of their service area residents. Their threats of what a society plagued by electricity shortages might look like was indeed dire, and they illustrated them for added impact: a boarded-up maternity ward; job seekers confronted with a closed door; a police officer standing guard as community members line up with their

---

31. Hughes, *Networks of Power*, 218–19; Goldstein, *Creating Consumers*, 209.
32. Lancaster, *Making Time*, 248–49; Graham, "Domesticating Efficiency."
33. Fraser, "Behind Marx's Hidden Abode."

electric cords in hand hoping to access the community outlet; a power plant engineer shutting off the big switch and, with it, everyone's power.[34] In linking fears about the future of society and the family in gendered and racialized ways, they drew on a wider trope of 1970s politics—even if PP&L "diversified" the figures in the drawings so Black and white residents lined up for access to the communal plug, while a white woman joined a group of men at the employment office.[35] But PP&L also insisted that electricity conservation in the home could help prevent this future from coming into being. To meet their energy conservation goals, PP&L once again turned to their home economists, the same people who had helped them to sell the region's women on all-electric living in prior decades.[36]

PP&L's business decision overlapped with a concurrent debate among home economists about what the energy crisis, and especially the advent of energy conservation, meant for their field. As industrialization of housework over the preceding century had replaced or reshaped much of the day-to-day muscle labor of the household with electricity, the relationship between the household and the broader electric power system was one of mutual dependency. As a result, home economists saw a special role for domestic labor in the nation's efforts to address the energy crisis. The development of new fuels, the opening of new reserves, or even the commercial development of renewable energy sources were all mid- to long-range solutions to problems with immediate consequences. According to the *Journal of Home Economics*, published by the American Home Economics Association and read by scholars, secondary educators, and practitioners in the field, "Home economists can help assist the nation through its immediate energy problems," while those in other fields dealt with the longer-range solutions.[37] "The family is an energy-driven ecosystem," wrote Beatrice Paolucci and M. Janice Hogan, two home economics professors, "and family members are inextricably linked to the environment through energy flows.... They are related to other social and economic groups by mutual access to particular energy sources."[38] Some home economists, taking their lessons from the women's movement, even tried out "energy consciousness-raising" activities.[39] But while home economists, in their professional forums, were more likely to focus on how families made energy decisions, or how energy choices shaped other driving concerns in their field, the utilities turned these insights and goals toward load management.

Unlike workplace discipline, which PP&L's management wielded in a manner consistent with other industries at the time, PP&L managed homemakers indirectly. Although utilities like PP&L *could*, in theory, cut or reduce service, imposed blackouts and brownouts were undesirable disciplinary tools because they opened private util-

34. Pennsylvania Power & Light, "Energy Crisis," ca. 1972–1973, PP&L Records, box 46: Corporate Communications 304.05, Annual Meeting 1973.

35. Zaretsky, *No Direction Home*; PP&L, "Energy Crisis."

36. Jack K. Busby, "We're No. 1," *PP&L Reporter*, February–March 1969, 1–5.

37. *Journal of Home Economics*, "Energy Crisis and Home Economics," 6.

38. Paolucci and Hogan, "Energy Crisis and the Family," 12.

39. *Journal of Home Economics*, "Energy Questionnaire," 34.

ities to public scrutiny and possible regulatory action. That was especially true in the years following the massive blackout of 1965 in the Northeast, which had infringed on the northern border of PP&L's service area.[40] By the mid-1970s, many Americans also felt they had a right to electric power.[41] Many of PP&L's users willingly tolerated localized blackouts during storms but complained if service went out for no discernible reason. PP&L advertisements to promote its 1970s building campaign captured the difficulty of walking back electricity access. "Try telling the lady she'll have to start washing by hand," one ad warned as a caricature of a woman, equal parts angry and defensive, stood in front of her washing machine, glaring back at the reader. The copy continued, "It's either make more [electricity] or tell the lady she can't have all the electricity she wants. An unthinkable idea to most people."[42] But if these arguments circulated in newspapers, leveraging a stereotype of an unreasonably demanding wife to explain and justify expensive building plans, the actual advice distributed to women in the form of energy conservation pamphlets told a different story.[43]

Not long after PP&L ran the ad featuring the glaring woman in its service area papers, the company also crafted a twenty-four-page advice book on conserving energy. It wasn't explicitly targeted at housewives, but it might as well have been. The book dedicated only one page to industrial and commercial conservation, and just five pages to masculinized activities like car maintenance. The guide on how to "dress smartly" was explicitly gendered, likely reflective of a projection of gendered experiences of climate control in office buildings.[44] The guide advised women to "STOCK UP!!" on pantyhose and to wear a sweater over their blouse and a jacket over that if needed.[45] The rest of the guide focused on energy use in the home and inadvertently revealed how much work energy conservation took and how much reorganizing of labor time it required—in a social context in which nearly all that work would have been done by women, much of which required her to be home at certain times of day to undertake particular activities.

In the section on limiting the use of energy for climate control, for example, the guide advised opening and closing curtains along with the movements of the sun; changing the direction of a clothes dryer's vent depending on the outside temperature; adding houseplants, which then required tending, to regulate humidity; dusting behind the thermostat to aid in its operation; and adding lining to drapery. Particularly telling was guidance on how to organize housework in the heat of the sum-

40. PP&L Records, box 2: Power Service—Northeast Power Outage, favorable replies, 1965 November and Power Service—Northeast Power Outage, unfavorable replies, 1965 November.

41. Nye, *Consuming Power*, 251.

42. "Try Telling the Lady . . . ," PP&L Records, box 46: Corporate Communications 101.0, Newspaper Advertising Correspondence 1970–72.

43. Jack K. Busby, remarks, Mechanicsburg Area Senior High School, April 28, 1971, transcription, 23–24, PP&L Records, box 46: Corporate Communications 304.05, Annual Meeting 1973.

44. Murphy, *Sick Building Syndrome*, 25–26.

45. PP&L, "The Energy Crisis: What Can We Do?," ca. 1973–74, PP&L Records, box 46: Corporate Communications 304.05, Annual Meeting 1974.

mer, especially if the household ran an air conditioner. The guide advised women to mop, wash dishes, iron, and launder clothes in the morning, during the coolest part of the day, and offered bulleted lists of tips on how to minimize electric energy use, whether from their appliances or from their electric heating and cooling systems.[46] Decades earlier, Lillian Moller Gilbreth and other domestic Taylorists had studied how women could reduce the number of steps needed to accomplish different tasks in the kitchen, and Gilbreth had coauthored a 1960 volume dedicated to helping home-makers live happier lives by limiting the physical energy spent on household tasks.[47] But now PP&L's guide advised women to organize their housework to conserve the appliances' energy rather than their own.

A survey by the Pennsylvania Electric Association (PEA), of which PP&L was a leading member, captured the gendered impact of energy conservation rhetoric. Around equal numbers of men and women agreed that they used more electricity in 1972 than they had five years prior. An overwhelming majority of men and women (92 percent and 93 percent, respectively) thought electricity was a pretty good value purchase. Slightly more women felt a power shortage was imminent than men. But when interviewers asked respondents to imagine the future, the largest gender gap in answers on the survey emerged. Only 35 percent of women thought they would be using more electricity in five years, compared to 53 percent of men who held the same belief.[48] Notably, this gap had already emerged well before the peak of the cri-sis. It was further amplified by PP&L-led efforts to directly target women with "con-sumer education" campaigns and home economics school programs beginning in 1972.[49] The 1974 energy conservation guide was almost certainly designed to be read in the gendered electrical world that PP&L had consciously created. While many women may have undertaken some of the guide's advice out of economic necessity or a genuine concern about the nation's energy future, these ads encouraged compli-ance not through threat of reduced service but through a gendered labor ideology that attached the quality of women's housework to their social value and that prior-itized energy for "productive" work outside the home rather than for the reproduc-tive labors of care within.

That shift concerned some home economists, even though members of their profession had also helped to develop the conservation guidelines. One home economist lamented that in a test house designed to incorporate solar power and reduce depen-dence on the grid, "the arrangement of the kitchen equipment shows no reference to time/motion studies."[50] Another asked, "If fuels and water are scarce resources... is it more important to save the homemaker's time and energy or use them as a human

46. PP&L, "The Energy Crisis: What Can We Do?"

47. Gilbreth, Thomas, and Clymer, *Management in the Home.*

48. Pennsylvania Electric Association, Statewide Survey Tabulations, March 1972, PP&L Records, box 52: PEA 1972 (2).

49. Recommendations for Public Relations Activities 1972–1973 for the Pennsylvania Electric Associ-ation, September 1972, PP&L Records, box 52: PEA 1972 (2).

50. Fairman, "Solar One," 31.

resource in the place of a scarce natural resource?"[51] They recognized that "energy waste" was really a question of values and, specifically, that energy conservation valued women's work in relation to the other components of the energy system. From the perspective of home economists, women's labor in the home wasn't a tangential part of the energy system—a place where (as PP&L public statements suggested) homemakers merely tapped into the grid as consumers. Instead, home economists conceptualized the home and the family, and the largely unwaged women's labor that sustained them, as the most foundational part of an energy system: the place where a society made decisions about how people should use their time, allocate their resources, and fulfill their human potential. Beatrice Paolucci emphasized this point in a teaching diagram that centered the family unit in an energy system, or as Paolucci termed it, a transformation system (fig. 2). Paolucci and other home economists who adopted this perspective could see the role of women and the home in the energy system differently precisely because they understood and valued the labor of housework.[52]

Paolucci's schema stood in marked contrast to the system maps and diagrams that informed utility company decision-making. Typical PP&L representations obscured residential electricity use, even as the utility clearly recognized the household's importance in preserving system operation whenever capacity shortages loomed. When management presented shareholders, investors, or regulatory boards with operating summaries and building plans, it almost always represented their service area system as a schematic diagram. An energy flow diagram from 1974 showed how energy inputs in a "conventional community" ultimately end up as "useful work" or "waste energy."[53] Shaded, winding arrows depict the movement of energy from input to outcome, their thickness representing the amount of energy flowing in a given direction. A careful examination by someone familiar with the operations of an electric power system would be able to infer the real-world movement of energy through time and space. In choosing this form of visual representation, PP&L radically simplified the complexity of their service area to make their business arguments legible. But diagrams, as Michael Marrinan and John Bender contend, are also situated objects, given meaning by a "chain of thoughts and gestures of attention."[54] In the case of the electric power system, those thoughts and attentions came from engineers and managers—and they were both revealing and perplexing. The diagram's creators made sure to list industrial and agricultural applications of energy as examples of useful work. Residential use went unnamed, despite constituting a large portion of the energy flows represented. It probably fell under the "etc." which followed industry and agriculture. Read alongside Paolucci's diagram, these representations of the energy system reveal the tension that sat at the heart of efforts to discipline house-

51. Field, "Energy Conservation," 24.

52. Bubolz, *Beatrice Paolucci*, 108.

53. Annual Flow of Energy in a Convential Community, PP&L Records, box 46: Corporate Communications 304.05, Annual Meeting 1974.

54. Marrinan and Bender, *Culture of the Diagram*, 19.

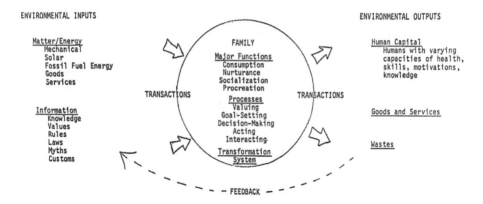

Figure 2. Beatrice Paolucci's conception of energy transformations in an ecosystem centered on families. Beatrice Paolucci Papers, box 2538, folder 24, University Archives, Michigan State University, East Lansing.

work as part of a residential conservation program. It is hard to imagine their conservation program would have been as detailed or effective without the work of home economists, but the same gendered ideology of labor that made housework an ideal target for conservation practices also made that labor harder to see and conceptualize as the system work of utility management.

Conclusion

How one perceives energy work reveals much about how understandings of electric power systems operate in conjunction with gender. Even as women's unwaged domestic labor, framed within a white, middle-class ideal, became a key target of electric discipline through multiyear utility energy conservation programs, the system-wide strike by PP&L's waged employees garnered much more attention and reporting. In part, this disparity reflected a wider devaluing and obfuscation of the socially reproductive labor performed largely by women. But it also had to do with ideologically gendered ways of categorizing energy practices, which labeled women's labors in the home as electricity consumption rather than energy work.

Even though utilities like PP&L had done much to obfuscate the labor involved in electrified housework by arguing electricity would free homemakers from drudgery, they recognized the energy work done by women in homes as key to the grid's stable operation. The company thus deployed energy conservation campaigns intended to indirectly discipline the labor of workers in the home, who overwhelmingly were unwaged women. In doing so, they revealed the complex social organization of work in electric power systems, which often defied easy categories of production or consumption. This wider history of energy work helps us better understand PP&L management's approach during the system-wide strike of waged employees in the summer of 1974. PP&L's reticence to tell service area residents to conserve power spoke as much to their relationship with unwaged workers in homes as it did to the public relations campaign targeted at their waged employees. To wield electric discipline unnecessarily might have sparked backlash—and thus reduced the effectiveness of energy conservation tools for balancing power demand over a longer term.

This case study, where an electric utility consciously, indirectly, disciplined unwaged labor while also denying the laborious character of that work also suggests that in writing the history of energy and work, we must critically engage actors' categories, and their attendant sociotechnical and scientific understandings of how their energy systems functioned. By looking at the ways that people work with electricity to make a power system, we can extend our understanding of energy as a scientific concept, of the electrical grid as a sociotechnical system, of the ways that different forms of power move through electric power systems, and of the tools we can use to contest them.

TRISH KAHLE is assistant professor of history at Georgetown University Qatar and project colead of the Energy Humanities Research Initiative at GUQ's Center for International and Regional Studies.

References

Adams, Sean. "Making Coal Sharp: Gendered Consumers and Users of Mineral Fuel in the 19th Century United States." *Journal of Energy History / Revue d'histoire de l'énergie* 6 (2021), http://energyhistory.eu/en/node/263.

Bhattacharya, Tithi, ed. *Social Reproduction Theory: Remapping Class, Recentering Oppression.* London: Pluto, 2017.

Boris, Eileen. *Home to Work: Motherhood and the Politics of Industrial Homework in the United States.* New York: Cambridge University Press, 1994.

Bose, Christine E., Philip L. Bereano, and Mary Malloy. "Household Technology and the Social Construction of Housework." *Technology and Culture* 25, no. 1 (1984): 53–82.

Bubolz, Margaret M. *Beatrice Paolucci: Shaping Destiny through Everyday Life.* East Lansing, MI: Paolucci Book Committee, 2002.

Cohn, Julie A. *The Grid: Biography of an American Technology.* Cambridge, MA: MIT Press, 2017.

Cowan, Ruth Schwartz. *More Work for Mother: The Ironies of Household Technology from the Open Hearth to the Microwave.* New York: Basic Books, 1985.

Daggett, Cara New. *The Birth of Energy: Fossil Fuels, Thermodynamics, and the Politics of Work.* Durham, NC: Duke University Press, 2019.

Dix, Keith. *What's a Coal Miner to Do? The Mechanization of Coal Mining.* Pittsburgh: University of Pittsburgh Press, 1988.

Dreilinger, Danielle. *The Secret History of Home Economics: How Trailblazing Women Harnessed the Power of the Home and Changed the Way We Live.* New York: W. W. Norton, 2021.

Dublin, Thomas, and Walter Licht. *The Face of Decline: The Pennsylvania Anthracite Region in the Twentieth Century.* Ithaca, NY: Cornell University Press, 2005.

Electric Light and Power, Transmission and Distribution Edition. "Alphabetical Listing of Company Performances." June 1973, 53.

Energy Information Administration. "US Electricity Retail Sales to Major End-Use Sectors and Electricity Direct Use by All Sectors, 1950–2020." *Monthly Energy Review*, March 2021, table 7.6. https://www.eia.gov/energyexplained/electricity/use-of-electricity.php.

Fairman, Honor. "Solar One." *Journal of Home Economics* 65, no. 9 (December 1973): 27–33.

Field, Anne. "Energy Conservation: A Challenge for Home Economists." *Journal of Home Economics* 65, no. 9 (December 1973): 23–26.

Fraser, Nancy. "Behind Marx's Hidden Abode: For an Expanded Conception of Capitalism." In *Critical Theory in Critical Times: Transforming the Global Political and Economic Order*, edited by Penelope Deutscher and Cristina Lafonte, 141–58. New York: Columbia University Press, 2017.

Frederick, Paul, and Don Zimmerman. "Clearfield County Taking Steps to Conserve Energy." *Clearfield (PA) Progress*, November 19, 1971.

Gilbreth, Lillian M., Orpha Mae Thomas, and Eleanor Clymer. *Management in the Home: Happier Living through Saving Time and Energy.* New York: Dodd, Mead, and Company, 1960.

Gimenez, Martha, and Jane Lou Collins. *Work without Wages: Comparative Studies of Domestic Labor and Self-Employment.* Albany: State University of New York Press, 1990.

Goldstein, Carolyn M. *Creating Consumers: Home Economists in Twentieth-Century America.* Chapel Hill: University of North Carolina Press, 2012.

Graham, Laurel D. "Domesticating Efficiency: Lillian Gilbreth's Scientific Management of Homemakers, 1924–1930." *Signs* 24, no. 3 (1999): 633–75.

Greenberg, Dolores. "Energy, Power, and Perceptions of Social Change in the Early Nineteenth Century." *American Historical Review* 95, no. 3 (1990): 693–714.

Greene, Ann Norton. *Horses at Work: Harnessing Power in Industrial America.* Cambridge, MA: Harvard University Press, 2008.

Greer, Eunice S. "Energy Consumption in American Households." In *Energy and the Way We Live*, edited by Melvin Kranzberg, Timothy A. Hall, and Jane L. Schreiber, 21–24. San Francisco: Boyd and Fraser, 1980.

Harrison Moore, Abigail, and R. W. Sandwell. *In a New Light: Histories of Women and Energy.* Montreal: McGill-Queens University Press, 2021.

Hirsh, Richard F. *Technology and Transformation in the American Electric Utility Industry.* New York: Cambridge University Press, 1989.

Hochschild, Arlie Russell, with Anne Machung. *The Second Shift: Working Parents and the Revolution at Home.* New York: Viking, 1989.

Hughes, Thomas P. *Networks of Power: Electrification in Western Society, 1880–1930.* Baltimore: Johns Hopkins University Press, 1983.

Jobson, Ryan Cecil. "Dead Labor: On Racial Capital and Fossil Capital." In *Histories of Racial Capitalism*, edited by Justin Leroy and Destin Jenkins, 215–29. New York: Columbia University Press, 2021.

Johnson, Bob. "Energy Slaves: Carbon Technologies, Climate Change, and the Stratified History of the Fossil Economy." *American Quarterly* 68, no. 4 (2016): 955–79.

Journal of Home Economics. "The Energy Crisis and Home Economics." 65, no. 9 (December 1973): 6.

Journal of Home Economics. "Energy Questionnaire." 65, no. 9 (December 1973): 34–35.

Lancaster, Jane. *Making Time: Lillian Moller Gilbreth, a Life beyond "Cheaper by the Dozen."* Boston: Northeastern University Press, 2004.

Lockwood, Robert. "Power Cut to Safeguard Reserves." *Morning Call* (Allentown, PA), June 11, 1974.

Marrinan, Michael, and John Bender. *The Culture of the Diagram.* Palo Alto, CA: Stanford University Press, 2010.

Marsh, Charles Franklin. *Trade Unionism in the Electric Light and Power Industry.* Urbana: University of Illinois Press, 1928.

Moccio, Francine A. *Live Wire: Women and Brotherhood in the Electrical Industry.* Philadelphia: Temple University Press, 2009.

Montaño, Diana J. *Electrifying Mexico: Technology and the Transformation of a Modern City.* Austin: University of Texas Press, 2021.

Murphy, Michelle. *Sick Building Syndrome and the Problem of Uncertainty.* Durham, NC: Duke University Press, 2006.

Noble, David F. *Forces of Production: A Social History of Industrial Automation.* New York: Routledge, 2011.

Nye, David E. *Consuming Power: A Social History of American Energies.* Cambridge, MA: MIT Press, 1999.

Nye, David E. *Electrifying America: Social Meanings of a New Technology, 1880–1940.* Cambridge, MA: MIT Press, 1991.

Palladino, Grace. *Dreams of Dignity, Workers of Vision: A History of the International Brotherhood of Electrical Workers.* Washington, DC: International Brotherhood of Electrical Workers, 1991.

Paolucci, Beatrice, and M. Janice Hogan. "The Energy Crisis and the Family." *Journal of Home Economics* 65, no. 9 (December 1973): 12–15.

Rabinbach, Anson. *The Human Motor: Energy, Fatigue, and the Origins of Modernity.* Berkeley: University of California Press, 1992.

Rosenberg, Robert. "Test Men, Experts, Brother Engineers, and Members of the Fraternity: Whence the Early Electrical Workforce?" *IEEE Transactions on Education* 27, no. 4 (1984): 203–10.

Schatz, Ronald W. *The Electrical Workers: A History of Labor at General Electric and Westinghouse, 1923–1960.* Urbana: University of Illinois Press, 1983.

Self, Robert O. *All in the Family: The Realignment of American Democracy since the 1960s.* New York: Hill and Wang, 2012.

Smith, Crosbie. *The Science of Energy: A Cultural History of Energy Physics in Victorian Britain.* Chicago: University of Chicago Press, 1998.

Stein, Judith. *Running Steel, Running America: Race, Economic Policy, and the Decline of Liberalism.* Chapel Hill: University of North Carolina Press, 1998.

Storch, Phil H. "First General Strike Hits PP&L—5,000 Out." *Morning Call* (Allentown, PA), May 20, 1974.

Taft, Chloe E. *From Steel to Slots: Casino Capitalism in the Postindustrial City.* Cambridge, MA: Harvard University Press, 2016.

Thompson, Kristen Moana. "Living Electrically with Reddy Kilowatt, Your Electric Servant." In *Animation and Advertising*, edited by Malcolm Cook and Kristen Moana Thompson, 127–44. Cham, Switzerland: Springer, 2020.

Tympas, Aristotle. "Perpetually Laborious: Computing Electric Power Transmission before the Electronic Computer." *International Review of Social History* 48, supp. 11 (2003): 73–95.

Zallen, Jeremy. *American Lucifers: The Dark History of Artificial Light, 1750–1865*. Chapel Hill: University of North Carolina Press, 2019.

Zaretsky, Natasha. *No Direction Home: The American Family and the Fear of National Decline*. Chapel Hill: University of North Carolina Press, 2008.

The ILO, the Politics of Statistics, and Changing Perceptions of Informal Work, 1970–Present

Sibylle Marti

According to recent estimates of the ILO (International Labour Organization/ Office), over 60 percent of the world's employed population make their living in the so-called informal economy. This number is based on data for more than one hundred countries across the globe, representing more than 90 percent of persons in employment aged fifteen years and older. Given this impressive finding, one might forget that the term *informal sector* was barely used before the 1970s and that reliable, directly measured, comprehensive, and comparable statistical data on informal employment was not available until a decade ago.[1] For the ILO, the development of statistics on the informal sector and informal employment has been an important political objective, justifying the organization's involvement in numerous international projects to generate data on informal work.[2]

This article brings the history of labor and the history of science into conversation by examining the development of statistics on informal work since the 1970s, and the use of quantification as an instrument to generate knowledge and exercise power. While statistical claims refer to objects that are real (e.g., workers), they are, at the same time, a construct reflecting social, political, and scientific conventions (e.g., the long-standing Western premise that women's household labor was not work worth counting). That is why the renowned historian of statistics Alain Desrosières has suggested to speak of "objectivation" instead of objectivity when explaining what statistics do and the scientific authority they convey.[3] In his and Sandrine Kott's understanding, to quantify refers to the process of making numbers (instead of just having words as before) from two distinct operations: first, agreeing on certain conventions, approaches, and definitions; and then, measuring.[4] The resulting numbers, conveyed

I would like to thank the reviewers for their helpful suggestions and Seth Rockman for his invaluable support.

1. ILO, *Women and Men in the Informal Economy*, 6.
2. For an overview see Charmes, "Brief History."
3. Desrosières, *Politics of Large Numbers*.
4. Desrosières and Kott, "Quantifier."

Labor: Studies in Working-Class History, Volume 21, Issue 1
DOI 10.1215/15476715-10948960   © 2024 by Labor and Working-Class History Association

in statistical form, both describe and create social reality, influencing the perceptions, interpretations, and meanings of the objects they represent. Yet for all their rhetorical authority, statistical descriptions are unstable, changing with the emergence of new methodologies and shifting with changing definitions of the phenomena they aim to picture.

In the case of labor and employment statistics, they have never simply depicted the social reality of working conditions or forms of work. Rather, they exemplify the "scientification of the social,"[5] the inherently political process that informs and influences common understanding of what counts and is counted as labor. Already starting in the nineteenth century but accelerating in the second half of the twentieth, labor has become a knowledge-based object, with international organizations like the ILO acting as prime sites of both the knowledge production and the accompanying efforts of standard setting on the international level.[6]

The decades-long attempts to develop statistics on the informal sector and informal employment reveal labor as an object of contingent (and contested) statistical definition; they also illuminate how actors representing informal workers mobilized statistical knowledge for political action. The ILO provided an important arena for negotiating processes of defining and measuring informal work. The term *informal sector* was coined as an alternative concept in development thinking, facilitated by research carried out under the ILO's World Employment Programme (WEP) in the 1970s, albeit without a coherent understanding of what it meant or how it could be defined. The ILO's preliminary attempts toward a feasible statistical definition started in the early 1980s and culminated, in 1993, in an internationally accepted definition of the concept. The spread of informal employment in industrialized countries during the 1990s paved the way for the broadening of the international statistical definitions at the beginning of the twenty-first century. Most recently, activist networks representing informal workers have mobilized statistics to propel policies of a formalization of the informal economy.

The Informal Sector as an Alternative Idea and Exploratory Field in Development

The concept of the informal sector emerged in development research in the early 1970s. At that time, development economics was in crisis, as traditional methods based on macroeconomic theories of modernization had largely failed. As a result, the interdisciplinary field of development studies emerged to better reflect the diversity and heterogeneity of developing societies with more concrete approaches.[7] In this context, the ILO launched the WEP in 1969 as a contribution to the second development decade of the United Nations (UN). The WEP aimed to develop strategies to create productive employment and reduce unemployment and underemployment,

5. Raphael, "Die Verwissenschaftlichung."
6. See Boris, *Making the Woman Worker.*
7. Speich Chassé, *Die Erfindung*, 210–21.

two major stumbling blocks to social development and poverty reduction. With the WEP, the ILO gained wide international recognition as one of the leading development agencies.[8]

The idea of the informal sector represented a welcome alternative in development thinking. The then-common distinction between a "modern" and a "traditional" sector was transformed into the dichotomy of "formal" versus "informal." The informal sector offered an alternative to conventional measurements of economic growth tied to gross national product, as well as to modernization theory's focus on formal employment.[9] For the ILO, the concept replaced the unsatisfactory notion of "disguised unemployment" with an operational measure to quantify employment insufficiency in developing countries, an objective the ILO had pursued since the postwar era.[10]

It was the British social anthropologist Keith Hart who coined the term *informal sector*. In the second half of the 1960s, Hart conducted a field study in Ghana of men and women in urban areas who provided services in trade, transport, housing, home manufacturing, shipping, and the like. Referring to the work of the renowned economist Joseph A. Schumpeter, he defined these men and women as "small-scale entrepreneurs."[11] Later, Hart conceptualized their economic activities as "informal income opportunities," "informal economic activities," "informal employment," and "informal occupation" taking place in an "informal sector."[12]

Crucial for the dissemination of the concept was the September 1971 conference titled "Urban Unemployment in Africa" at the Institute of Development Studies at the University of Sussex,[13] then a leading hub for interdisciplinary, alternative approaches to redistribution and poverty.[14] Hart's idea of the informal sector stimulated "fruitful discussions,"[15] with some conference participants adopting an "unorthodox" view of the informal sector as an important factor for future economic progress; no longer was the lack of formal employment understood as the biggest obstacle to development.[16] John Weeks, a lecturer in economics at the University of Sussex, presented "broadly similar ideas."[17] One year later, he participated in one of the WEP's comprehensive employment missions, codirected by Hans W. Singer and Richard Jolly, two eminent development researchers also based at the influential Institute of Development Studies.[18]

---

8. On the WEP see Maul, *International Labour Organization*, 171–81.

9. Bangasser, *ILO and the Informal Sector*; McNeill, "Informal Sector"; Macekura, *Mismeasure of Progress*, 138–65.

10. Benanav, "Origins."

11. Hart, "Small-Scale Entrepreneurs," 106.

12. Hart, "Informal Income Opportunities."

13. The conference papers were published as special issue in *Manpower and Unemployment Research in Africa* 6, no. 2 (1973).

14. Macekura, "Dudley Seers," 58.

15. Institute of Development Studies, *Fifth Annual Report*, 29.

16. Shaw, *Sir Hans Singer*, 160; Weeks, "Introduction," 3, 4.

17. Weeks, "Introduction," 4.

18. On Hans W. Singer see Shaw, *Sir Hans Singer*.

During this 1972 mission to Kenya, the concept of the informal sector was tested and played a dominant role in the chapters for which Weeks was primarily responsible in the mission's widely received report.[19] Social scientists from the Institute of Development Studies at the University of Nairobi also contributed, suggesting that "a new school of analysis may be emerging," as the Kenya report put it.[20] The report appraised the informal sector rather positively as a potential prosperity factor, characterizing informal economic activities by "ease of entry," "family ownership of enterprises," "small scale of operation," and "unregulated and competitive markets," among others.[21]

Existing literature distinguishes between "job-based" and "enterprise-based" definitions of informality, with Hart's description belonging to the first definition and the Kenya report to the second.[22] It must be emphasized, however, that the representation of informal workers as "entrepreneurs" had played a key role in Hart's understanding and was thus central to the concept from the beginning. In the following years, the notion of the informal small-scale entrepreneur would become appealing to neoliberal celebrations of free enterprise.[23]

The new concept of the informal sector, as the ILO proudly noted, gained "wide currency" in development thinking in the 1970s.[24] The definition and meaning of the term remained elusive, however, prompting further ILO research and a reorientation of the WEP's "Urbanisation and Employment" subprogram toward the informal sector.[25] The research was led by US economist Harold Lubell, who arrived at the ILO in 1971. He was joined two years later by S. V. Sethuraman, who would become one of the ILO's leading experts on the informal sector. Together they launched a series of survey studies that became known as "the urban informal sector programme."[26] The first three studies covered the cities of Calcutta, Dakar, and Bogotá, followed later by surveys in other cities in Asia, Africa, and Latin America.[27] Although exploratory in nature, the surveys designed by Sethuraman and then adapted for each city represented a first attempt to systematically collect information on the informal sector.[28]

Sethuraman defined the informal sector as a subsector of the urban economy consisting of "small-scale units engaged in the production and distribution of goods and services,"[29] excluding agricultural activities.[30] The perception of informality as

19. Shaw, *Sir Hans Singer*, 289.

20. ILO, *Employment, Incomes and Equality*, 6.

21. ILO, *Employment, Incomes and Equality*, 6.

22. Charmes, "Brief History," 15, 18.

23. See Marti, "Shadow Economy."

24. Sethuraman, "Concepts, Methodology and Scope," 12, 13.

25. For an overview on ILO's informal sector activities in the 1970s see ILO, *Urbanisation, Informal Sector and Employment*.

26. Bangasser, *ILO and the Informal Sector*, 11–12.

27. Summaries of these studies can be found in Sethuraman, *Urban Informal Sector*. Full-length versions were published earlier as WEP Working Papers in the WEP 2–19 Series.

28. Sethuraman, "Concepts, Methodology and Scope," 23.

29. Sethuraman, "Concepts, Methodology and Scope," 17.

30. Bashir, "Statistics concerning the Urban Informal Sector," xiv.

an urban phenomenon was built into the concept from the outset. Like the Kenya report, the urban informal sector studies chose enterprise as the observable unit. However, ILO official Sethuraman acknowledged that this term was "perhaps inappropriate," since shoeshine boys, street vendors, building caretakers, or parking attendants "can hardly be called an enterprise."[31] Nevertheless, he considered an enterprise-based approach most likely to support the ILO's goals of improving employment and income conditions in the informal sector.[32]

The urban informal sector studies faced several definitional difficulties, beginning with fitting the observed economic activities into existing classification schemes such as the International Standard Industrial Classification of All Economic Activities and the International Standard Classification of Occupations. The activities studied did not appear in these international classifications because, as one ILO paper noted, "some of the informal sector occupations and activities seem to be unique to developing countries."[33] The greatest difficulty, however, was defining a sample frame. The survey studies' general approach was to construct a sample frame consisting of the eligible units in the whole city or selected sectors of it. But it was not easy to determine what constituted an eligible unit because the smaller the economic unit, the greater the likelihood that it was not recorded anywhere in official records. Therefore, it proved extremely difficult to assemble a meaningful sample that could be studied. If, for a given city, it had been known, for example, that most informal workers were found in certain occupations or activities, the informal sector could have been defined to include only those occupations or activities, but such preexisting information was generally not available.[34]

The survey studies of the WEP's urban informal sector program hence revealed considerable inadequacy in statistically representing the social reality of informal work in developing countries. As comprehensive statistics seemed crucial to support the assertion of the informal sector's growth potential,[35] the ILO pressed ahead with projects on the feasibility of informal sector statistics with the aim of establishing international standards.

Toward an International Statistical Definition of the Informal Sector

At the beginning of the 1980s, the ILO reeled under financial pressure due to the earlier withdrawal of the United States. Moreover, with the rise of neoliberalism and structural adjustment policies, other international organizations, notably the World Bank and the International Monetary Fund (IMF), were gaining prominence on issues of economic growth and labor.[36] At the same time, the ILO was confronted

---

31. Sethuraman, "Concepts, Methodology and Scope," 23.
32. Sethuraman, "Concepts, Methodology and Scope," 13–15.
33. Bashir, "Statistics concerning the Urban Informal Sector," xvi.
34. Bashir, "Statistics concerning the Urban Informal Sector," xiv–xvi.
35. Bashir, "Statistics concerning the Urban Informal Sector," xiii.
36. Benanav, "Origins," 121.

with profound changes in the world of work and sought to adapt its recommendations on employment policy accordingly.[37]

It was against this backdrop that the Thirteenth International Conference of Labour Statisticians (ICLS) met in 1982 to revise its recommendations concerning statistics on the labor force, employment, unemployment, and underemployment. In a report prepared for the conference, the ILO explained that especially for developing countries, existing protocols were "neither easy to apply nor particularly meaningful."[38] A resolution adopted by the Thirteenth ICLS therefore called to "account for the informal sector activities, both in developed and developing countries," among other things.[39] Notably, in acknowledging the prevalence of informal work in developed countries, the resolution reflected the public and political attention given to the so-called hidden economy, whose existence advocates of neoliberalism in the early 1980s attributed to overregulation of the formal sector.[40]

The ILO Bureau of Statistics subsequently commissioned two methodological surveys, one in Kerala in India and one in San José in Costa Rica, to test alternative question formulations and to examine the application of the 1982 ICLS resolution "in different cultural settings."[41] The surveys were designed by ILO officials, while the fieldwork was done by the Kerala Statistical Institute and the Dirección General de Estadística y Censos in Costa Rica, but little progress was made in developing statistics specifically on the informal sector.[42]

At the Fourteenth ICLS in 1987, the ILO devoted a chapter of its general report to the informal sector,[43] and the ICLS supported an oral resolution from the delegate of Mexico "to measure employment outside the formal sector."[44] The informal sector was then placed on the agenda of the next ICLS in 1993 as "the first completely new topic" since 1949 to be discussed with the aim of standard setting.[45] As informal work at the time was no longer seen as a phenomenon limited to developing countries, the ILO carefully ensured that these countries' perspective was not overshadowed by the voices of industrialized countries. Preferably, a person from a developing country would chair a committee presenting its findings to the 1993 ICLS. Ralf Hussmanns, responsible for the work on the informal sector at the ILO Bureau of Statistics, noted that the "ideal candidate would be a person from an important Latin American country."[46]

---

37. See the discussions at the ILC in 1983 and 1984 on the Recommendation No. 169 concerning Employment Policy.

38. ILO, *Statistics of Labour Force*, 15.

39. ILO, *Report of the Thirteenth ICLS*, I/8.

40. See Marti, "Die 'Entdeckung.'"

41. Hussmanns, Mehran, and Verma, *Surveys of Economically Active Population*, vi.

42. ILO Archives, Geneva (ILOA), ST 69 Jacket 1, R. Turvey to Rafael Trigueros, December 3, 1982, Mehran to Clara Jusidman, February 24, 1983.

43. ILO, *General Report to the Fourteenth ICLS*, 8–19.

44. ILO, *Report of the Fourteenth ICLS*, 9, 83.

45. ILO, *Report of the Fifteenth ICLS*, 31.

46. ILOA, ST 73 Jacket 2, Ralf Hussmanns to Maria Martha Malard Mayer, December 16, 1991.

A chair from Latin America reflected a pivot away from Africa toward Latin America for studying the informal sector.[47] The ILO's Regional Employment Programme for Latin America and the Caribbean had introduced the concept of the informal sector to Latin America at the beginning of the 1970s and contributed to a Latin American theory of informality.[48] More importantly, the 1986 publication of the Peruvian economist Hernando de Soto's bestseller *The Other Path* made the informal sector something of a cause célèbre for neoliberals who imagined small-scale entrepreneurs as the driving forces of a free-market revolution from below.[49] De Soto's book was disseminated in foundations, think tanks, development agencies, and international organizations advocating for neoliberal policies.[50] Even the ILO could not avoid de Soto as a reference, although his arguments were grist to the mill of the World Bank and IMF structural adjustment policies that the ILO fought against.

Maria Martha Malard Mayer, head of the Department of Employment and Income at the Brazilian Institute of Geography and Statistics, chaired the resulting committee.[51] Their definitions, adopted in a resolution by the Fifteenth ICLS, were included in the 1993 version of the System of National Accounts, the internationally agreed-upon recommendations for measuring economic activity.[52] According to the resolution, the informal sector consisted of "units engaged in the production of goods or services" aimed at "generating employment and incomes." These units usually operated "at a low level of organization" and "on a small scale" and had "the characteristic features of household enterprises." Enterprises could be marginal, with no clear distinction between production activities and other activities, such as subsistence or reproduction activities of the owners; or they could be larger and thus include occasional or even permanent contributing family workers or employees. The common feature of all these heterogeneous manifestations of household enterprises was that their operational relations were based on "casual employment, kinship or personal and social relations rather than contractual arrangements with formal guarantees."[53] With this description, what gave the informal sector its informality might be called "extra-legal regulation."[54]

This formulation reflected the ILO's limited scope of the informal sector as confined to units that produced for the market. Accordingly, informal sector activities or enterprises had to meet the criteria of production and the categories of household market enterprises as established in the System of National Accounts. Household enterprises engaged exclusively in nonmarket production for own final consumption and unpaid domestic services were therefore excluded.[55] Housework, care work, and

47. Benanav, "Origins," 122.

48. Vergara, "'Trabajadores pobres e informales.'"

49. De Soto, *The Other Path*.

50. Dommann, "Informelle Ökonomie," 179–80.

51. ILOA, ST 73 Jacket 2, Report on a mission to Rio de Janeiro, November 24–29, 1991.

52. Commission for the European Community et al., *System of National Accounts 1993*.

53. ILO, *Report of the Fifteenth ICLS*, 51–64.

54. Mayer-Ahuja, "Labor, Insecurity, Informality," 260.

55. ILO, *Measurement of Employment*, 28–30.

volunteer work, as well as do-it-yourself activities, were seen as noneconomic and thus uncounted, although they had often been included in conceptualizations such as the British sociologist Jonathan Gershuny's theory of the self-service economy,[56] and feminists' insistence that reproductive labor be recognized and measured as work. Within the ILO, development feminists involved in the "Programme on Rural Women" overcame the distinction between housework and productive work based on research about informal subsistence labor by rural women, but it would take until 2013 for the ICLS to recognize unpaid reproductive labor as "'own-use production'" and thus as "'work.'"[57]

Although the 1993 ICLS resolution aimed to set an international standard for all countries, the concept reflected the particular social reality of developing countries. But as Ralf Hussmanns recalled, since "the developed countries...were well represented in the committee and engaged actively in the discussions," the relationship between the concept and measurement of the informal sector and the underground economy was again discussed for "considerable time."[58] The idea that informal work might equate to hidden production or concealed employment, however, was mainly a Western view. As a journalist from the internationally distributed *Colors* magazine asked, did employment in the informal sector now primarily mean "unreported economic activities" and "unlicensed work"?[59]

This had indeed become the emphasis in industrialized countries thanks to advocates of neoliberal ideas, arguing that the hidden economy was an escape route from overregulation. Calls for tax reduction, liberalization, privatization, deregulation, and a flexibilization of labor were echoed in pronouncements by the World Bank, the IMF, and the Organisation for Economic Co-operation and Development (OECD) and contributed to a new branch of macroeconomic research to calculate the underground economy's share of the gross national product. However, because these macroeconomic approaches did not utilize interviews or questionnaires and limited themselves to indirect metrics, the nature of the hidden economic activities remained obscure.[60] The ILO was also interested in quantitative data on the informal sector but considered the usual, direct methods of employment statistics more appropriate to capture it. At the same time, these survey techniques made it possible to learn more about the informal sector as a specific place of production and employment. The ILO therefore insisted on distinguishing between the informal sector and the hidden economy because they reflected "a different socio-economic concern with its own measurement objective" that accordingly required different approaches to quantification and statistical coverage.[61]

56. Gershuny, *After Industrial Society?*; Gershuny, "Informal Economy."

57. Boris, *Making the Woman Worker*, 122–54, 229; Betti and Boris, "Feminised Work," 136–37.

58. ILOA, ST 73 Jacket 4, Ralf Hussmanns to Mr. S. M. Vidwans, April 6, 1993.

59. ILOA, ST 73 Jacket 4, Jean Decker Mathews to F. Mehran, March 29, 1993.

60. Marti, "Die 'Entdeckung,'" 17–18.

61. ILO, *Measurement of Employment*, 7–8.

The 1993 ICLS largely followed this argument by emphasizing that informal sector activities "are not necessarily performed with the deliberate intention of evading the payment of taxes or social security contributions, or infringing labour or other legislations or administrative provisions."[62] An earlier terminological suggestion to speak of "business under the open sun"[63] underlined that most work in the informal sector was not intentionally concealed but remained absent in official records whether because informal sector entrepreneurs were unaware of existing laws and regulations or could not afford the cost and time required to comply with them, or authorities lacked the resources to enforce existing legal, administrative, or technical regulations.[64] For these reasons, the ILO considered (il)legality "of limited relevance in defining the informal sector, particularly in the context of developing countries."[65] The issue had featured in earlier contributions such as the 1972 Kenya report,[66] but with its goal of creating employment and income opportunities, the ILO was more interested in the "operational characteristics" than in the legal-administrative aspects of informal sector enterprises and their relations to public authorities.[67] Nonetheless, in order to accommodate developed countries, the ICLS resolution included non-registration as a possible criterion for defining informal sector enterprises.[68] Overall, however, the informal sector resolution of the Fifteenth ICLS in 1993 was a success for both the developing countries and the ILO. While the developing countries established a concept of work that reflected social realities, the ILO successfully made informal work an internationally recognized labor concept and integrated it into the System of National Accounts. In contrast to calculations of the hidden economy, but in line with ILO policy objectives, the informal sector should be statistically captured from a perspective related to income and employment.

The Global Spread of Informality and the Broadening of Definitions

The 1993 ICLS resolution advocated an "enterprise-based" definition of informal work, as the observable unit that provided the basis for the first international statistical definition was (small-scale) enterprises. The notion of informal sector enterprise seemed reasonable because it fit into existing classifications. But while the ICLS was establishing this definition, the ILO was addressing what it called the "dilemma of the informal sector," namely whether to promote further employment in the informal sector or to plead for more protection and social security at the risk of reducing informal employment possibilities.[69] The ILO was thus well aware that "enterprise" was a blunt euphemism for a heterogeneous informal sector in which workers mostly

62. ILO, *Report of the Fifteenth ICLS*, 52.
63. ILO, *Report of the Fourteenth ICLS*, 8.
64. ILO, *Statistics of Employment*, 8.
65. ILOA, ST 73 Jacket 4, R. Hussmanns to Jean Decker Mathews, April 1, 1993.
66. ILO, *Employment, Incomes and Equality*, 504.
67. ILO, *Measurement of Employment*, 36.
68. ILO, *Report of the Fifteenth ICLS*, 53–54.
69. ILO, *Dilemma*.

lived and toiled in precarious conditions. Renana Jhabvala, the secretary of the Self Employed Women's Association (SEWA), a respected and influential association of women informal workers in India,[70] wrote to the ILO director-general to express her concern "with the limited understanding of the informal sector," given the "wide variety of workers and types of economic activities," in "both rural and urban areas."[71] Against the backdrop of such criticism, the understanding of informality expanded in the 1990s.

A decade of neoliberal labor market policies had already led to a worldwide decline in so-called standard or formal employment. This trend was exacerbated in the 1990s, transforming the prevalence and the perception of the problem of informality. As a 2002 ILO report pointed out, a large proportion of new employment opportunities in developing countries as well as those transitioning away from socialism was in the informal economy. In addition, trends toward decentralization, outsourcing, and subcontracting had increased informal employment in industrialized countries. As a result, the ILO called for "decent work along the entire continuum from the informal to the formal end of the economy."[72] The International Labour Conference (ILC) adopted a resolution that now allowed the "informal economy" to encompass "all economic activities by workers and economic units that are—in law or in practice—not covered or insufficiently covered by formal arrangements."[73] Notably, just as the formal economies of industrialized countries were now subjecting workers to atypical, nonstandard, and often precarious employment, the ILO and the ILC universalized the need for decent work.

This sea change in perception also led to a change in the statistical definition of informal work. In 2003, the Seventeenth ICLS discussed new guidelines to complement its 1993 definition. A veteran of the 1993 meeting, French statistician Jacques Charmes, chaired a committee that recommended the recognition of informal work within formal economies. "Informal employment" carried out "in formal sector enterprises, informal sector enterprises, or households" now complemented the conceptual framework.[74] Adding a job-based definition of informal employment to the existing enterprise-based definition also made "the total number of informal jobs" an observable unit.[75] The expanded 2003 ICLS definition no longer referred only to production units; now it referred explicitly to workers as well. Thus, in addition to enterprise relations, labor relations became a focus of statistical analysis.

The new guidelines also recognized two important categories of informal labor: agricultural and domestic workers. They urged countries to develop "appropriate definitions for informal jobs in agriculture."[76] Agricultural activities had not

70. On SEWA see Bonner, Horn, and Jhabvala, "Informal Women Workers."

71. ILOA, ST 73 Jacket 4, Renana Jhabvala to Director General, June 22, 1993.

72. ILO, *Decent Work and the Informal Economy*, 4.

73. ILC, *Ninetieth Session*, 53.

74. ILO, *Report of the Seventeenth ICLS*, 11, 13.

75. ILO, *Report of the Seventeenth ICLS*, 13.

76. ILO, *Report of the Seventeenth ICLS*, 14.

been included in the 1993 ICLS definition due to fears that doing so would greatly expand the scope and cost of conducting surveys, especially as many countries already had established systems of agricultural censuses and surveys.[77] A decade later, deteriorating working conditions in agriculture were a major concern of the ILO.[78] In the new context of promoting decent work, it now viewed obstacles to data collection as political rather than practical problems.

Regarding paid domestic workers, the guidelines recommended that they should be treated "separately as part of a category called 'households.'"[79] Under the 1993 resolution, such workers had not been consistently included in informal sector statistics because the ICLS could not reach agreement on the topic.[80] This indecision reflected a common belief that women's labor in intimate workplaces such as private households was incomparable to other occupations. However, the 2003 creation of the separate category of households suggested that commodified forms of household and care work would receive more recognition in the new millennium. In 2011, the ILC adopted a convention on domestic work.[81]

In sum, the ICLS's expanded conceptual framework encompassed both the notion of the informal sector and that of informal employment; the latter was of particular interest to developed countries.[82] The spread of informal employment in informal as well as formal economies had made informal work into a global problem, affecting developing, transition, and developed countries alike. Suggestions to speak of "unprotected employment" instead of informal employment reflected a change in the perception of informality.[83] Although the ICLS rejected this idea, the discussion clearly showed the new focus on the precariousness of informal work and decent work deficits.

Instrumental in the expanded statistical definition of informality was a statistical expert body known as the Delhi Group. The Delhi Group was established in 1997 by the UN Statistical Commission,[84] after the informal sector had been identified as one of the "critical problems in economic statistics" and the measurement of informal sector activities as "a most pressing need" for policymaking, especially in developing and transition countries.[85] The Indian Central Statistical Organization, which had gathered a wealth of information on statistical methods for designing surveys and collecting data in the informal sector, offered to host: hence, the Delhi Group.[86] Participants were some two dozen experts from statistical offices around

---

77. ILO, *Statistics of Employment*, 30–31.

78. ILO, *Decent Work in Agriculture*, 5.

79. ILO, *Report of the Seventeenth ICLS*, 13.

80. ILO, *Report of the Fifteenth ICLS*, 35.

81. See Boris, *Making the Woman Worker*, 193–228.

82. Hussmanns, *Measuring the Informal Economy*, 2.

83. ILO, *Report of the Seventeenth ICLS*, 12.

84. UN Statistical Commission, *Report on the Twenty-Ninth Session*, 5.

85. UN Statistical Commission, *Expert Group on Critical Problems*, 1, 11.

86. UN Statistical Commission, *Reports on Selected Critical Problems*, 31.

the world, especially from developing countries. Members also included international bodies like the Asian Development Bank, the Economic and Social Commission for Asia and the Pacific, the Statistical Institute for Asia and the Pacific, the UN Statistics Division, and the ILO (represented with its senior statistician Ralf Hussmanns), along with NGOs, think tanks, research institutes, and organizations representing informal workers such as SEWA.[87]

The Delhi Group helped advance statistical inquiry toward the insecurity and precarity of informal work. In 2001, reacting to the inability of an enterprise-based definition to capture all aspects of the increasing informalization of work, they concluded that "the definition and measurement of employment in the informal sector needs to be complemented with a definition and measurement of informal employment."[88] They also recommended that countries test the new concept of informal employment and the job-based definition, respectively. Subsequently, several countries—Georgia, Brazil, Mexico, India, and the Republic of Moldavia—followed this recommendation, and, as one ILO report noted, "the results of the tests were encouraging."[89] The operational criteria used to define informal jobs—no employment contract, no social security coverage, no paid annual or sick leave, no protection against arbitrary dismissal, and the casual nature of the work—clearly elucidate the difference from the earlier concept of the informal sector, which mainly emphasized enterprises' small size and possible nonregistration.[90] The Delhi Group contributed to a chapter titled "Informal Aspects of the Economy" in the 2008 System of National Accounts,[91] and it initiated and collaborated on a 2013 manual that remains the main source of technical and practical guidance to national statistical offices and other producers of statistics on the informal sector and informal employment.[92]

Statactivism and the Formalization of the Informal Economy

Beyond the global spread of informal employment and the broadening of statistical definitions, new global activist networks emerged in the 1990s to provide visibility and support to workers in the informal economy. Particularly influential is Women in Informal Employment: Globalizing and Organizing (WIEGO), which was heavily involved in the work of the Delhi Group.[93] WIEGO uses statistics as a political strategy and successfully lobbies at the international level to improve and further disseminate statistics on informal work. Its founding members include Harvard lecturer Martha Chen, SEWA's Renana Jhabvala, statistical expert Jacques Charmes, and former ILO official S. V. Sethuraman. WIEGO came out of the 1996 fight on the ILO

87. UN Statistics Division, "Delhi Group on Informal Sector Statistics."

88. Government of India/Ministry of Statistics and Programme Implementation, "Report of the Fifth Meeting."

89. ILO, *General Report to the Seventeenth ICLS*, 53.

90. ILO, *General Report to the Seventeenth ICLS*, 53.

91. Commission for the European Community et al., *System of National Accounts 2008*.

92. ILO, *Measuring Informality*.

93. On WIEGO see Bonner, Horn, and Jhabvala, "Informal Women Workers."

convention on home work, as activists had learned through the process that statistics mattered in the making of global labor standards and for the visibility of workers.[94]

From the beginning, WIEGO's founders recognized "the power of statistics" to draw attention to the scope and situation of workers in the informal economy and to provide statistical data for informal workers to use in their discussions with policymakers.[95] As WIEGO "seeks to mainstream" the measurement of the informal economy in official statistics, it strives to improve classifications, concepts, and methods for data collection, as well as the availability, reliability, and international comparability of data.[96] It also advocates for countries to include informal employment in their statistical programs, tries to find donors for statistical activities, and provides training on informal economy statistics to statisticians and data users. In addition, WIEGO works with organizations of informal workers and their networks, including SEWA and several associations of street vendors, home-based workers, domestic workers, and waste pickers.[97]

WIEGO's statistical experts and consultants engage in "scientific political activism."[98] They are highly decorated scientists who contribute expertise to their special field of knowledge but at the same time use their scientific authority to pursue very determined political objectives. An evaluation report of WIEGO's statistics program in 2009 therefore emphasized that "the use of statistics to drive arguments is not uncommon among activists, but to place it at the forefront of their work agenda is rare."[99] This mobilization of statistics has been called "statactivism," a neologism to point to social movements' use of statistics as a form of contentious and/or emancipative action.[100]

WIEGO's statactivism is based on the belief that statistics are key to drive policy initiatives. "Numbers are needed to influence policy and change the situation for women around the world," observes Joann Vanek, senior adviser on statistics and former director of the WIEGO Statistics Programme.[101] A first and crucial step is accessibility to statistical knowledge: "In fact," one WIEGO working paper noted, "many countries began to collect data on the informal sector and informal employment because international definitions became available which they could use."[102]

Since its founding in 1997, WIEGO's statactivism has relied on collaboration with such bodies as the UN Statistics Division and the Delhi Group,[103] but its most important partner in its statistical endeavors has been the ILO. One of WIEGO's first contacts within the ILO was the ILO Bureau of Statistics, to which it offered

94. See Boris, *Making the Woman Worker*, 155–89.

95. WIEGO, "Statistics Programme."

96. WIEGO, "Statistics Programme."

97. WIEGO, "Statistics Programme."

98. Germann, Held, and Wulz, "Scientific Political Activism."

99. Mehran, *WIEGO Impact Evaluation*, 1.

100. See Bruno, Didier, and Vitale, "Statactivism," and the identically named special issue.

101. WIEGO, "Joann Vanek."

102. Vanek et al., *Statistics on the Informal Economy*, 32.

103. WIEGO, "Statistics Programme."

its expertise.[104] Some WIEGO statistical experts, in particular Jacques Charmes, had been involved in the development of informal sector statistics from the outset. In the new millennium, WIEGO has consistently played an important role in the development of statistics on all aspects of the informal economy and has joined together with the ILO to produce a flagship publication on the size, scope, and types of informal work across the globe, titled *Women and Men in the Informal Economy: A Statistical Picture*. The most recent edition in 2018 included differentiated data for more than one hundred countries, as mentioned at the beginning of this article.[105]

Statactivism has also led WIEGO to expand its influence through the exchange of know-how and expertise. In 2008, for example, WIEGO's Statistics Programme organized an expert workshop at Harvard University to explore data collection on all forms of informal and nonstandard employment in OECD countries. The main goal of such efforts is to raise awareness of the ongoing informalization of work around the globe, which affects both developing and developed countries, and to design statistical approaches accordingly. Following the workshop, WIEGO successfully advocated with a workshop participant at the Eighteenth ICLS in 2008 for a revision of the International Classification on Status in Employment to better reflect the changing structure of the labor force.[106] The ICLS subsequently made this topic a priority for ILO work on labor statistics.[107]

In 2015, the ILC adopted a recommendation to formalize the informal economy with the aim to "facilitate the transition of workers and economic units from the informal to the formal economy," "promote the creation, preservation and sustainability of enterprises and decent jobs in the formal economy," and "prevent the informalization of formal economy jobs."[108] In the process leading to the recommendation, WIEGO together with SEWA not only participated in the ILO's preliminary expert meeting in 2013 but also organized regional workshops in Africa, Asia, and Latin America where informal workers could give their input to develop a platform, which subsequently was shared at the ILC 2014.[109] In 2015, WIEGO supported a delegation of thirty-two representatives of informal workers to participate in the ILC discussion on the adoption of the recommendation "to ensure that their voices were directly heard again."[110] The ILO, which called the recommendation "the first international labour standard specifically for the informal economy,"[111] believes that the regular collection of statistical data on the size and composition of the informal economy is a key element in monitoring and assessing progress toward formalization.[112] WIEGO

---

104. ILOA, ST 73 Jacket 6, Marty Chen to Ralf Hussmanns, May 7, 1998.

105. ILO, *Women and Men in the Informal Economy*, 6.

106. Carré and Heintz, *Toward a Common Framework*, 18.

107. ILO, *Report of the Eighteenth ICLS*, 20.

108. ILC, *104th Session*, 10-1/6.

109. WIEGO, "Formalizing the Informal Economy."

110. WIEGO, "Formalizing the Informal Economy."

111. ILO, "ILO News."

112. ILC, *104th Session*, 10-1/20, 10-1/22.

thus not only supported and represented informal workers in their fight for an international labor standard but also contributed to develop the statistical knowledge that underpins the recommendation and will assess its impact. WIEGO's statactivism continues, as it is currently involved in the revision of the statistical standards on informality, the proposal for which is to be submitted to the ICLS in 2023.

WIEGO mobilizes statistics because it believes that what counts and is counted as (informal) work is foundationally a matter of numbers. One could argue that the current perception of informality as a common problem of developing and developed countries alike has much to do with the availability of numbers based on international statistical standards that make it possible to compare and relate phenomena of informality and informalization on a global scale.

Statistics (of informal work) are inherently political because they enable certain perceptions and interpretations about the social world (of work) and make others less plausible. That is, numbers help make a particular argument more robust because, as objectifications, they are a way of making things "real." Or, to put it another way, numbers make it harder to ignore a particular social phenomenon. Accordingly, statistics open up scope for political action. Statistics can change the perception of reality simply by their presence, and when they do, they become a powerful rhetoric and a transformative tool. In this regard, WIEGO has recognized the importance of quantification from the beginning, emphasizing the power of statistics and the influence of numbers on policy.

At the same time, statistics tend to hide the complex epistemic, social, and political contexts and the contentious negotiation processes that made their production possible in the first place. Numbers often evoke immediate evidence and seem to speak for themselves. Statistics' supposedly apolitical and neutral image has much to do with this disappearance of their coming-into-being. The scientific expertise and authority required to produce the numbers, in turn, commonly reinforce the trust in them. For this reason, WIEGO has taken advantage of its close relationships with renowned scholars and leading institutions and has invested heavily in becoming a valued collaborator with international bodies that also deal with the production of statistics on the informal economy, particularly the ILO.

However, mobilizing statistics requires significant effort to make a difference in the social world. Even if the numbers seem to speak for themselves, to be politically effective they must be widely disseminated and recognized. The example of WIEGO is illuminating because it shows what statactivism looks like in practice: It is not limited to producing numbers. Rather, the numbers must be actively circulated and used to lend plausibility to and advance political demands. To achieve this, access to and credibility with influential actors and institutions are essential. This is the reason why WIEGO has actively offered its statistical expertise to political authorities and international organizations from the very beginning.

Studying statactivism and the development of (labor or employment) statistics is instructive because statistics, as instruments of knowledge and power, capture and at the same time transform social realities and perceptions (in the world of work).

This means that statistics are both indicators and factors of social change. Engaging in conversation with the history of science in order to analyze and historicize the process of the creation and impact of statistical data in the social world is therefore a worthwhile endeavor for labor historians.

SIBYLLE MARTI is currently working on her second book on the history of informal and precarious work since 1970, funded by an Ambizione grant from the Swiss National Science Foundation at the University of Bern. Her research is situated at the intersection of the global history of work, the history of knowledge, and the history of capitalism. Research stays have taken her to the International Institute of Social History in Amsterdam and the International Research Centre "Work and Human Life Cycle in Global History" (re:work) in Berlin, among others.

References

Bangasser, Paul E. *The ILO and the Informal Sector: An Institutional History.* Geneva: ILO, 2000.

Bashir, K. M. "Statistics concerning the Urban Informal Sector." *Bulletin of Labour Statistics* (1st quarter 1980): xiii–xxvi.

Benanav, Aaron. "The Origins of Informality: The ILO at the Limit of the Concept of Unemployment." *Journal of Global History* 14, no. 1 (2019): 107–25.

Betti, Eloisa, and Eileen Boris. "Feminised Work after Fordism: The New Precarity." In *The Routledge Handbook of the Gig Economy*, edited by Immanuel Ness, 131–44. London: Routledge, 2022.

Bonner, Chris, Pat Horn, and Renana Jhabvala. "Informal Women Workers Open ILO Doors through Transnational Organizing, 1980s–2010s." In *Women's ILO: Transnational Networks, Global Labour Standards and Gender Equity, 1919 to Present*, edited by Eileen Boris, Dorothea Hoehtker, and Susan Zimmermann, 176–201. Geneva: ILO; Leiden: Brill, 2018.

Boris, Eileen. *Making the Woman Worker: Precarious Labor and the Fight for Global Standards.* New York: Oxford University Press, 2019.

Bruno, Isabelle, Emmanuel Didier, and Tommaso Vitale. "Statactivism: Forms of Action between Disclosure and Affirmation." *Partecipazione e conflitto: The Open Journal of Sociopolitical Studies* 7, no. 2 (2014): 198–220.

Carré, Françoise, and James Heintz. *Toward a Common Framework for Informal Employment across Developed and Developing Countries.* 2009. Reprint, Manchester: WIEGO, 2013.

Charmes, Jacques. "A Brief History of 50 Years of Conceptualisation and Measurement of the Informal Economy." In *Dimensions of Resilience in Developing Countries: Informality, Solidarities and Carework*, edited by Jacques Charmes, 13–36. Cham, Switzerland: Springer, 2019.

Commission for the European Community—Eurostat, IMF, OECD, United Nations, and World Bank. *System of National Accounts 1993.* Brussels: Commission for the European Community, 1993.

Commission for the European Community—Eurostat, IMF, OECD, United Nations, and World Bank. *System of National Accounts 2008.* Brussels: Commission for the European Community, 2008.

De Soto, Hernando. *The Other Path: The Invisible Revolution in the Third World*. New York: Harper and Row, 1989. Spanish original, 1986.

Desrosières, Alain. *The Politics of Large Numbers*. Cambridge, MA: Harvard University Press, 1998. French original, 1993.

Desrosières, Alain, and Sandrine Kott. "Quantifier." *Genèses* 58, no. 1 (2005): 2–3.

Dommann, Monika. "Informelle Ökonomie: Hernando de Soto. El otro sendero (1987)." In *Deregulation und Restauration: Eine politische Wissensgeschichte*, edited by Monika Wulz, Max Stadler, Nils Güttler, and Fabian Grütter, 178–97. Berlin: Matthes & Seitz, 2021.

Germann, Pascal, Lukas Held, and Monika Wulz. "Scientific Political Activism—eine Annäherung an das Verhältnis von Wissenschaft und politischem Engagement seit den 1960er Jahren." *NTM Zeitschrift für Geschichte der Wissenschaften, Technik und Medizin* 30, no. 4 (2022): 435–44.

Gershuny, Jonathan. *After Industrial Society? The Emerging Self-Service Economy*. London: Macmillan, 1978.

Gershuny, Jonathan. "The Informal Economy: Its Role in Post-industrial Society." *Futures* 11, no. 1 (1979): 3–15.

Government of India/Ministry of Statistics and Programme Implementation. "Report of the Fifth Meeting of the Expert Group on Informal Sector Statistics (Delhi Group)." https://mospi.gov.in/5.2-delhi-group (accessed May 1, 2023).

Hart, Keith. "Informal Income Opportunities and Urban Employment in Ghana." *Journal of Modern African Studies* 11, no. 1 (1973): 61–89.

Hart, Keith. "Small-Scale Entrepreneurs in Ghana and Development Planning." *Journal of Development Studies* 6 (1970): 103–20.

Hussmanns, Ralf. *Measuring the Informal Economy: From Employment in the Informal Sector to Informal Employment*. ILO: Geneva, 2004.

Hussmanns, Ralf, Farhad Mehran, and Vijay Verma. *Surveys of Economically Active Population, Employment Unemployment and Underemployment: An ILO Manual on Concepts and Methods*. Geneva: ILO, 1990.

ILC. *Ninetieth Session: Provisional Record No. 25*. Geneva: ILO, 2002.

ILC. *104th Session: Provisional Record No. 10-1*. Geneva: ILO, 2015.

ILO. *Decent Work and the Informal Economy*. Geneva: ILO, 2002.

ILO. *Decent Work in Agriculture*. Geneva: ILO, 2003.

ILO. *The Dilemma of the Informal Sector*. Geneva: ILO, 1991.

ILO. *Employment, Incomes and Equality: A Strategy for Increasing Productive Employment in Kenya*. Geneva: ILO, 1972.

ILO. *General Report to the Fourteenth ICLS*. Geneva: ILO, 1987.

ILO. *General Report to the Seventeenth ICLS*. Geneva: ILO, 2003.

ILO. "ILO News: ILO Adopts Historic Labour Standard to Tackle the Informal Economy." June 12, 2015. https://www.ilo.org/ilc/ILCSessions/previous-sessions/104/media-centre/news/WCMS_375615/lang—en/index.htm.

ILO. *Measurement of Employment in the Informal Sector*. Geneva: ILO, 1991.

ILO. *Measuring Informality: A Statistical Manual on the Informal Sector and Informal Employment*. Geneva: ILO, 2013.

ILO. *Report of the Thirteenth ICLS*. Geneva: ILO, 1982.

ILO. *Report of the Fourteenth ICLS*. Geneva: ILO, 1988.

ILO. *Report of the Fifteenth ICLS*. Geneva: ILO, 1993.

ILO. *Report of the Seventeenth ICLS*. Geneva: ILO, 2003.

ILO. *Report of the Eighteenth ICLS*. Geneva: ILO, 2008.

ILO. *Statistics of Employment in the Informal Sector*. Geneva: ILO, 1992.

ILO. *Statistics of Labour Force, Employment, Unemployment and Underemployment*. Geneva: ILO, 1982.

ILO. *Urbanisation, Informal Sector and Employment: A Progress Report on Research, Advisory Services and Technical Cooperation*. Geneva: ILO, 1984.

ILO. *Women and Men in the Informal Economy: A Statistical Picture*. Geneva: ILO, 2018.

Institute of Development Studies. *Fifth Annual Report*. Brighton: Institute of Development Studies, 1972.

Macekura, Stephen. "Dudley Seers, the Institute for Development Studies, and the Fracturing of International Development Thought in the 1960s and 1970s." *History of Political Economy* 52, no. 1 (2020): 47–75.

Macekura, Stephen J. *The Mismeasure of Progress: Economic Growth and Its Critics*. Chicago: University of Chicago Press, 2020.

Marti, Sibylle. "Die 'Entdeckung' der Schattenwirtschaft: Informelle Arbeit und neoliberale Politik in den 1980er Jahren." *Geschichte und Gesellschaft* 48, no. 4 (2022): 551–83.

Marti, Sibylle. "The Shadow Economy and Ideas of Freedom: Debates and Policies on Informal Work in 1970s and 1980s West Germany and Beyond." *Moving the Social: Journal of Social History and the History of Social Movements* 69 (2023): 51–72.

Maul, Daniel. *The International Labour Organization: 100 Years of Global Social Policy*. Berlin: De Gruyter Oldenbourg / Geneva: ILO, 2019.

Mayer-Ahuja, Nicole. "Labor, Insecurity, Informality." In *Capitalism and Labor: Towards Critical Perspectives*, edited by Klaus Dörre, Nicole Mayer-Ahuja, and Dieter Sauer, 257–68. Frankfurt: Campus, 2018.

McNeill, Desmond. "The Informal Sector: Biography of an Idea." In *Global Institutions and Development: Framing the World?*, edited by Morten Bøås and Desmond McNeill, 41–55. London: Routledge, 2004.

Mehran, Farhad. *WIEGO Impact Evaluation—Evaluator's Assessment Report: Mainstreaming the Measurement of the Informal Economy in Labour Force and Economic Statistics*. Manchester: WIEGO, 2009.

Raphael, Lutz. "Die Verwissenschaftlichung des Sozialen als methodische und konzeptionelle Herausforderung für eine Sozialgeschichte des 20. Jahrhunderts." *Geschichte und Gesellschaft* 22, no. 2 (1996): 165–93.

Sethuraman, S. V. "Concepts, Methodology and Scope." In Sethuraman, *The Urban Informal Sector in Developing Countries*, 10–27.

Sethuraman, S. V., ed. *The Urban Informal Sector in Developing Countries: Employment, Poverty and Environment*. Geneva: ILO, 1981.

Shaw, D. John. *Sir Hans Singer: The Life and Work of a Development Economist*. Basingstoke, UK: Palgrave Macmillan, 2002.

Speich Chassé, Daniel. *Die Erfindung des Bruttosozialprodukts: Globale Ungleichheit in der Wissensgeschichte der Ökonomie*. Göttingen: Vandenhoeck & Ruprecht, 2013.

UN Statistical Commission. *Expert Group on Critical Problems in Economic Statistics (E/CN.3/1997/2)*. New York: United Nations, 1996.

UN Statistical Commission. *Report on the Twenty-Ninth Session (E/CN.3/1997/29)*. New York: United Nations, 1997.

UN Statistical Commission. *Reports on Selected Critical Problems in Economic Statistics (E/CN.3/1997/3)*. New York: United Nations, 1997.

UN Statistics Division. "Delhi Group on Informal Sector Statistics." https://unstats.un.org/unsd/methodology/citygroups/delhi.cshtml (accessed May 1, 2023).

Vanek, Joann, Martha Alter Chen, Françoise Carré, James Heintz, and Ralf Hussmanns. *Statistics on the Informal Economy: Definitions, Regional Estimates and Challenges.* Manchester: WIEGO, 2014.

Vergara, Ángela. "'Trabajadores pobres e informales': Economistas, organismos internacionales y el mundo del trabajo en América Latina (1960–1980)." *Revista latinoamericana de trabajo y trabajadores* 4 (2022): 1–25.

Weeks, John. "Introduction." *Manpower and Unemployment Research in Africa* 6, no. 2 (1973): 3–7.

WIEGO. "Formalizing the Informal Economy." https://www.wiego.org/our-work-impact/themes/formalization (accessed May 1, 2023).

WIEGO. "Joann Vanek." https://www.wiego.org/specialists/joann-vanek (accessed May 1, 2023).

WIEGO. "Statistics Programme." https://www.wiego.org/our-work-impact/core-programmes/statistics (accessed May 1, 2023).

Strong Winds and Widow Makers: Workers, Nature, and Environmental Conflict in the Pacific Northwest Timber Country
Steven C. Beda
Urbana: University of Illinois Press, 2023
312 pp.; $110 (cloth), $24.95 (paper), $14.95 (e-book)

Following several decades of intermittent wars of conquest against Indigenous peoples and war and negotiation with rival European claimants, the American government asserted sovereignty over western parts of North America around the middle of the nineteenth century. Such assertions became concrete mainly through possession and occupation. In *Strong Winds and Widow Makers*, Steven Beda explores aspects of the history of occupancy and industry in one such claimed space, focusing on Oregon, Washington, and British Columbia. Here as in many other parts of North America, a central aim for state and capital alike was to profit by commodifying nature. In the context of the Pacific coast, vast forested areas were the focus, and by the last years of the nineteenth century the main strategy for this region was to transform trees into lumber, reaping immense returns in realized value by selling this product in markets in North America and beyond. As Beda shows, felling and moving the trunks of ancient trees across the land and into sawmills, and from the region to the wider world, was a herculean task. It required technological expertise, logistical capacity, and much labor power. Capitalists' profits varied inversely with the rates paid for labor employed. Accordingly, the waves of migrants who populated camps and communities in the western woods endured highly dangerous working conditions in return for meager remuneration.

Others have described the danger and exploitation central to timbering and other extractive industries. Beda does not revisit well-worn ground for its own sake. Instead, he explores links between exploitation, community, place, and the origins of a class-based environmental consciousness. He argues that in his study area, rates of pay were insufficient to afford working families a satisfactory subsistence. Accordingly, hunting, gathering, and growing vegetables, among other activities, supplemented wages as families bridged the gap between insufficient earnings and income requisite for an acceptable existence. Vibrant forests, then, were essential to survival, and Beda argues that workers developed a strong impulse to steward spaces and resources on which personal and communal well-being depended. The lean years of the 1930s were important in crystalizing these links for workers in the region, with the desperation of the Depression years underscoring the connection between vibrant forests and vibrant communities. From that point until the postwar years, the stewarding of the forests was central to workers and their organizations in the region. Beda argues that such a disposition remains central to many timber workers and other working-class residents of timber country. He also sees a diminishing of the class basis of environmentalism in the timber industry, as a cadre of small-scale capitalists share a commitment to the preservation of the forests and the rural communities and lifeways dependent on them.

According to Beda, this vernacular, industry environmentalism is underappreciated. Blindness to it reflects shifts in popular understandings of rural working people in the later twentieth century, and the rise of a new movement-oriented environmentalism at about the same time. Often urbanites, and often more accustomed to standing desks than stands of trees, movement-oriented environmentalists disparaged timber workers and others in the timber industry, insisting on the principle of the preservation of forests in an untouched state. Beda claims that this approach to environmentalism misunderstands the forests and leads to counterproductive approaches to their management. Forests, he reminds, have never been pristine places. Lightning has struck in the past, just as it strikes now, resulting in forest fires and a cycle of destruction and regeneration. The region's Indigenous peoples had also long conducted controlled burns to encourage the different flora and fauna that occurred at different stages of the regenerative process. Proceeding as though long-standing forests should remain unchanged or untouched, forest managers may prevent or delay the destruction of trees. They also, however, do not allow for the vibrancy and diversity that Indigenous residents had encouraged through burning. Fires also are not indefinitely staved off, and in a context of a warming climate, a buildup of tinder results in more catastrophic conflagrations. Pointing to his case study, Beda counsels that the most effective systems of forest management included those who lived and worked in the woods. In his estimation, any effective system of management going forward will draw on such people as well.

There is much to recommend this book. Thoroughly researched and well written, it provides much insight into changing technologies and labor processes in the timber industry in the coastal Pacific region. It also offers a nuanced account of the social history of timbering communities, highlighting the importance of place for working people and their movements. Beda admirably weaves these details together with wider developments in the international capitalist order. Finally, his vivid descriptions of people and places make clear that Beda has explored the territory he writes about and that he has taken the time to know those who have and do live there. He displays a deep respect for both.

That said, this work is not without faults. Beda cogently explains how US policymakers on different scales have shaped life and labor in timber country. The same cannot be said of the Canadian parts of his study area. At times these sections of the book seem like afterthoughts. Perhaps more serious is the manner in which Indigenous peoples figure in this account. The author mentions Indigenous inhabitants and their practice of controlled burning periodically (e.g., 58, 71, 220). At one point he connects timber workers' vocabulary to language forms partly derived from Indigenous peoples (95). In terms of the more general theorization of capitalism, class, and community formation central to this book, Indigenous people disappear from the scene. Settlement and dispossession are two halves of the same coin. In this age of reconciliation, surely we must acknowledge that a fulsome account of the former requires that we conceptualize and explore its history as necessarily premised on the latter.

Kurt Korneski, *Memorial University of Newfoundland*

DOI 10.1215/15476715-10948973

Workers of the Empire Unite: Radical and Popular Challenges to British Imperialism, 1910s–1960s
Edited by Yann Béliard and Neville Kirk
Liverpool: Liverpool University Press, 2021
xviii + 331 pp.; $143 (cloth)

This is an important book. Editors Yann Béliard and Neville Kirk have laid out the groundwork for a complete reworking of the collapse of modern imperialism. Focused on the fall of the British Empire, this book is situated at the crossroads of two sets of historiographies: an older historiography, dating back to the nineteenth century, on the British Empire; and a more recently resurgent historiography on labor. The former largely ignored the latter, engaged instead with great debates on the merits and demerits of the empire, on the flows of power within that empire, and the role of these factors in the empire's rise and fall. Labor historians, on the other hand, have found the empire more central to their writing for several decades now. This book builds on the fruitful labor of these historians, acknowledging Antoinette Burton, E. P. Thompson, the Subaltern Studies Collective, Frederick Cooper, and the more recent transnational histories emerging out of the International Institute of Social History to make an important claim: that it is now possible to write "a People's History of British Decolonization" (3–21, 287).

This book provides us with the outlines of just what such a history might look like. Three women play important parts: Annie Besant, Sylvia Pankhurst, and Ellen Wilkinson. Besant is probably the best-known, with an illustrious political career in India that made her a name that virtually every Indian is familiar with, even today. All three socialists identified anti-imperialism as critical to the emancipation of workers in Britain and across the British Empire. Pankhurst and Wilkinson made the additional claim that anti-imperialism was imperative for the emancipation of women, especially in Britain's colonies. Besant and Wilkinson traveled to India, while Pankhurst tried to bring the empire down through her work for the *Workers' Dreadnought* (47–80, 115–32, 25–46).

Other individuals emerge as well. They include the brilliant M. N. Roy, founder of the Communist Party of India and indefatigable organizer of expatriate Indians in Europe against the British Empire; the British Communist Fenner Brockway, who forged connections with the Frenchman Marceau Pivert in an Anglo-French alliance to bring down their respective empires; and, finally, Albert Fava, whose activism proved too much for British authorities in his native Gibraltar and led to his deportation in 1948. All these individuals played important roles in inspiring and organizing political opposition to the power of British imperialism (81–114, 133–63, 197–216).

This "people's history of British decolonization" also includes collective action by vast swaths of organized working-class labor and Communist Parties across the British Empire. Some of the strongest chapters in the book discuss heroic struggles in British Africa, specifically in Sudan, where organized civil servants, dockworkers, and railway workers struck repeatedly through the 1940s and 1950s in an inspiring struggle to bring down the British Empire. Their bravery, in the face of brutal repression from the Brit-

Labor: Studies in Working-Class History, Volume 21, Issue 1
© 2024 by Labor and Working-Class History Association

ish Imperial machinery, was matched by comrades in Kenya's tea plantations. Collective action turned the colony's profitable plantation economy into a significant pressure point on the bourgeois section of the Kenyan nationalist project. Their action in the form of a series of crippling strikes threatened a smooth transition from British colonial rule to an independence dominated by a new comprador Kenyan ruling class. Finally, Communist Parties in Australia and South Africa resisted the imperialist project by an honorable and refreshing commitment to antiracism in the otherwise virulently racist politics of white settler colonies (167–96, 217–72).

Neville Kirk, in his conclusion, lays out an eight-point theory on the role of labor and the end of the British Empire. The essays in this book lead Kirk to correctly identify the inspiring internationalism and unequivocal commitment to anti-imperialism and antiracism of individual actors as well as organized labor. They also lead to the more dispiriting conclusion of the limitations and failures of both individual as well as collective action (273–86). Some of this, however, is a function of the geographical focus of the essays in the book. A "people's history of British decolonization" must necessarily be written with geographical focal points located in the empire's colonies, in India, Nigeria, and South Africa. This is imperative, as the research in the book demonstrates that imperialism was far too entrenched, and capitalism far too developed in the metropole, for socialists and communists to successfully challenge. Success was more likely in the colonies, where imperialism was contested and capitalism still weak. A "people's history of British decolonization" can provide a much more meaningful focus on the achievements of the British Empire's subjects in its colonies than on the limited successes of its citizens in the metropole.

These chapters are critical starting points necessary to writing such a history. Collective action, especially in the colonies, played a far more important part in the unraveling of the British Empire than has been chronicled. Their decisive intervention was downplayed in favor of the national bourgeoisie that eventually came to power across the Third World. Historians, therefore, must rework the history of the fall of the British Empire by placing labor in its correct, central place in this project. My own forthcoming work on the million-strong organized railway workers in British India outlines their important part in this history. Béliard and Kirk, through this timely book, have laid out an architecture that points out the possibilities of a "people's history of British decolonization."

Indeed, the timeliness of this book lies not only in its rescue of labor and imperial history, as suggested by Paul Pickering in his foreword, but also in the return of labor politically around the world. In 2022, two hundred million laborers struck in India, the culmination of two decades of mobilization against the ugliness of neoliberal capitalism. Their collective action mirrors on a larger scale repeated industrial action by NHS workers in Britain. Indeed, a resurgent organized working class was on full display across continental Europe on May Day 2023. A people's history of anti-imperialism is imperative as a source of inspiration for millions of workers the world over today.

Aniruddha Bose, *Saint Francis University*

DOI 10.1215/15476715-10948986

Vendors' Capitalism: A Political Economy of Public Markets in Mexico City
Ingrid Bleynat
Stanford, CA: Stanford University Press, 2021
xiv + 246 pp.; $120.00 (cloth), $30.00 (paper)

One of the central facets characterizing life in Mexico City has been its vibrant commercial activity within markets and on the streets. This book endeavors to shed light on the transformations experienced by these vendors between 1867 and 1966, coinciding with shifts in the economy and the gradual consolidation of capitalism. The research comprehensively traces a century-long trajectory of the intricate relations between vendors and authorities, encompassing their modes of challenging authority, organizational structures, and the consequential changes witnessed in public markets amid the rapid urbanization of one of the world's most densely populated capital cities.

This scholarly work makes a contribution to the existing literature on commercial activity among numerous self-employed women and men who operated in buildings specifically constructed during this period to accommodate their entrepreneurial endeavors, as well as in the bustling streets surrounding the public markets. These public spaces served as workspaces for many individuals who lacked the financial resources to lease shops or obtain licenses.

Ingrid Bleynat's research delves into the intricate position of these vendors within the political economy. The author observes that "they endured exploitation through exchange" (2). The book discusses with specialists on the economic and social setting of Mexico during the studied period, including figures such as John Womack Jr., Ariel Rodríguez Kuri, John Lear, and Pablo Piccatto, and addresses the interplay between politics and commercial activity. Broadly speaking, the book presents a comprehensive account of the attitudes exhibited by the political and economic elites toward these activities, drawing on archives in Mexico as well as newspapers throughout five major periods, each corresponding to a chapter within the book.

For the initial two periods spanning the so-called Restored Republic and the first decade of the twentieth century, the author focuses her attention on the attitudes adopted by political and intellectual elites, as well as the relevant authorities (primarily the Ayuntamiento [city council] and the government of the Federal District) regarding public markets and street vendors (*viento* vendors). Throughout this period, the author argues with historiography that has addressed the contentious relations between the ayuntamiento and the central government in terms of regulating these activities. Given the inherent challenge in granting visibility to the vendors themselves, Bleynat primarily investigates paternalistic attitudes, which she posits are a consequence of religiously tinged "compassion" toward the urban poor. The author posits that vendors built their legitimacy on the foundation of a moral economy. However, due to the scarcity of sources or the absence of the vendors' own voices, the book does not provide comprehensive support for this argument. The author could have engaged in a more extensive dialogue with the historiog-

Labor: Studies in Working-Class History, Volume 21, Issue 1
© 2024 by Labor and Working-Class History Association

raphy on markets or research on the perspectives of vendors during the late nineteenth century and the early decades of the twentieth.

Bleynat discusses how market vendors gained empowerment during the Mexican Revolution, subsequently incorporating the advocacy of their rights, which reflects existing historiography. The book contributes to this scholarship by examining the formation of early vendor organizations in the 1920s, which actively opposed rent, fee, and tax increases. It provides an insight into the nascent collective actions undertaken by these vendors and their varied forms of protest. Nevertheless, a more comprehensive analysis of this period would have enriched the work by emphasizing the consolidation of these organizations and highlighting the distinctions between salaried workers and these self-employed sectors. These distinctions only emerge when the author highlights the contrasting attitudes of workers and sellers regarding the demand for Sunday rest in 1923.

The book also examines the expansion of markets into other areas of the burgeoning city and the exponential growth of commercial activity on the streets during the postrevolution period, the Mexican miracle and developmentalism, spanning from 1930 to 1966. The author elucidates how vendors' organizations underwent politicization and became integrated within the corporatist framework of the official party, initially the Partido de la Revolución Mexicana (PRM) and subsequently the Partido Revolucionario Institucional (PRI). Bleynat prioritizes two crucial aspects: the quotas and taxes imposed on vendors within markets, and the impact of price control policies. Drawing from the existing historiography on clientelism in Mexico, this book highlights the political maneuvering of repression in controlling street commerce, while simultaneously seeking to incorporate vendors into the party base through their affiliation with organizations controlled by politicians, such as the Confederación Nacional de Organizaciones Populares or the federations and associations of vendors that emerged during this period. The remarkable expansion of this economic sector broadened the pool of potential voters, who were both courted and rewarded during specific junctures. This final segment of the book offers an in-depth and densely researched study of clientelist relations between 1930 and 1966.

Undoubtedly, this book makes a valuable contribution to the historiographical landscape by introducing new sources and providing insights into the construction of clientelist relationships within a visible segment of the population in the Mexican capital. Covering a long period carries the risk of leaving many processes only sketched out or inadequately explaining certain assertions. Several topics remain unresolved, demanding further analysis by the author. These include the moral economy of vendors in the late nineteenth century, the incorporation of the vendors' perspectives in studies of political economy, the relationship between compassion and paternalism, the significance of urban self-employment in Mexico amid the advance of capitalism, and a more seamless dialogue with the growing bibliography on street vendors in the mid-twentieth century. As with all rigorous research, this work effectively opens up avenues for future discussion and exploration.

Mario Barbosa-Cruz, *Universidad Autónoma Metropolitana*
DOI 10.1215/15476715-10948999

Working in the Magic City: Moral Economy in Early Twentieth-Century Miami
Thomas A. Castillo
Urbana: University of Illinois Press, 2022
xiii + 274 pp.; $110.00 (cloth), $28.00 (paper), $19.95 (e-book)

Miami is a hard place for working people. Second in the nation in income inequality, the Miami metro area also has the ninth-highest poverty rate in the nation. Employment tends to be seasonal and labor markets volatile. The largest sector, tourism, employs thousands of low-wage workers who must endure difficult working conditions while wearing a smile for outsiders on whose largesse they depend. Meanwhile, the political and social climate are both hostile to organized labor. Thomas A. Castillo's study of early twentieth-century Miami demonstrates that the city's workers have long dealt with these conditions and that, for an equally long period of time, they have demanded a political economy that would provide them a "competency ... the right to a pleasurable life, with access to recreation and decent living conditions" (5). That Miami has seldom if ever made room for this vision, he concludes, is the result of the power of capitalists, not the failure of workers to challenge them.

Across seven chapters, Castillo explores the labor history of Miami prior to World War II. Skillfully using a mix of obscure and scant sources to reconstruct a picture of Miami's early twentieth-century workers, he describes the matrix of class and race in the rapidly growing city. Elites, a group he largely leaves undetailed, envisioned a tropical paradise that simultaneously exploited white and Black workers and rendered them invisible or at least made them appear docile to wealthy tourists through significant social controls.

Castillo demonstrates workers were anything but invisible or docile and pushed back against capitalist visions for Miami's development with their own. He focuses on three major struggles: control of the chauffeuring business, employers' demand for the open shop in construction, and access to jobs for local workers (as opposed to transient workers) during the Great Depression. In these cases, he argues, working-class Miamians, white and Black, spoke in the language of a "class-harmony discourse" that, recognizing the deleterious effects of labor strife for everyone involved in tourism and real estate, eschewed open conflict against the bosses (5). This lack of confrontation was rooted neither in an acceptance of the capitalist order nor in a lack of class identity, Castillo argues; instead it was a strategy for gaining leverage to create a moral economy for workers. That this strategy led workers to punch other workers instead of their bosses—and especially white workers to punch Black workers (and in one case to dynamite the Oddfellows Hall in what was then Colored Town)—was, according to Castillo, not evidence that they rejected class politics or of simple white working-class racism but the result of having to struggle in an economy of scarcity maintained by the city's elites. Pushed hard in an economy already segmented by Jim Crow, workers had little room for organizing across the color line or utopian politics if they hoped to maintain a livelihood. "The social democratic project of unionism often operated in the context of scarcity and competi-

Labor: Studies in Working-Class History, Volume 21, Issue 1
© 2024 by Labor and Working-Class History Association

tion," Castillo explains, "placing workers with difficult decisions and, sometimes, unfair outcomes" (8).

Castillo is no doubt on to something with the reminder that the capitalist structure of Miami's political economy kept workers from making the world as they pleased. His final two chapters, both set in the era of the Great Depression and focused on the work of activist Perrine Palmer and the Dade County Unemployed Citizens' League, suggest that the changed circumstances of the 1930s opened the door for a broader, more-inclusive politics that culminated in the elimination of Florida's poll tax. Widespread scarcity, as well as a changing local and national political environment, made room for different approaches. The context, Castillo shows, matters.

Of course, there is a difference between contextualizing and exonerating. White chauffeurs who terrorized Black chauffeurs to maintain a stranglehold on the market, whites-only building trades unions that embraced antiradicalism and racism to fight off the open shop, and local workers who sided with elites in their use of the "Hobo Express" to expel unhoused job seekers, lived in circumstances that were not of their making; nevertheless, they made choices that other workers (particularly Black workers) did not make. It would be a massive condescension for historians to judge them too much. But it would also be historical malpractice to explain away their actions as products of their own time.

Evan P. Bennett, *Florida Atlantic University*
DOI 10.1215/15476715-10949012

Becoming Free, Becoming Black: Race, Freedom, and Law in Cuba, Virginia, and Louisiana
Alejandro de la Fuente and Ariela J. Gross
Cambridge: Cambridge University Press, 2020
xiv + 281 pp.; $25.95 (cloth), $16.95 (paper and e-book)

In *Becoming Free, Becoming Black* coauthors de la Fuente and Gross intervene fruitfully in long and sometimes contentious debates among twentieth- and twenty-first-century historians about whether legal and cultural traditions of European colonizing powers or the demographic and economic characteristics of their colonies were most influential in determining the perceived severity of enslavement and the possibility of enjoying freedom before and after abolition. In their explicit counter to earlier comparative approaches, de la Fuente and Gross state, "It was not society's recognition of slaves' humanity, nor its racial fluidity, that marked the differences.... It was how successfully the elites of that society drew connections between blackness and enslavement, on the one hand, and whiteness, freedom, and citizenship on the other" (5).

Labor: Studies in Working-Class History, Volume 21, Issue 1

Building on the work of Rebecca Scott and many others, the authors return to an emphasis on the importance of law and culture in their comparisons of Cuba, Virginia, and Louisiana using "the tools and approaches of cultural-legal history close to the ground" (8–9). They seek to "move old comparative debates into new territory... to recover slaves' lives and actions, and to be attentive to change across time" (xi). They have succeeded admirably in doing so.

A major argument of the book is that "the law of freedom" rather than "the law of slavery" was "the most crucial for the creation of racial regimes in law" (4). Thus, each of the five chapters discusses an aspect of freedom in the three sites—the "process of legal race making" in the early European settlement period, manumission and freedom suits before and during the Age of Revolution, and the efforts to constrain Black freedom, interracial relationships, and free Black communities in the mid-nineteenth century (16).

The process of defining race in law began in Cuba in the sixteenth century, in Virginia in the seventeenth century, and finally in Louisiana in the eighteenth century. The last is included as a hybrid case that developed under French, Spanish, and, finally, US rule from 1700 to the mid-1800s. At the time of colonization in the Americas, Spanish law already allowed manumission and self-purchase of freedom but also tied Blackness to slavery and debased status in statute and practice. Rather than seeing these possibilities for freedom as evidence of a "softer" and more fluid Iberian slave system, de la Fuente and Gross argue that "the practical effect of Iberian legal and social precedents was to arrive even more quickly at hardened racial distinction in the law" (16). At the same time, the authors show how enslaved people used legal rights such as self-purchase to press for a set price, payments in installments, and the right to the portion of their freedom that they had already purchased. All three practices became customary rights over time and helped create a growing free population of color from the mid-1500s onward, despite the early imposition of racial difference.

For the authors, the equation of slavery and Blackness was most "unsettled and open to interpretation" in Virginia, at least for the early colonial period in the 1600s (16). Here the authors follow the outline of Edmund Morgan's argument about increasing legal restrictions against Africans and their descendants growing from elite fears of alliances between Blacks and poor whites, though they see this explanation as incomplete. The authors agree with Morgan that elite Virginians expanded rights for free whites and "limit[ed] legal opportunities for freedom, and even [changed] the meaning of freedom along racial lines" (59). Yet they contend that the shift was more gradual and that "the interaction of demographics and economics, on the one hand, and politics and law, on the other" best explains the constraints placed on Black freedom by the eighteenth century (59). As enslavers' ability to manumit declined, the authors show how freedom suits increasingly sought to claim "a free female ancestor" often Indigenous or white, because the law now determined enslavement at birth by a mother's status (63).

De la Fuente and Gross contend that the Age of Revolution from 1763 to 1820 was the "era of greatest commonality across all three" sites (129). French settlers in Louisiana in the early eighteenth century had adopted restrictions on manumission and interracial marriage developed in the French Caribbean colonies, unlike either early Virginia or Cuba. Revolutionary-era elites in all three sites adopted "legal reforms... to protect their slave systems" by briefly allowing more paths to freedom (129). Some enslaved men who fought for various powers during the wars of the revolutionary era attained freedom, though the authors don't discuss this. Overall manumissions increased and in all three areas the free population of color grew. A key distinction across these sites was whether Black freedom remained an accepted legal and social reality into the 1800s.

By the mid-nineteenth century, Cuba, Louisiana, and Virginia were all "mature slave societies" (219). After 1840, in the face of slave rebellion and abolitionism, elites in all three sites attempted to constrain Black freedom and even expel free people of color. The authors argue that elites in Cuba were least successful in these endeavors in part because Black freedom had been accepted in law and practice for centuries. The new slave code of 1842 enshrined in law the previously customary practice of *coartación* (self-purchase by installments), perhaps the clearest example of claims by the enslaved shaping law. Free Cubans of color continued to participate in civic life and marry across racial boundaries. The size of their communities made wholesale expulsion impossible. On the other hand, by the mid-nineteenth century in Virginia and Louisiana race had become an "impassable barrier," limiting rights and citizenship to whites (224). But as de la Fuente and Gross demonstrate so convincingly, enslaved and free people of color in all three sites "ferociously contested" efforts to restrict Black freedom and sometimes succeeded in claiming it (224).

Becoming Free, Becoming Black will reframe debates on comparative slavery and freedom as well as scholarship on Cuba, Virginia, and Louisiana. The book may be most useful to scholars and graduate students, as the historical context of each region and time period is only briefly sketched out. At the same time, the book is a fine example of the insights possible through deep archival research and the benefits of collaborative scholarship in addressing complex historical questions.

Evelyn P. Jennings, *St. Lawrence University*
DOI 10.1215/15476715-10949025

Our Veterans: Winners, Losers, Friends, and Enemies on the New Terrain of Veterans Affairs
Suzanne Gordon, Steve Early, and Jasper Craven
Durham, NC: Duke University Press, 2020
xxi + 330 pp.; $104.95 (cloth), $24.95 (paper)

Military veterans occupy an honored yet ambivalent place in American culture. They are hailed as exemplars of cherished social values (e.g., patriotism, sacrifice, selflessness) but often neglected or ignored once they reenter civilian life. In part, this ambivalence reflects public dissatisfaction with post–World War II conflicts that resulted in stalemate (Korea) or defeat (Vietnam and Afghanistan) or victories that have proven either short-lived or pyrrhic (the wars in Iraq). Also, the creation of a volunteer army has relegated the experi-

Labor: Studies in Working-Class History, Volume 21, Issue 1
© 2024 by Labor and Working-Class History Association

ence of military service to a much smaller group of Americans. These developments have tended to isolate veterans and limit expressions of pride and recognition that typically accompany military service or achievements on the battlefield. And, as Suzanne Gordon, Steve Early, and Jasper Craven describe in *Our Veterans*, vets find that the principal institution designed to meet their needs, the Veterans Health Administration (VHA), suffers from dwindling resources and a steady shift toward privatization.

The book rests on several premises: ill-advised "forever" wars and an often toxic military culture have created "the most disabled generation of veterans in American history" (232); the new terrain of veterans affairs is denying many veterans the quality care they deserve; and division among veteran advocacy groups has complicated efforts to bolster the VHA, which the authors describe as a "a unique culture of empathy and solidarity . . . that has no counterpart in American medicine" (17).

The authors' story begins with the sobering assertion that military service encompasses a "collection of very dangerous occupations" whether in combat or noncombat roles (29). The wounds of war include damage to body and mind, exposure to toxic materials, and sexual harassment and assault resulting in the phenomenon of military sexual trauma. These wounds compound the difficulties many veterans face in their adjustment and reintegration into postmilitary life. Although the military touts a seamless transfer of veteran skills to the civilian job market, the authors find that many vets (outside those in the officer class) have difficulty finding secure and remunerative employment. And for some veterans, their alienation from the world they reenter leads to substance abuse, troubles with the law, and even suicide. In the authors' view, these challenges underscore the need for comprehensive veterans' services, which the VHA is uniquely equipped to provide. As a national public health care system that is often staffed by veterans, heavily unionized, and able to provide accessible and coordinated care, the authors view VHA as a "homegrown model for socialized medicine" that urgently needs political support (238).

Historically, veterans service organizations (VSOs) such as the American Legion, Veterans of Foreign Wars, and Disabled Veterans of America have advocated for veterans' interests. These organizations have been joined by an array of VSOs that emerged following the Vietnam War and more recent conflicts in Iraq and Afghanistan. Spanning the political spectrum from the right-leaning Concerned Veterans for America, which is funded by the Koch brothers, to Veterans for Peace, a left-leaning group founded after the Vietnam War, these organizations have struggled to speak with a common voice. The authors assert that some of the newer organizations' reliance on corporate funding has muted their support for VHA. These corporate connections complicate efforts by VSOs to contest a "manufactured scandal" over waiting times for services that has allowed the political right to defame the VHA as "socialized medicine at its worst" (127). This orchestrated campaign has led Congress and the executive branch to accelerate the outsourcing of VHA functions, a move Gordon, Early, and Craven see as lowering the quality of care while enriching private interests.

The authors note that the number of veterans currently serving as members of Congress (18 percent in the House, 17 percent in the Senate) falls far below their 70 percent representation in the early 1970s. Over the past two decades, Democrats and Republicans have intensified their recruitment of military candidates, calculating that swing and independent voters will find them attractive. However, the authors lament that most veterans in Congress, regardless of party affiliation, hold centrist views and are unwilling to question military spending, the direction of US foreign policy, or efforts to outsource VHA functions. Moreover, although the percentage of veterans voting for Donald Trump dropped somewhat during the 2020 election, this ardent advocate of VHA privatization still won over 50 percent of veterans' votes. Noting the defeats of well-funded former officers running as moderates in key 2020 Senate races, Gordon, Early, and Craven suggest that greater support for working-class veteran candidates and stronger progressive stances on domestic and foreign policy might have achieved a different result.

The book combines impressive research, deep knowledge of the world of veterans' care, and attentiveness to social and historical context. The authors consistently allow veterans' voices to be heard, lending their argument a sense of authenticity and credibility. However, the evidence they present highlights a gap between their advocacy of a radical reorientation in American military and foreign policy and the more conservative attitudes of many veterans and VSOs. Their determination to defend VHA as the bridge to creating a system of universal health care coverage, however laudable, also faces obstacles in garnering veterans' support. One promising approach the authors outline involves deepening ties between veterans' groups and labor organizations, potentially creating a broader alliance better positioned to support VHA and advance a progressive political agenda. This book can serve as an invaluable resource for such efforts and prompt a much-needed public conversation about how the nation meets its obligations to "our veterans."

Bob Bussel, *University of Oregon*
DOI 10.1215/15476715-10949038

The Bosses Union: How Employers Organized to Fight Labor before the New Deal
Vilja Hulden
Urbana: University of Illinois Press, 2023
350 pp.; $125.00 (cloth), $30.00 (paper), $19.95 (e-book)

This is an extraordinarily well-researched and informative history of how US employers' associations sought to impede unions before the New Deal era. Significantly, it is also a history of the "closed shop," the main target of early twentieth-century union-fighting employers, which sets it apart from previous work on organizations such as the National Association of Manufacturers (NAM) and the National Civic Federation (NCF) during this era.

I have always found it odd that NAM aimed its most calculated fire not at the Wobblies or various socialist or anarchist groups but, rather, at the most "conservative" union of the day, the AFL, whose leader forthrightly endorsed the capitalist system and its mythology of individual liberty and progress. NAM was laser-focused on destroying

Labor: Studies in Working-Class History, Volume 21, Issue 1
© 2024 by Labor and Working-Class History Association

AFL head Samuel Gompers because Gompers sought to secure power for unions via the "closed shop," a gatekeeping policy/strategy that required all workers in a workplace to be union members and abide by union rules. As Hulden shows and insists, the closed shop was the only way labor could hope to have any role in governing and controlling the workplace. Therefore, it was a real threat to employers' power and, according to Hulden, a truly radical policy that is as necessary today as it was in the early twentieth century.

Hulden acknowledges that the closed shop affirmed union hierarchies, overrode individual workers' choices (liberty), disciplined rulebreakers, and discriminated against racial minorities and women—all charges that NAM and employers raised in their public relations campaigns against it. But she also helps us understand and balance these shortcomings, excavating the closed shop's long history and evolution, its possibilities and reasoning, its surprising allies and enemies. We learn that abolitionists (like employers) were suspicious of craft traditions rooted in community and coercion rather than individual liberty and impersonal markets. Like NAM, nineteenth-century abolitionists and progressives equated "free labor" with "freedom of contract," which craft traditions and the closed shop seemed to resist. Hulden counters that construction by comparing craft unions' attempts to create and enforce rules about credentialing and training to modern professional associations (for doctors and historians, for instance), which likewise sought to gatekeep who got into their "unions." This is a highly textured and detailed history, which provides excellent context for understanding employers' strategies to uphold the "open shop."

The book focuses on the two largest and most famous employers' organizations, the NCF and NAM. There is an extensive historiography on these organizations from both labor and business perspectives, and Hulden usefully draws from them. But what sets her work apart is her nuanced, objective consideration of every issue and policy in terms of the history, costs, and benefits for each group. Allergic to overgeneralization, she rigorously identifies exceptions to her broader claims.

She also revisits old questions with surprising new insight. In just one example, historians have long argued about why some industrialists gravitated toward the NCF, with its seemingly enlightened acceptance of unions and even the closed shop, while others went to the combative and vitriolic NAM. A common assessment is that the largest, most rationalized, publicly owned enterprises went with the NCF for public relations reasons, while smaller, privately owned proprietorships went with NAM. Hulden affirms that business leaders in the NCF were in highly rationalized mass production industries. But then she suggests that employers in these industries were more open to unions and the closed shop because agreements with those unions made labor markets more uniform and predictable for them. Unions in those industries were strong and could guarantee worker compliance via the closed shop, whereas NAM members were overrepresented in the metal industries, which were not yet rationalized mass producers but, rather, "batch producers" (100). There was little deskilling and a myriad of unions, none of them large or strong enough to deliver compliant workers. Thus, the closed shop offered no benefits for employers in these industries. Hulden provides a useful chart to map this contention with data taken from NAM membership rosters.

In addition to this original analysis and insight, Hulden deploys digital technology to map out the data in her sources. St. Louis, for instance, was home to a thriving "open shop" movement with many NAM member employers. Using data from various St. Louis social and business registers, Hulden digitally maps the social networks of NAM members, identifying overlapping memberships in social clubs, business organizations, and neighborhoods and providing evidence of the collective unity of employers. While it is hardly news that employers occupied the same social networks and class, this digital methodology is promising for mapping other connections and networks that are not so obvious. Hulden provides similarly thick analyses of how these associations navigated the courts, public relations, and Congress, taking the reader to the triumph of welfare capitalism and the "open shop" in the 1920s.

There is plenty that one may quibble with in this book, which is only to be expected in any thoughtful, ambitious work. But one leaves thoroughly impressed by its high level of historical research and argumentation.

Jennifer Delton, *Skidmore College*
DOI 10.1215/15476715-10949051

Transatlantic Radicalism: Socialist and Anarchist Exchanges in the 19th and 20th Centuries
Edited by Frank Jacob and Mario Keßler
Liverpool: Liverpool University Press, 2021
vii + 264 pp.; $185.97 (cloth), $143.00 (e-book)

Transatlantic Radicalism: Socialist and Anarchist Exchanges in the 19th and 20th Centuries is a collection gathered together from the 2017 symposium "Transatlantic Anarchism and Socialism in the Nineteenth and Twentieth Centuries" held in Würzburg, Germany. It includes findings from a generationally diverse group of scholars who have academic positions in five different countries. Taken as a whole, the book offers a series of surprises in analytical and anecdotal form.

Transatlantic Radicalism's strongest chapters include innovative contributions in which the authors rethink figures, topics, and themes that have been at the core of labor and working-class history for decades. Editors Frank Jacob and Mario Keßler lay out the central foundations of the book in their argument that individuals matter in the history of radicalism. The book's point of view, including the symposium and the written volume, was a response to Constance Bantman's (and others') call to reassess transnationalism as a field of study and as a tool of analysis. Ultimately, Jacob and Keßler suggest that transnationalism's scale has meant that scholars have not sufficiently included the "individual" as subject and agent of change. Indeed, the editors argue that their work and its reification of the individual sheds light on what they deem "the understudied ties between radicals in the European and American contexts" (14). The five chapters in each of the two parts are connected by the project's methodological commitment to privilege the "singular" over the social to explain the meaning, experience, and significance of transnationalism in the late nineteenth and early twentieth centuries.

Carlo Romani and Burno Carréra de Sá e Benevides illuminate the symbiotic relationship between anarchists from Italy and the anarchist communities in Brazil; each were changed by the contact. The authors document the ideological landscape of anarchism and tease out the connections of anarchist individualism (which most Italians in their study adhered to upon their arrival in Brazil). The authors provide the best example of the benefits of this narrow lens. As they argue, "A plural understanding of how Italian anarchism . . . put together different practices of organization appropriate to each specific need" was the result of individuals like Felice Vezzani, Oreste Ristori, and Alessandro Scopetani (61). Their commitment to anarchism never wavered, but it did change from stringent "individualist positions" to a more fluid form of anarchist thought and practice (68). These men moved "themselves among different positions inside anarchism, from a more individualist defense of freedom to more coordinated organization inside the union" (78).

Hillary Lazar also focuses on individuals who were part of the transnational anarchist exchange of ideas. She looks at the seven-year run of *Man!*, the editors of which were more individualist than syndicalist. The paper included regular lessons in anarchist theory, which became more practical over time. Out of necessity, *Man!* included strategy to support its editor, Marcus (Shmuel) Graham, and other associates who faced increased harassment and eventual deportation from the United States. Lazar's analysis invests in the book project's methodology by focusing on *Man!*, a single source.

James Michael Yeoman provides complementary findings by looking at individualist anarchist print culture in Panama during the construction of the Panama Canal. The newspapers *Tierra y Libertad* and *Acción Libertaria*, published in Spain, dedicated space to conditions Spanish anarchists faced in Panama. The former, the first and most significant publication of anarchist individualism, Yeoman argues, helped to sustain "libertarian ideas, [which] had arrived with the first Spanish migrants" to Panama (105). But it was the "idiosyncratic figure" M. D. Rodriguez who used "the paper . . . to advance an abrasive, minority view of anarchism, which was out of step with the prevailing trends within the international movement" (105). Yeoman includes a critical discussion of the formation of the Confederación Nacional del Trabajo during this period and the increased support of syndicalism (over individualist anarchism), which would carry important weight in the battle against fascism in the Spanish Civil War. Unlike the impact that Brazil had on Italian anarchist individualists, which resulted in a more fluid and less rigid ideological form, the same was clearly not true in Panama, a connection one wishes the authors and editors had made themselves.

The geographical tracings of transnational radicals are carried through in Steven Proffitt's chapter on the rapid rise and eventual fall of the Knights of Labor, indelibly linked to one leader: Terence Powderly. That argument in itself is less innovative than the author's argument about Powderly as a transnational figure. Proffitt lays the groundwork for more studies of Powderly from a global perspective. Frank Jacob also follows the rise and fall of an ideal. Instead of an individual (as in the case of Proffitt) or the case study of a source (as in the case of Lazar), Jacob offers a place as "case": the Kusbas. The Soviet Union banked on the Kusbas, a planned community of industrial production, to draw in needed skilled workers, deliver production goals to the new state, and fulfill the Marx-ist vision, "from each according to their abilities, to each according to their needs." The environmental reality of Siberia, transnational transplants soon realized, would prevent the dream from coming true. Jacob's study includes well-known individuals like Emma Goldman and Big Bill Haywood, but the bulk of his focus is on everyday workers. Ford autoworker Herbert Calvert and Ruth Kennell from San Francisco, for example, relo-cated to the Kusbas to support the USSR's success. Jacob narrates the hope, transforma-tion, disillusionment, and tragedy of the Kusbas and its migrant population. The author's particular skill is in narrating life cycle turning points and relaying the trauma they wrought in the material and spiritual psyche of those who had put so much hope in the enterprise. Georg Leidenberger also focuses on individuals in his biographical sketch of a man, "unlike most exiles" (173). Meyer was a professional architect and integrated into the country, unlike other contemporary political and economic exiles. Leidenberger sug-gests that the ability to transcend the ethnic enclave of an exile community "illustrates the multivalence of the exile experience of the European Left" (187). That's a tenuous argu-ment, given the author's narrow focus on one man, but Leidenberger offers intriguing points of reference for future studies.

The two other chapters in the book are interesting but have weaknesses. Using a "method of 'reconstructivism,'" Ricardo Altieri provides a visualization of the personal, political, and ideological networks two individual radicals traveled through (182). Like other German exiles in the period, Rosi Wolfstein and Paul Frölich altered their world-view as a product of their transnational experiences. From Social Democrats to "radical and internationalist Communist Party" activists, they documented their transformation in letters that Altieri incorporates into the text (191). In fact, the lengthy letter excerpts take up 20 percent of the chapter—too much to go undigested (there is no discussion or interpretation of these important sources). Lack of full engagement in his sources and lit-tle explanation of "reconstructivism" make it challenging to fully assess Altieri's claims. Mario Keßler, meanwhile, provides a biography of a man, Ossip K. Fleichtheim, and a field. The author (and volume editor) does not really develop the claim that the life of Fle-ichtheim "offers more than just an interesting biography" (222).

Lutz Häfner introduces a new methodological weakness: lack of historical accu-racy. The author's topic, the fluctuating transatlantic public's perception of terrorism as a tactic, is fascinating. Allies and sympathizers of resistance movements, who lived outside the targeted state, were apt to be sympathetic to terrorism and violence against autocratic regimes. The main individual that Häfner uses to follow this argument is Katherine Breschkovsky, an individual with "intense personal networks" that were transnational in scope (40). Häfner uses her transnationality and "versatility" to explain how Ameri-cans (temporarily) accepted terrorism against the Russian regime in the early twentieth century (38). Breschkovsky strengthened ties with activists in the US women's move-ment, Häfner writes. Yet when Häfner dubs one of the elements in the networks the "women's liberation movement," it reveals a lack of context or knowledge about the field (40). Read in the most generous light, this erroneous detail is anachronistic. The "wom-en's liberation movement" came out of a specific series of organizing efforts, experi-ences, and splits within the feminist movement in the latter half of the twentieth century.

Citing Alice Stone Blackwell's 1919 *The Little Grandmother of the Russian Revolution* alongside her unpublished 1905 piece, rather than historiography, points to part of the problem.

This gaffe both instills doubt about the chapter and shines a light on the project's gender trouble. As a note from the editors reads,

> The obvious gender imbalance of the present volume was not intended by the editors. However, since neither the open call for a workshop in Würzburg, Germany, in 2017 nor the further recruitment attempts for the volume could solve this problem, the editors eventually decided to publish this volume in its current form. We nevertheless wish to emphasize that there are many female colleagues working in the field of anarchist studies and the history of the international labor movement as well, whose important and often extraordinary works deserve to be acknowledged. (14n66)

The point confounds gender and sexual identity with the scholarly community and is problematic for that reason alone. Assuming the editors meant the latter, one wonders whether the lack of response from scholars in the field of women's and gender history explains a conceptual issue that should be addressed more fully. Perhaps if women authors had been consulted and included in the design of the project, the "gender imbalance" would have been eradicated. Furthermore, it's not clear whether the problem is the gender identity of the contributors or the lens through which the topics are viewed. But it's problematic either way and reflects a larger dialogic error in the book. *Transnational Radicalism* is a volume with little cohesion or discussion between its contributors themselves, let alone the field as a whole. There is no reference in any of the chapters to other authors in the volume, which is emblematic of the project's overall conceptualization. The study of the individual by individuals who work in separate satellites marks a particular type of history that does little service to essays in this volume or to the wider field of labor and the working class.

Caroline Waldron, *University of Dayton*
DOI 10.1215/15476715-10949064

Divorce, American Style: Fighting for Women's Economic Citizenship in the Neoliberal Era
Suzanne Kahn
Philadelphia: University of Pennsylvania Press, 2021
viii + 327 pp.; $55.00 (cloth), $55.00 (e-book)

What constitutes a good divorce or, rather, a fair divorce? This question animates Suzanne Kahn's eye-opening book—and impelled the generation of "feminist divorce reformers" at the heart of her study. As divorce rates doubled in the United States between 1967 and 1979, a generation of women who had entered marriages with the assumption of lifetime economic dependence on a male breadwinner found themselves cast out into the cold. Measly alimony (if any at all) wasn't even the worst of it. After years of caring for children and homes, dismal job prospects awaited them, and their dedication to family counted for nothing in the division of marital assets. Credit cards—granted on their exes' credit—were cut up the moment they were no longer wives. Generous employer-sponsored health insurance was terminated the day divorce papers were signed. Lucky divorcées held on to the spouse's less generous portion of Social Security. Pensions were a different matter: divorcing men walked away with their pensions intact. Not surprisingly, the country had a lot of motivated, angry women on its hands. Kahn argues that the feminist movement offered them answers and an outlet to channel their discontent.

In drawing out the campaigns divorce reformers embarked upon from the 1970s to the 1990s, Kahn simultaneously illuminates histories of marriage and of the welfare state. At stake was women's economic citizenship, which divorce activists sought to rewrite through two claims: First, marriage was an economic contract, in which wives were equal partners, and for which they deserved state entitlements independent of their husbands. Second, marriage was also a status, which made wives worthy citizens, deserving of social and state recognition. Divorce reformers' often quite explicit counterpart to this worthy wife was the less meritorious unmarried woman on need-based public assistance.

Painful compromises accompanied some remarkable wins as deeply ingrained male-breadwinner ideology, welfare state retrenchment, and conservative political ascendance blocked divorce reformers' most ambitious visions. The result, Kahn asserts, was that wealthier women, with private resources to divvy up, gained access to a range of family property. Lower-income women, whose primary household assets lay in access to selective entitlements like Social Security, still depended on meager and unequal distribution of dependent benefits by the state.

Kahn lays out the step-by-step process by which this outcome emerged. The book opens with the no-fault divorce revolution. No-fault divorces were far easier to obtain, but they eliminated the presumption that wives merited ongoing support from their former husbands and left divorcing women at the mercy of judges in property distributions and with limited-duration "need-based maintenance" (32). The women who mobilized in response were largely middle class and white. When political compromises inevitably became necessary, they frequently clashed with lower-income women and women of color, as their backgrounds shaped their priorities. A grassroots push from below brought feminist organizations like the National Organization for Women and the Women's Equity Action League on board. Divorce reformers sustained this grassroots feminist energy through the 1970s; by the 1980s, political leaders and experts took the place of on-the-ground activists, nurturing a feminist agenda long past the conventional end point assigned to second-wave feminism.

The middle chapters of the book follow debate over ten national laws targeted to divorced women's economic status that Congress enacted between 1974 and 1986. Kahn highlights how "functional equality" rather than "strict formal equality" was divorce reformers' goal (63). Among their desiderata were equal access to consumer credit, recognition of their unpaid household labor in property divisions, rights to their former husbands' employer-provided health insurance, equitable division of both private and federal-provided pensions, and restructuring of Social Security to give divorcing women adequate benefits independent of their ex-partners.

The 1974 Equal Credit Opportunity Act (ECOA) is illustrative. Divorcing women lost access to credit built up during marriages (it went to husbands), faced sex and marital-status discrimination in applying for new credit, and could not get child support and alimony counted as income. The ECOA rectified those barriers. Two years later, Congress added race, national origin, and receipt of public assistance as further protected categories. A major victory for feminists, the legislation broke "coverture's long hold on the credit industry" (94). However, the ECOA guaranteed only equal *access* to credit. Poorer women (like the welfare rights activists also fighting for credit reform in these years) still struggled to prove their *creditworthiness*. Efforts to reform Social Security are also revealing. Feminists envisioned multiple means for wives to get out from under the dependent-driven structure of Social Security benefits, but in the end they won only changes that broadened their entitlements as formerly *married* women. As Kahn effectively demonstrates, divorce reformers succeeded with laws "mandating that private institutions treat married women as equals and partners"; they failed in "instilling this understanding of married women into the public social insurance system" (95).

Broad reluctance to abandon selective entitlements anchored in marriage combined with conservative political power to whittle away at feminists' ambitions. By the end of the 1980s, divorce reformers returned their attention to states and led campaigns to replace common law with community property regimes. They renewed pressure on judges to count women's unpaid contributions in property settlements. Slowly, divorce reform energies faded as feminists shifted attention to better benefits for working women. Kahn observes that in the 1990s children replaced the divorced "displaced homemaker" as the citizens deserving of welfare state entitlements.

Divorce, American Style would have benefited from drawing more fully on recent scholarship on the women's movement that has shown that divorce reformers were not alone in making the arguments Kahn uncovered. ERA advocates, general feminist Social Security reformers, wages for housework campaigners, and legal feminists all shared common ground with feminist divorce activists. Together, they reinforce Kahn's important reframing of the 1960s–80s feminist movement and demonstrate that formal workplace equality was never activists' single, or even primary, concern. Kahn rightly concludes that feminists were not able to win the egalitarian vision they imagined. Her study reveals how path dependency and a tradition of awarding entitlements to the worthy meant that marriage remained entrenched in the US welfare structure to the detriment, mostly, of poorer and working-class Americans.

Kirsten Swinth, *Fordham University*
DOI 10.1215/15476715-10949077

Everyday Communists in South Africa's Liberation Struggle: The Lives of Ivan and Lesley Schermbrucker
Alan Kirkaldy
Cham, Switzerland: Palgrave Macmillan, 2022
xviii + 386 pp.; $129.99 (cloth), $129.99 (paper), $99.00 (e-book)

Alan Kirkaldy has written a lively account of the careers of two Communist activists in twentieth-century Eastern Cape, South Africa: the labor organizers and movement fundraisers Ivan and Lesley Schermbrucker. He was granted full access to the family and incorporated a partial manuscript biography of Ivan by Lesley. An experienced historian, Kirkaldy has crafted a tribute with depth and genuine surprises.

Black African workers organized by the Communist Party (CP) successfully struck on the gold mines in 1946, and Africans fought against deferred payment, racist grain markets, rural labor abuse, and restrictions on residential rights in a massive political union, the Industrial and Commercial Workers Union. The Communist Party had been oriented mostly toward white workers before the war, incorporating some Black men (and a few women) from the 1920s on, vying with anarchists and socialists in meetings on the Witwatersrand. The Schermbruckers were working-class Jews. Ivan, born in 1921 in Ngqeleni, a small town in the Eastern Cape, spoke isiXhosa as a boy with his friends. He left school for the military in part because his parents could not afford university fees and went to North Africa and Italy during World War II. Fred Carneson, later of Cape Town's Communist Central Committee, recruited Ivan when he, Wolfie Kodesh, and Ivan were serving in Tunisia—with Brian Bunting, also later a Central Committee member, stationed "nearby." The three men worked together in the Italian port of Ancona in contact with partisans and the Italian CP (51).

A difficulty Kirkaldy faces is providing a context. "Everyday Communists" is a double-entendre title meaning "full time" and "middle rank." Still, the Schermbruckers were white, as were most of their intimate colleagues (Bram Fischer, Winnie Kramer, Arnold Selby, etc.), and as such were privileged. There were some Africans and South Asian South Africans, and so on, in the party, but there were also many whites, and the vast bulk of the working class in South Africa in the twentieth century was Black under white union-member supervision. Ivan worked for a while for the Department of Native Affairs, the government organ devoted to administering Africans under apartheid, but he quit during the general replacement of liberals by apartheid officials.

The chronology jumps around a bit, but the solution is to use Ivan's and Lesley's *life* (or lives together) as the context(s) for national and local political events, rather than vice versa. Ivan and Lesley met in 1946, and by all accounts had a great marriage, and this book chronicles their professional work as active organizers against apartheid, zooming back and forth a bit. In places, their ordinariness suggests a different vision of reform from that espoused by their revolutionary colleagues. As the state closed in on the African National Congress (ANC) and Pan Africanist Congress (PAC) inside South Africa in the early 1960s—the now-illegal party was renamed the South African Communist Party—African nationalists carried the day within and outside the SACP and organized violence on a larger scale. Thousands of PAC (and Poqo) members were arrested on the verge of *their* plan for violence, and then Umkhonto we Sizwe (MK) stepped up recruitment of scores of new members for their ranks. Nelson Mandela's vanguard force, MK people, were funneled out via the border post at Lobatse to be trained and sent back in with arms—another venture that the state destroyed in embryo.

The tight-knit connections between and among top Communists, including future apartheid state's witnesses like Piet Beyleveld, constitute a hidden theme in the book. Kirkaldy is aware that the interactions, texts, and even photographs in the Schermbrucker family allow him to speak more freely about those who intersected with them, people woven together in heritage, military service, social and Communist Party connections, and marriage. There he shines a bright light. The generous biographies lodged in the endnotes (another unusual structural decision) mostly focus on White comrades, via the Schermbruckers' documented associations, but not entirely. That the Schermbruckers went on holiday to Plettenberg in 1960–63, as they did every other year, more than their race, emblematizes their distance from the vanguard. The catastrophic defeat of MK in '63 is elided into exile and prison. True, life went on for organizers and soldiers, in and out of prison, or squalid MK camps, or London hotels.

The ordinary Communists of various backgrounds did not always agree with each other in or out of prison. The Schermbruckers later said they confronted the reality of Stalinism, and so focused most on the local (South African) mobilization against apartheid and the National Party, and not the international proletarian dimension. Joe Slovo and others in the party failed to make this recalculation so clearly but also supported the ANC's embrace of revolutionary violence: it became entirely symbolic after 1963, until the 1980s. The union movement, its organizers cannibalized by MK, did not recover from the '60s collapse until the early 1970s, in Durban.

Episodic evocations of the Schermbruckers' quiet work in passing funds through their "Arnold's Christmas Hamper" club, along with their efforts at the *Guardian*, and discussions of the way they mixed with, as Lesley said, "all peoples of every color and background" and of their job in facilitating Bram Fischer (Communist Party chairman) during his brief underground period, all are quite interesting (110).

No one was spared when the arrests came in the 1960s, and Ivan (after being tortured by the "statue" method) went to jail for a long time, while others suffered exile, house arrest, "banning" (from public associations with political groups, etc.)—and hanging. With Ivan in jail, authority was taken up by women, such as Jean Middleton (Strachan), and Lesley, including for MK. As the active efforts went into an eclipse, in jail, Ivan became a kind of parental figure to other prisoners, both political and common cons; he was laid back but tough. As Hugh Lewin put it, he was "Ivan fucking Schermbrucker, especially to himself" (287).

One notes that Canon Collins of the Anglican Church (who often worked with Tambo) directed MK and party representatives on a committee he worked with to merge with an existing Johannesburg underground committee known only by Collins, in order to receive all world Protestant church monies—including the Quakers'—in one place. The committee pledged to use the funds only to support detainees' families. One notes that the committee was composed of active MK people: Gertrude Shope (wife of Mark Shope, MK), Tshintshing Caroline Mashaba (wife of Andrew Mashaba, MK), James Ngwenya, and two others, including one pastor; and that Tambo later admitted he had at times taken funds earmarked for civilian actions in South Africa and used the money to support the ANC's MK soldiery in Tanzania and Angola (261).

Multiple personal relationships, not all of them amicable, are set into the urban and international scope of the party. In this way, Kirkaldy draws the picture of "Everyday Communists" responding to the singular problem of South Africa in a quotidian manner, more like social democrats than Bolsheviks. Still, though, in pursuing those aims unwaveringly, they gave their lives and offer their legacies now.

Paul S. Landau, *University of Maryland (and Senior Fellow, University of Johannesburg)*
DOI 10.1215/15476715-10949090

Monetary Authorities: Capitalism and Decolonization in the American Colonial Philippines
Allan E. S. Lumba
Durham, NC: Duke University Press, 2022
232 pp.; $102.95 (cloth), $26.95 (paper), $26.99 (e-book)

The publication of Amy Kaplan and Donald E. Pease's *Cultures of United States Imperialism* exactly thirty years ago heralded a new wave of US empire studies. Emerging in the shadow of the Persian Gulf War and through the 2003 US invasion of Iraq and subsequent occupation, this collection of essays identified the United States as an empire and drew connections between American culture and projections of US power in the world. The book and much work that followed bucked enduring views—academic and popular—of US overseas aggression circa 1898 as an aberration and US imperialism as exceptional and incomparable to European forms. In *Monetary Authorities: Capitalism and Decolonization in the American Colonial Philippines*, Allan E. S. Lumba builds on this scholarship while also advancing a distinct framework for his subject.

Labor: Studies in Working-Class History, Volume 21, Issue 1
© 2024 by Labor and Working-Class History Association

Drawing on the insights of decoloniality, Lumba approaches "economic experts" and their work of building and controlling a monetary and banking system in the colony as part of a broader history of decolonization. In making decolonization—not imperialism writ large—his conceptual frame, Lumba follows American Studies scholar Manu Karuka's provocative analysis of the United States' "countersovereignty" vis-à-vis Indigenous nations. Lumba sets US colonialism in the Philippines in relation to an "American tradition of reactionary logic" manifest in a continental history of settler colonialism (3). Economic experts from both the United States and the Philippines designed a colonial currency, established a Postal Savings Bank system that stretched across the archipelago, managed the operations of the Philippine National Bank, and communicated visions of economic nationalism during the Philippines' transition from colony to commonwealth. None were efforts to realize what Lumba terms "unconditional decolonization"—the undermining of a colonial system of racial capitalism and the development of a fundamentally fairer and more just collective life (8). Experts applied their monetary authority as part of a "counter-decolonization" strategy or, in the case of Filipino nationalist elites, toward a form of merely "conditional decolonization" (3, 13–14).

Lumba sources his account primarily in "the archives of experts"—the official reports, academic articles, and correspondence where university-trained men made and claimed knowledge about the capitalist market (5). Among these money and banking experts were Americans Charles Conant and Edwin Kemmerer. Conant addressed currency problems that troubled the early years of the US military occupation. Accepting the view that Filipinos' racial capacity did not yet rise to the measure of modern, civilized societies operating on the gold standard, Conant adjusted his commitment to "a world smoothed out by one unified gold standard" and proposed a new colonial currency—a silver coin called the Philippine peso (58). Its value would be the same as a "theoretical gold peso" (58). This "ghostly" and hierarchical monetary system signaled recognition of the colony's class and racial order and preserved it, Lumba argues (60).

Meanwhile, "money doctor" Edwin Kemmerer, who had helped to design the US Federal Reserve system, was brought aboard to improve the adoption of the new currency. Like Conant, Kemmerer drafted policy premised on Philippine peoples' supposed incapacity and the benignity of American racial paternalism. To encourage Filipinos on a path toward financial probity, he helped to establish a Postal Savings Bank system that operated across the colony. Encouraged to save their money in these banks, Philippine people practiced a new relationship to money and to the colonial state.

To their promoters, the currency and banking systems provided Filipinos with a much-needed education. By assigning the power of seigniorage to the colonial state, the currency plan was also profitable to the colonial government. Capital accumulated in making and maintaining the currency system funded colonial infrastructure projects and labor and supplies and thus lent material support to the military pacification of the colony. Colonial currency and banking also performed ideological work, teaching people within the colony and beyond to see the US government as a protector of capital investment and safeguard against commercial insecurity. In all these ways, the currency and banking reforms were rooted in and entrenched racial capitalism and constituted elements of "counter-decolonization." Monetary authorities "materially and ideologically bound [the Philippines] to the U.S. Empire and capital. To demand decolonization would be to demand the destruction of such a relationship and to lose present and future wealth" (92).

Filipino political and economic elites also come under scrutiny in Lumba's study. His first chapter, set primarily in the Spanish colonial period, concludes with a consideration of the Malolos Republic, the government created by members of the revolutionary movement to overthrow Spanish colonialism and then the US occupation. In pursuing national sovereignty, political recognition from within and outside the Philippines, and loans to underwrite their operations, Filipinos at the helm of the Malolos Republic shelved problems of economic inequality and labor exploitation. They pursued the "conditional decolonization" that Lumba goes on to associate with the positions of nationalist leaders like Sergio Osmeña and Manuel Roxas. They challenged US imperial sovereignty but not the strictures of capitalism in the Philippines. Nationalists like these accepted a colonial currency that kept wages low; they viewed workers' strikes and unrest as impediments to national sovereignty; and in the 1930s, they repressed radical movements led by the Philippines' Communist Party and the Sakdalistas.

Lumba's framing of the colonial Philippines as a long history of decolonization is novel and foregrounds the anxieties and tensions that beset the Spanish and US colonial government. Economic experts fretted over the instabilities triggered by the circulation of forces perceived as foreign to the colony or beyond their control whether in the form of the Mexican coin (in the Spanish colonial period), embodied by Chinese workers and capital, or expressed in workers' intractability. Economic experts idealized sovereign markets yet also claimed the right to structure markets in ways that advantaged colonialists and preserved the racial and class status quo. Lumba's decolonization framework also helps him avoid an essentializing parable of imperial aggressors versus champions of national independence. Lumba is attentive to the capitalist ordering of the world that Filipino nationalists embraced or, in some instances, may have accepted pragmatically.

By the end of *Monetary Authorities*, lineaments of an "unconditional decolonization" finally come more sharply into view. Writing on the Depression-era Philippines, Lumba describes peasants and farmers practicing "new modes of collective survival" and discusses Crisanto Evangelista, a founder of the Partido Komunista ng Pilipinas (the Communist Party of the Philippines), who countered a narrow vision of national sovereignty with one of "radical internationalism" (139, 140). A history framed by decolonization invites this and arguably even more attention to the alternative forms of collective life practiced by historical actors and their social and political imaginaries. We might also wonder about historical subjects whose actions, ideas, and beliefs over time blurred the binary of "conditional" and "unconditional" decolonization. Perhaps some of them suggest still other complex and contingent paths toward a world more just.

Rebecca Tinio McKenna, *University of Notre Dame*
DOI 10.1215/15476715-10949103

A Liberal-Labour Lady: The Times and Life of Mary Ellen Spear Smith
Veronica Strong-Boag
Vancouver: University of British Columbia Press, 2021
288 pp.; CA $89.95 (cloth), CA $32.95 (paper), CA $32.95 (e-book)

The inversion of "Life and Times" in the title of Veronica Strong-Boag's insightful biography of Mary Ellen Spear Smith speaks to a historical truism that individual lives can only be understood in context. This seems to be particularly so in the case of Mary Ellen Smith. Her story speaks to the particular conjunction of class and gender politics in Britain and Canada in the decades spanning the turn of the twentieth century. Remembered as the first female member of the British Columbia legislature and the first woman cabinet member in the British Empire, her significance is based in her struggle to expand the democratic rights of workers and women. But, as Strong-Boag argues, settler-colonial privilege shaped her legacy in a number of troubling ways.

Her story is remarkable. She was born Mary Ellen Spear into a poor mining community in Devon, England, although the family soon moved to the relatively more prosperous coal mining region of Northumberland in northern England. There she married miner Ralph Smith. Although wages were better in Northumberland than elsewhere, this was a dismal place with cramped, rudimentary housing, slag heaps and smoke, and the raft of dangers and disease that plagued mining towns. But the community possessed a deep culture of self-improvement, reflected in well-organized unions, a strong cooperative movement, and a commitment to education and temperance rooted in Methodism. Such sentiments aligned with those of members of the radical wing of the Liberal Party, who were interested in building collaborative alternatives to class conflict and socialism. Northumberland was the center of the resulting Labour-Liberalism, a politics of consensus between employers and workers. While Mary Ellen was busy raising young children, Ralph Smith was a vocal advocate of "Lib-Labism."

The couple brought this ideology to the coal mines of Nanaimo, on British Columbia's Vancouver Island. Ralph again took center stage, emerging as a leader of the local, independent miners' union, arguing that the precarious union needed a strategy of "reason, conciliation and arbitration" to succeed (49). His rise was meteoric. Starting in 1898, he was successively a member of the provincial legislature, president of the Trades and Labour Congress of Canada, and member of Canada's federal parliament. Defeated following two terms as MP, he returned to the British Columbia legislature. Although pushing for labor reforms, his opposition to socialism alienated him from the British Columbian labor movement, and he grew increasingly close to the mainstream of the Liberal Party.

Mary Ellen's own talents became increasingly clear as she came to play leading roles in an impressive range of community activities as well as the local Women's Christian Temperance Union and the Ladies' Liberal League. When the family moved to Vancouver, she organized a local branch of the Imperial Order of the Daughters of the Empire, led the Women's Canadian Club, and worked for the Pioneer Political Equality

Labor: Studies in Working-Class History, Volume 21, Issue 1
© 2024 by Labor and Working-Class History Association

League. As this suggests, she rose relatively freely into British Canadian society, not just as the spouse of a member of parliament but as someone with significant political and oratorical skills. The *Ottawa Citizen* declared her "one of the best informed women on matters political" in the country (60).

Mary Ellen shone in the local and national spotlight. Her uncanny ability to inhabit elite social networks, hosting teas and parties, dressing spectacularly, and often soft-selling her message made her an acceptable face of the progressive New Liberalism. And she functioned well among middle- and upper-class women in the suffrage movement. After Ralph's death in 1917, Mary Ellen continued the fight on her own. The following year, in the wake of women's enfranchisement, she ran as an independent women's candidate and claimed Ralph's seat in the British Columbia legislature. She rallied nonpartisan sentiments and women's votes in the tumult following World War I. And it allowed her, in Lib-Lab fashion, to distance herself both from the growing radicalism of British Columbia's unions and the antilabor and antifeminist leadership of the provincial Liberal Party. Once elected, Smith, with her feminist allies, pushed the Liberal government to adopt a number of reforms, particularly those enhancing women's well-being, suggesting the possibilities of a more statist New Liberalism in British Columbia.

It was not, however, to be. Despite some immediate gains, the 1920s proved to be a decade of reaction, both against labor and against women's political gains. British New Liberalism failed to gain a foothold in Canada, and further efforts at reform floundered. The Liberal government hoped to placate Smith, and to gain from her popularity, by appointing her as a cabinet minister without portfolio. Despite its historic status, the appointment was a pyrrhic victory, as it came with no power, so she resigned, refusing to remain "an ornament" (156). Indeed, she spent the remainder of her political career frustrated, frozen out by a Liberal Party uninterested in progressive reform, an increasingly belligerent capitalist class, a union movement highly critical of the kind of class collaboration Lib-Labism promised, and feminists who lost interest in Mary Ellen's increasingly ineffective politics.

For all Mary Ellen Smith's defense of democracy and championing of labor and feminist causes, Strong-Boag clearly notes the ways in her worldview was marked by prejudice. She (and Ralph) persistently campaigned to exclude Asians from Canada and sought to replicate British institutions within the context of empire. Issues of Indigenous dispossession seemed not to register throughout their political careers. This, then, is a story that Strong-Boag tells with nuance. As Mary Ellen fought for women's political inclusion, she fought against that of others.

Operating within a "political caste system that feared independent women," Mary Ellen was challenged at every turn, relying on her remarkable set of skills to rally broad support as well as on tactics to ingratiate herself among the more powerful (143). This volume fits well into Strong-Boag's impressive oeuvre of studies of early twentieth-century feminism, which wrestles effectively with the complexities of class and race, particularly within the suffrage movement. *A Liberal-Labour Lady* adds another layer, enlightening our understanding of the complexities of the suffrage movement, the weight of settler colonialism, and the fate of Lib-Labism in Canada.

James Naylor, *Brandon University*
DOI 10.1215/15476715-10949116

Red Harvests: Agrarian Capitalism and Genocide in Democratic Kampuchea
James A. Tyner
Morgantown: West Virginia University Press, 2021
180 pp.; $99.99 (cloth), $29.99 (paper), $29.99 (e-book)

Between 1975 and 1979 the infamous Red Khmers ruled over Cambodia, causing the death of about a quarter of the country's population either through executions or through famines and exhaustion. This genocide goes beyond comprehension. Genocide studies, the academic field that studies the causes and context of such horrific chapters of human history, will probably have decades of work ahead.

James Tyner tries to understand the broader context of this genocide in terms of what exactly the Khmer Rouge aimed to destroy and for what purpose. The apparent answer is the destruction of cities, of everything intellectual, religious, and creative, to instill a complete obedience to the central leadership of the Khmer Rouge. Pervasive also was the collectivization of agriculture and the abolition of currency as part of a policy to eradicate traditional rural life, with its family farms, and turn the countryside into one big work camp. But why, and what did this have to do with the professed communist ideology of the Khmer Rouge?

Tyner addresses these questions by writing "a political economy of the Cambodian genocide" (114). He applies the conceptual lens of *state capitalism*, which means the state, ruled by a single party, controls the country's entire economy to generate surplus value. The state takes over the role of capitalist enterprise in order to generate revenue, usually to be reinvested in industrialization. This happened despite the Marxist-Leninist rhetoric of the Communist Party of Kampuchea (CPK) and contradicts how scholars have described the democratic Kampuchea as "pure communism" or "agrarian socialism." Tyner argues therefore that we need to study the rural transformation of Cambodia under the Khmer Rouge from the perspective of the history of *capitalism* and its many different manifestations. In this case, the CPK leadership aimed for independence from outside investments through massive exploitation of the countryside to generate the economic surplus needed for industrial investments.

The draconian policies of the Khmer Rouge originated in the civil war between 1970 and 1975. The US bombardments helped to generate support for the Khmer Rouge, legitimize its policy of depopulating towns and villages under their control, and reorganize the countryside. Not surprisingly, the CPK rapidly lost popular support, setting in motion a vicious cycle of oppression, distrust, and large-scale executions. The only way out for leaders of the Khmer Rouge was to set Cambodia on a trajectory in which "the meaning of socialism changed from self-emancipation of the working class to national economic development" (33). The example of the Soviet Union and the emphasis of the Non-Aligned Movement on self-reliance provided the ideological and historical legitimation for an autarkic course. Whereas in classical Marxism the emancipation of the working class was only conceivable at a world scale, since the rise of the Soviet Union it had been believed that a socialist utopia could be achieved within national boundaries. The only route toward such a paradise, however, was by squeezing all surplus capital from the countryside and investing it in sectors that would generate the economic growth necessary to catch on with the wealthier countries in the world.

The Khmer Rouge set the economic goals of technical advance of agriculture and import substitution. Official contacts of the CPK leadership with a number of Non-Aligned countries may have helped to achieve such a modernization, as did Tanzania at that time, for example. But Khmer Rouge leaders failed to obtain the necessary development aid to modernize the agricultural sector. Instead, Tyner argues, the Khmer Rouge engineered a project of *original accumulation*, turning the country into one big commodity frontier. This policy failed too.

Tyner does not directly address the question why the agricultural exports obtained at such a high price did not lead to investments that generated higher agricultural productivity and more agricultural surplus. The answer is more or less hidden in the book: it was the betrayal of the country by the big powers that facilitated the paranoid and totally incompetent leadership of the Khmer Rouge coming to power. Moreover, after years of extreme violence the country was deeply traumatized. Marx and Engels would never have agreed with a violent imposition of a communist regime, and they would have been even more appalled by the idea that such a transformation would be orchestrated by guerrilla bands. While it is clear that what the Khmer Rouge did had nothing to do with the emancipation of the working class, I am not sure whether this was the result of fundamental contradictions in Marxist-Leninist ideology that produced the oxymoron of state capitalism, as Tyner suggests. What I read in his book is that in a country ravaged by war, internationally isolated, and taken over by guerrillas there was no basis for whatever government to start a healing process without structural outside help.

Ulbe Bosma, *International Institute of Social History, Amsterdam*
DOI 10.1215/15476715-10949129

Labor Power and Strategy
John Womack Jr., edited by Peter Olney and Glenn Perušek
Oakland: PM Press, 2023
208 pp.; $16.95 (paper), $8.95 (e-book)

In a recent Supreme Court case, *Glacier Northwest v. International Brotherhood of Teamsters Local 174*, a concrete company won a claim against its union for material costs caused by a strike. Prior to walking out, workers had left wet concrete in some mixing trucks. When it hardened, the concrete was ruined; the trucks themselves were preserved from damage only by swift company action. Fruitlessly, the union argued that this was the exercise of workers' economic power in its ordinary form and did not constitute a tort justiciable in the court system—leave it to the National Labor Relations Board. For workers to identify and exploit a material vulnerability in the production process is merely to strike effectively. But to hold unions responsible for economic damages from strikes has been a dream of employers since the 1930s, and the court system is now ready to oblige. Although the ultimate decision did not go as far as it might have—the justices attempted instead to construct a conceptually untenable distinction between deliberate sabotage and legitimate economic action—it nonetheless marks a clear move back in this direction.

The *Glacier* case thus illustrates both the possibilities and the challenges that arise out of the analysis and exploitation of vulnerabilities in production processes. Such analysis and exploitation has long been the lodestar of the historian John Womack Jr. and is the topic of discussion and debate in the new volume *Labor Power and Strategy*. Womack, a historian of Mexico, is the author of a famous essay in Spanish, "Posición estratégica y fuerza obrera" ("Strategic Position and Workers' Power"), which has circulated by word of mouth in the United States both in Spanish and in translation for nearly two decades. In that essay and across much of his career, he rejects the interest of the "new labor history" in workers' culture, instead emphasizing the decisive importance of leverage at the technical seams and bottlenecks of the production process. The new book *Labor Power and Strategy*, edited by Peter Olney and Glenn Perušek, does not include Womack's original essay. Rather, its heart is a lengthy dialogue about the topic of strategic position between Womack and Peter Olney, the retired organizing director of the International Longshore and Warehouse Union; this is followed by ten brief responses from organizers and scholars including Jane McAlevey, Bill Fletcher Jr., and Jack Metzgar.

In a certain way, Womack's approach is excitingly open-ended. While he is especially interested in industries like logistics (hence the dialogue with a veteran of the ILWU), he believes any large-scale process of production involves moments where workers must work the interface between different technical systems—the "hubs, nodes, and vertices" (36).

> Where are the docks or doors for deliveries and shipping? Where is motive and light power, the switchboard? Where are the generators? Where are the server room, the air-conditioning, and humidification? And the moving parts: Where are their connections, simultaneous and sequential, who tends them, who maintains them all, and where is their tool room, the HELP room? What's the shift plan? What are the various schedules and productive routes inside and out? (35)

Anyone who has organized a workplace and discovered the seemingly spontaneous self-confidence of skilled workers at such positions recognizes the force of this insight. At the same time, Womack somewhat dilutes the power of this analysis by his eagerness to fold almost any branch of production into it—describing the leverage of food service workers and janitors, for example, in terms of strategic position (56). As in the logic of the *Glacier* decision (ironically), the power to inflict costly damage on vital technical processes loses some of its distinctiveness against the larger backdrop of workers' power more generally in *Labor Power and Strategy*. After all, every worker employed by capital is employed for an economic reason of some kind. The concept of "strategic position" initially engages in a bit of admirably icy discrimination, paying equal ethical respect to all workers' struggles without granting them equal economic or political significance. But Womack, quite understandably, seems not quite willing to sustain such a coldblooded posture. Rather, he is appropriately eager to identify the kernels of possibility in the heroic and one-sided struggles of the working class, stretching his concepts in the process. But it is not clear how well concepts forged in the conceptual world of industrial production and transportation translate into less capital-intensive contexts.

This question—the slippery definition of strategic position—shapes the central debate of the volume. Along with Olney and the respondents, Womack is drawn into a discussion that translates "strategic position," or what he sometimes calls "the power to wound," into the concept of "structural power," as contrasted with "associational power," a term coined by sociologist Erik Olin Wright (30–31). Associational power describes the power workers may wield through their relational position in society rather than in the accumulation process. Womack acknowledges the significance of associational power but insists that it is causally secondary to structural power, around which he expects the former to gather.

But is the relationship so linear? As Katy Fox-Hodess observes in a response in the volume (following her writing with Camilo Santibañez Rebolledo), and as Michael Billeaux Martinez has written recently in this journal, certain social preconditions must exist in order for workers to withstand the pressure that will come if they attempt to exploit powerful technical leverage. The Teamsters at Glacier Northwest had structural power aplenty. The problem was the greater power that came down on them when they tried to use it.

It is true that workers are generally quicker to trust each other if they can see they have something to win. But that trust must still be earned, and the relationships that embody it must still be built. Even if the needed relationships of solidarity correspond to long-standing everyday workplace social relationships, there remains no guarantee that one will translate easily into the other. How many millions of long-standing work friendships have been broken when one friend struck and another scabbed? Solidarity is always at least somewhat uncertain. Often, moreover, the relationships that are strategically necessary are not the same as those that are socially available. Some work functions lend themselves easily to social connection, while others isolate workers from each other; this distinction often has little to do with position in relation to capital's technical vulnerabilities. Indeed, it can easily be the case that the most replaceable workers are the most connected ones: in many large multifunction service providers, the largest department is a "shared services" call center. With its relatively high number of workers relative to managers, it is often a relatively ideologically militant shop, because a more independent workers' culture has a chance to develop there. Yet call center workers have little strategic power in the technical sense, since they are quite easily replaced—except in the sense that all workers perform functions that employers require. Consideration of replaceability thus adds an important nuance to the meaning of strategic power, in this sense.

Moreover, some forms of leverage are so strong that they are difficult or impossible to employ, at least directly, without risking major retaliation. Womack suggests that health-care workers enjoy structural power, an intuitive idea that arises from their connection to matters of life and death (147). But they can never use this power: nurses' strikes are planned to ensure that the hospital continues to operate. The social breach otherwise would be so great as to represent nihilism. Instead, then, what nurses do is force administrations to continue to operate the hospital by employing travel nurses. This can still be costly and can still generate significant leverage (as McAlevey points out in the collection), but it stresses a much less sensitive seam in the garment of capital (111).

The return of debates about strategy to academic labor studies (particularly history) is an extremely welcome development, and one that owes a good deal to Womack. The vitality of the discussion within the volume and its reception thus far indicates how much appetite there is for a discussion for which we have been somewhat starved. There is much to figure out, particularly as labor markets continue to change rapidly.

Gabriel Winant, *University of Chicago*
DOI 10.1215/15476715-10949142

We Kept Our Towns Going: The Gossard Girls of Michigan's Upper Peninsula
Phyllis Michael Wong
East Lansing: Michigan State University Press, 2022
224 pp.; $19.95 (paper), $19.95 (e-book)

Phyllis Michael Wong joined her husband at Northern Michigan University when he was president from 2004 to 2012. In Marquette, on the shores of Lake Superior, she learned about the "Gossard Girls," women of all ages who worked for H. W. Gossard Company in the Upper Peninsula (UP). Teenage girls, young single women, married mothers, and widows sewed apparel, mostly undergarments, and processed paperwork from 1920 until both Michigan factories closed in 1976. Wong's interest started with a 2007 club project to celebrate "women who made a difference." She researched Geraldine Gordon Defant, an organizer with the International Ladies' Garment Workers' Union (ILGWU) who was at Gossard in the 1940s.

In 2010, Wong spoke at a Women's History Month event where several former Gossard workers shared differing perspectives on the same past situations. Wong realized she could gather their "collective voices" and artifacts and help create an archive at the local history center. Over several years, she conducted ninety-six oral histories and facilitated the making of a memorial quilt. She also pursued the publication of *We Kept Our Towns Going*, which serves as an homage to the women's contributions to the UP and as an effort to broaden labor history. Wong emphasizes that women took pride in their skills, income, and economic role in a region that usually highlights its mining history. She also wants to expand the history of women in the textile and apparel industry to include these workers in the UP, who have not often been part of labor studies.

With these as goals, the book reads like a work of mainstream public history—a preservation of the women's oral histories and reportage from local newspapers that are Wong's core primary sources. It is not a scholarly monograph that attempts to place this history into conversation with particular historians or frameworks; rather, it is an

Labor: Studies in Working-Class History, Volume 21, Issue 1
© 2024 by Labor and Working-Class History Association

endeavor to claim a presence and value for the Gossard Girls. As a labor historian with interests in gender theory, racialized class formation, intersectionality, organizing strategy, and global trade, I wanted more. As an educator who has spent as much of my career outside the university as in it, I admired the book's desire to open space for women's voices, share locally grounded stories, and expose more readers to women's labor history.

The book begins with a foreword by Lisa Fine, professor of twentieth-century labor history at Michigan State University. It provides a succinct scholarly framing that places the book with Tamara Hareven and Randolph Langenbach's *Amoskeag: Life and Work in an American Factory City* (1978) and Jacqueline Dowd Hall et al.'s *Like a Family: The Making of a Southern Cotton Mill World* (1987). All three rely on oral histories and center workers and their conceptualizations of their daily lives. The foreword is also the only part of the book with notes. The author and publisher made the decision to simply list sources at the back, most likely to appeal to nonacademic readers and save cost and time. It is unfortunate that they were not able to create a notes section that listed sources used by page numbers, but we know the realities of current press budgets. The book also does not cite where the oral histories are located. I searched online and found thirty-six listed under "Gossard Interviews" in the John M. Longyear Archives at the Marquette Regional History Center. The archivist believes Wong most likely kept the other sixty transcripts because those women did not give her permission to make them fully public.

We Kept Our Towns Going then advances through an introduction and nine chapters before closing with a helpful glossary, sources, and index. Each chapter covers a set span of history, starting in the 1920s and culminating with contemporary memories of the factories and Gossard Girls. Each chapter concludes with a brief biographical summary of two or three women who contributed oral histories. These honor the women workers, speak to general readers, and share personal life details that a regional labor history cannot include. The book's specific information about the towns of Ishpeming and Gwinn, illumination of the thoughts and decisions of women workers, and counternarrative to the traditional history of the Iron Range are valuable contributions to labor history. The book offers new primary sources and ideas for labor historians who study women, the textile and apparel industry, and mining. It also makes reference to Canada and migration, raising questions about border relations and the dynamics between the UP, the upper Midwest, and Canada.

Most scholars will have frustrations. Wong makes little attempt to balance the oral histories and local newspapers with more diverse primary sources, including union papers. Although the newspapers have titles like *Mining Journal* and *Iron Ore*, Wong presents their reporting without interrogation. She uses several letters and reports from the ILGWU Chicago Joint Board Records at the Kheel Center, but only to tell her general history of organizing at Gossard in the 1940s. With few references to local, state, or national politicians, political parties, or labor law, the ILGWU appears to be acting in a void.

I hope *We Kept Our Towns Going* leads readers deeper into labor studies and materials that include gender and feminism, race, and global trade. Instructors who assign the book for undergraduates will have to guide them to engage with it critically while respecting its contributions. In addition, nostalgia permeates the book, as it does much local public history with its mission to connect visitors or viewers to place-based stories. Using it as a foundation for a seminar, an instructor could lead discussion in ways that help students to appreciate the women's labor and quest for financial stability, autonomy, or friendship while also provoking questions about memory-making and culture. Chapter 8, "Remembering the Gossard," is particularly rich for this purpose.

The book is a generative and illuminating collection of stories and descriptions that can pull historians in new directions and prompt questions about women manufacturing workers of the UP and the Canadian-US border. It is also a tribute to Wong's decision to use her status and access to resources to collaborate with the women of the UP on this regional labor history.

Aimee Loiselle, *Central Connecticut State University*
DOI 10.1215/15476715-10949155

Keep up to date on new scholarship

Issue alerts are a great way to stay current on all the cutting-edge scholarship from your favorite Duke University Press journals. This free service delivers tables of contents directly to your inbox, informing you of the latest groundbreaking work as soon as it is published.

To sign up for issue alerts:

1. Visit **dukeu.press/register** and register for an account. You do not need to provide a customer number.

2. After registering, visit **dukeu.press/alerts**.

3. Go to "Latest Issue Alerts" and click on "Add Alerts."

4. Select as many publications as you would like from the pop-up window and click "Add Alerts."